Hearing
Grasshoppers Jump

Hearing Grasshoppers Jump

THE STORY OF
RAYMOND ACKERMAN
AS TOLD TO
DENISE PRICHARD

DAVID PHILIP
CAPE TOWN

First published 2001 by David Philip Publishers (Pty) Ltd,
208 Werdmuller Centre, Newry Street, Claremont 7735,
Cape Town, South Africa

© 2001 Raymond Ackerman

ISBN 0-86486-382-9

Page design by Sarah-Anne Raynham
Page layout by Claudine Willatt-Bate
Printed by Clyson Printers, 11th Avenue, Maitland

FOR MY GRANDCHILDREN — AND ANY STILL
TO COME — FOR ALL THE PLEASURE THEY BRING ME,
AND FOR ALL THE YOUNG PEOPLE OF SOUTH AFRICA,
BECAUSE THEY ARE OUR FUTURE

Contents

PREFACE   ix

PROLOGUE   1

PART ONE: GROUNDINGS

1   An Assassination and an Ousting   9

2   Beyond the Pale   12

3   Adieu Ackermans   23

4   Hard Lessons   31

5   New Experiences   37

6   Marilyn Monroe Marketing   49

7   Fired   63

PART TWO: SETTING THE TABLE

8   90 Percent Guts, 10 Percent Capital   75

9   Into Battle   81

10   Down Diagonal Street   87

11   Ironic Expansions   94

12   Stores Do Burn   103

13   The Boundaries of Loyalty   110

14   Hatching Hyper Mania   120

15   'Extramural' Activities   131

Contents

16   After Soweto   139

17   Political Twists and Turns   146

18   Policy and Pragmatism   159

PART THREE: NUTS AND BOLTS, NODS AND WINKS

19   Building a Pyramid   169

20   Going Down Under   179

21   What, No Rubicon?   191

22   Coming of Age   211

23   Darkest Before Dawn   224

24   The Beginning of the Beginning   232

PART FOUR: THE DECADE OF DEMOCRACY

25   Against All Odds   245

26   Birth of a Dream   260

27   Without the Yeast, There Will Be No Cake   276

28   A Silent End   288

29   The New South Africa   308

30   The Crown is No Heirloom   315

CONCLUSION   334

INDEX   337

Preface

As soon as I finally decided that I must find time to set down an account of my life, something I had thought about and been encouraged to do for years, events at Pick 'n Pay took such a dramatic turn over the company's future structure that I was on the very brink of packing the project away again – perhaps for years, perhaps for ever.

However, after my wise and loyal secretary June Hanks had first shaken her head over the pages of my crammed diary, wondering when I could possibly fit in a project of such magnitude, she advised me, not without trepidation, to go ahead regardless.

Denise Prichard and I started work on what has become *Hearing Grasshoppers Jump* in April 1999. Since then, my daily diaries, spanning more than thirty years, have been retrieved from archives and consulted. Hours, stretching over two years, have gone into recalling and setting down the events forming the fabric of my personal and business life. When all the pieces were put together, the person most surprised by the story which emerged was myself!

I would like to thank Denise for the endless hours she has spent on researching and writing this book, and for interpreting my thoughts and words so well. I have a very deep sense of gratitude to her.

To Wendy and my children, and to all my colleagues at Pick 'n Pay – I thank you so much for your contribution and for keeping me company on the amazing journey we have shared.

Prologue
1994

They greeted us like conquering heroes, the summer evening in January 1994 when we came home in triumph bearing Cape Town's official nomination as candidate city for South Africa's 2004 Olympic bid.

When we stepped off the chartered plane that brought us back to Cape Town, the air was electric with excitement. I had never known such a feeling, such an upsurge of warmth for anything I had been involved with before. Excitement had been running at fever pitch since the early afternoon announcement that Cape Town had beaten competing cities Durban and Johannesburg. Looking for a way to express their jubilation, people had spontaneously made their way to the airport to give us this welcome fit for conquering heroes.

The release of Nelson Mandela and South Africa's painful but determined journey towards democracy had caught the imagination of the world, and the timing for our bid to host the 2004 Olympics was absolutely perfect. South Africa's self-motivated move towards democracy had heroic overtones on a continent notorious for backward rather than forward political slides. In 1994 we were pre-eminently the best-placed nation on the African continent to host an Olympic meeting. It was our turn.

I have chosen to open my story with an account of events in 1994 because, although there is hardly an *uneventful* period in my life to record, that year of nerve-stretching intensity, when drama piled upon drama and I was forced to re-examine some of my most dearly held beliefs, shared with events in South Africa a roller-coaster ride that skimmed intrigue and division, hope and despair, all at break-neck pace.

At the time of our triumphant return to Cape Town with the city's bid nomination secured, South Africa was travelling a rough road on the final four-month run-down to the first democratic election. We had been handed hope, but hope cost dearly. The transformation which was the solution to the racial confrontation that would otherwise have brought civil war to South Africa as sure as night follows day, did not proceed easily.

In one two-month period at the beginning of 1994, 29 acts of sabotage were reported up and down the country. People across the political spectrum died execution-style and the country held its breath after a black Monday when gunmen fired on a crowd of Inkatha marchers in Johannesburg's economic heartland.

But, despite hiccups and horrors, and a huge build-up of tension between Mr De Klerk and Mr Mandela, South Africa did arrive, bruised, battered but still buoyant, at election day in April 1994.

Within weeks of Mr Mandela's inauguration, while everyone was still aglow with goodwill, annual wage negotiations at Pick 'n Pay broke down. Although it seemed on the surface as though wage negotiations with South African unions were merely about wages, other issues bubbled and simmered below. To black people, unions had become forums for political expression because no other form of expression existed prior to 1994.

After the 1994 election, union leaders became impatient with what they saw as slow implementation of the new dispensation. They wanted higher wages and better jobs for their members *now*, not at some nebulous time in the future. The unions were in no mood for conciliation, and even my personal attempts at negotiation with workers were to no avail. The most debilitating strike in the thirty-year-long history of the Pick 'n Pay group began to run its sad course.

That the strike should have come at a time of such euphoria and optimism was in itself distressing. More distressing still was that it should have happened to us at all. By 1994, forty to fifty percent of our managers were black. I had grown adept at interpreting the 'nods and winks' of apartheid's governors over the years, which had allowed us to defy legislation demarcating jobs and housing according to race. But the union hierarchy had reached a collective decision. They had decided that certain high-profile organisations should be 'targeted' through strike action designed to demonstrate the strength of the unions to the new ANC-led government. Pick 'n Pay was one of the chosen targets.

As daily press reports and TV news bulletins night after night reported striking Pick 'n Pay workers rioting, smashing stores and assaulting customers, I was devastated by the viciousness and violence. It seemed as though the culture of customer care and courtesy I had spent years building up was in tatters. When things were at their darkest I sat alone in my office and seriously wondered whether this was the end for Pick 'n Pay.

I spent every waking moment working furiously, desperately trying to hold things together. The phone calls, the meetings, the press conferences, the acrimonious confrontations with union representatives and sadly worried ones with my management demanded every iota of energy I could muster. I was frequently exhausted and felt ill with worry. Scenes of looting in our Bophuthatswana store sickened me.

As the strike seethed and sucked away at the profits of Pick 'n Pay and the pockets of strikers, I began to receive telephonic death threats. Strain piled on strain. I felt I was doing very well indeed if I managed to sleep four hours out of twenty-four. At precisely this traumatic time, the clash between Sam Ramsamy, head of the National Olympic Committee of South Africa (NOCSA), and the Bid Committee I led stepped up. The concentrated attempt to undermine me as head of the committee coordinating Cape Town's 2004 Olympic bid ground into gear – sadly, soon after the triumph of our nomination as South Africa's bid city.

With the campaign against my leadership escalating, I continued pouring in the millions of my own money which would be spent on Cape Town's bid, and tried desperately to hold firm against the onslaught. I attempted to concentrate on the fact that there was, or should have been, a common goal – winning the 2004 Olympic Games for Cape Town – until Sam Ramsamy's refusal to put NOCSA's signature to the contract endorsing

Cape Town's candidature under the leadership of my committee ended any further pretence of a common interest.

By now, word was reaching us from the headquarters of the International Olympic Committee in Lausanne that the disunity within the Cape Town bid was seriously jeopardising our hitherto unassailable position in the 2004 competition. Also, to my utter dismay, there was beginning to be talk of asking government for a vastly increased contribution towards funding Cape Town's bid.

As the ugly confrontation between strikers and Pick 'n Pay reached a climax, years of positive growth were destroyed, delivering the company's first drop in profits in thirty years. The strikers, too, sacrificed millions in wages that they could ill afford to lose. We were all hurt. The strike knocked down morale in our company and sullied our reputation.

I was plagued by tension headaches, permanently exhausted, yet continuously on my mettle as the campaign of disruption within the Cape Town Olympic bid continued in tandem with the strike. The long process that would ultimately end with the announcement that Cape Town had lost the 2004 Olympics to Athens – a contest we came closer to winning than the public of South Africa yet know – ground on.

I tried desperately to find some equilibrium. But the sudden resignation of my stalwart Managing Director, Hugh Herman, a man who had been through trials of fire with me over many years, precipitated yet another crisis. It was then that I decided to appoint outside consultants to look at the ills that time and the strike had visited on Pick 'n Pay. Things had gone fundamentally wrong. Ultimately, the clear-eyed views of these wise professionals led Pick 'n Pay to a rebirth and to momentous changes in the leadership of the company.

While I waited – tired and dispirited but still convinced that the company would turn vital corners – for the consultants to start work, news of the death of a cherished family member, the fifth we had suffered during 1994, came through, casting our lives even deeper into shadow.

Just when it seemed my energies could be stretched no further, I was nominated to the position of Chairman of an international organisation of retailers, the CIES, which at that time operated in 41 countries, representing members whose combined retail trading volume exceeded US$750 billion. I saw the appointment as a symbolic end to South Africa's isolation from the wider world of business and commerce and decided, despite unremitting pressure, to gratefully accept. I also figured that my chairmanship of the CIES would provide incomparable opportunities to get into global boardrooms and make influential friends for Cape Town's Olympic bid, which it did, although finally to no avail.

At the end of 1994 I thought back on the series of dramatic events that had affected my company, my country and myself. I thought how, in retrospect, these events emphasised the magnitude of transformation that had happened to South Africa and would have to happen to breathe fresh life into Pick 'n Pay. Doors had opened but, as I tried to put the events of 1994 into perspective, I had to remember that I had only come to that point – reached a stage in my business career when my company was a national institution employing thousands of people and I was able to take on the demands of an Olympic bid – because, once before, another door had slammed resoundingly shut in my face.

PART ONE

GROUNDINGS

'If you can meet with Triumph and Disaster
And treat those two impostors just the same ...'
– Rudyard Kipling, 'If'

CHAPTER 1

An Assassination and an Ousting

I could still detect an atmosphere of edginess and uncertainty among the crowds on the streets of downtown Johannesburg as I headed, unusually late, for my office at the headquarters of Checkers. It was almost a month since the afternoon of 6 September 1966 when, in South Africa's House of Assembly, the Prime Minister, Dr Hendrik Frensch Verwoerd – grand architect of apartheid – was assassinated. At 2.30 p.m., the time the Assembly was to have convened, Verwoerd was carried from Parliament on a stretcher to be certified dead on arrival at Groote Schuur Hospital.

Here, in Johannesburg – the economic heartland of South Africa – the stock market remained volatile and unstable following Verwoerd's assassination, and the appointment of B. J. Vorster as Verwoerd's successor was viewed with trepidation by most black South Africans, and many whites too. On Vorster's accession, in October 1966, it was just six years since the shots at Sharpeville had reverberated around the world and two years since Nelson Mandela and his fellow accused had been sentenced to life imprisonment for treason after the Rivonia trial.

It was the energetic implementation of Verwoerdian race laws that caused me to be hurrying along late for work, on the morning of Monday 3 October 1966. A gardener who had worked for my family for nearly 12 years had fallen foul of the Group Areas Act when he was caught out working in Johannesburg without the required permit. I had been at the City Pass Office, where such matters were dealt with, and by 10.00 a.m. the necessary rubber stamp was on the piece of paper that would keep our gardener out of jail.

As well as the annoyance of the tasteless Pass Office interlude, I had plenty of other things on my mind that morning. At 35, I was General Manager of 85 Checkers supermarkets, the jewels in the profit crown of department-store group Greatermans. I had worked incredibly hard to build the Checkers chain which, as the original dedicated company man, I saw as my life's work. Also much on my mind that morning was my wife Wendy, who was very ill in her fourth pregnancy. The doctors still feared she might lose the baby, so I had spent the weekend taking care of her and our three small children.

Since I was in close daily touch with the Chairman and Managing Director of the Greatermans Board, Norman Herber, over the affairs of Checkers, it was no surprise to be summoned to his office when I arrived at work that morning. I beat an unhurried path to his door after giving my secretary some letters and casting my eye over the day's mail. The man I found waiting for me was in a terrible state. His knuckles were all bandaged, blood seeped through from the raw dermatitis beneath, and tension radiated from every fibre of his body. I was immediately concerned – he seemed so strange, ill. I asked him what was wrong. After staring at me in silence for a few quivering moments, he delivered a bombshell that nearly knocked me off my feet with shock. Yelling almost hysterically, he said that he and his co-directors had had enough of me. To my utter astonishment, he told me I was fired.

I suppose my response must have sounded pathetic. I kept babbling on about building Checkers, about my loyalty as a company man, about our fathers having been colleagues who trusted one another. There was history between us, we were friends …

Today, not even the humblest employee could be summarily dismissed the way it happened to me in 1966. Then, however, no niceties of labour law applied. When I refused to sign a bogus letter of resignation, drawn up I am sure so that it could be flashed around to absolve the Greatermans

Board from any implication in my leaving, I was told to go and clear my desk and get out there and then. The pitch of Norman Herber's voice rose to screaming point again; he was almost inarticulate with rage. Through the outpouring of anger, I gathered there was a plan to move Checkers in a new direction and, because I was so difficult and always wanted to do things my way, I was not part of that plan.

Very strangely, about three nights previously, I had dreamed that I was sitting in front of Norman Herber and the whole Greatermans Board and they were telling me I was out. I even told my wife about the dream at the time. What I'd had was clearly a premonition – no other warning, hint or clue preceded the actual incident.

It was to be quite a time before I was able to identify one of the prime reasons behind my dismissal from Checkers. Norman Herber had fired me because he didn't have the courage to give me more freedom. If he had, I could have built Checkers the way I've built Pick 'n Pay. There would not even have been a Pick 'n Pay.

When I reeled out of the Greatermans building, all I could think about was breaking the news to my ill and stressed wife. With lightning speed I had gone from being the high-flying head of a booming food chain to an unemployed, 35-year-old father of almost four.

I headed for Zoo Lake and walked round and round and round. I thought about my whole life up to that awful day, about the beginnings of our family in South Africa. I thought a lot about my father and his tribulations.

Every time I tried to think forward, nothing came up. All I could see was a grey mist, with Wendy, the children and me milling around in confusion. I had absolutely no idea where I was supposed to go from there – other than home, when I could put it off no longer, to tell my wife I had been fired.

CHAPTER 2

Beyond the Pale

The tall, dark man whose features showed his Lithuanian origins hurried along a cobbled street of Montmartre in early twentieth-century Paris, clutching a swatch of ostrich feathers. Every so often he anxiously consulted a fob watch pulled from his waistcoat pocket. This was my paternal grandfather, Meyer Ackerman, late for a rendezvous with the high-kicking girls of the *Folies Bergère* because he had been detained over-long at the salon of his previous client, an *émigré* Prince. Such were the colourful clients the enterprising Meyer served when he set off from his home in the Cape Colony, carrying cases of ostrich feathers for the fashion-conscious ladies of Europe.

Meyer Ackerman had been among eager audiences of Jews, resident in the Russian Pale of Settlement in the nineteenth century, who listened entranced to rumours of fabulous fortunes being made in farming giant geese in the Cape Colony of southern Africa.

Interest among those harried individuals would have been heightened immensely when they learned that the industry built on the prized plumes of great flightless birds – ostriches, in fact – was centred on a place where Jews were not persecuted, where they could worship freely and live without restrictions. At that time, the Jewish population of the Pale were subjected to severe restrictions which did not allow them to travel – let alone live – outside designated areas without special authority.

Daily existence within the Pale was a struggle governed by a vast body of official 'Jewish' regulations which applied restrictively to trade and occupation, culture, education and religion, as well as residential rights. In addition, many had experienced at first hand the horrors of pogroms and dreaded a resurgence.

Small wonder, then, that when they heard about Oudtshoorn, the Karoo town at the centre of the ostrich industry in the Cape Colony, they named it the Jerusalem of Africa. My grandfather joined the thousands of Jews – although his wife was not one of them, having refused to go with him – who fled the combined forces of anti-Semitism and Imperial Russia's 'organisation' of Jews out of Lithuania into the Cape Colony. Two generations later, in the country of my grandfather's sanctuary, I too went into young adulthood toughened by encounters with anti-Semitism and at the beginning of a modern exercise in social engineering – the one called apartheid. On many occasions when I've confronted bureaucratic dictates legislating where races could or could not work and live in South Africa; what positions people could or could not hold; where, in which commodities and at which prices we could or could not trade, the parallels with my grandfather's Lithuanian past have been striking.

By February 1892 Meyer Ackerman was a naturalised citizen of the Cape Colony and an established ostrich feather buyer, one of around forty thousand refugee Jews who arrived in South Africa from Eastern Europe up until the time of Union in 1910.

Ostrich farming had begun in Oudtshoorn in the 1860s, about the time that the discovery of the Kimberley diamond fields began transforming South Africa into a modern economy. The ostrich feather industry went through a series of slumps and booms, reaching a peak between 1903 and 1913 before plunging to terminal depths. In boom times some of the ragged Jewish refugees from Europe travelled a real rags-to-riches route, becoming notorious for affluent antics like lighting cigars with £10 notes and bathing in brandy. Meyer Ackerman, however, never reached such heights of ostentation. He operated on the fringes of the industry as a *smous* – or hawker – paying low prices for feathers that had been rejected by the mainstream clothing industry and selling them on to smaller clothing manufacturers or makers of feather dusters.

But Meyer Ackerman had a natural talent for trading and an inborn inclination to think big. Soon he was travelling overseas selling feathers to showgirls and princes. After divorcing his childless first wife who had remained in Lithuania, Meyer married my grandmother Esther, who had been brought out to Africa as an orphan. My father, Gustave, or Gus, was born in 1894. A second son, Mitchell (always called Mick), arrived a few years later.

In 1902, the year the Treaty of Vereeniging formally ended the South African (Anglo-Boer) War, Meyer Ackerman suddenly died, leaving his wife and two small sons almost destitute. My grandmother took what meagre savings she had and headed with the children for Cape Town, where she thought she would be better able to provide for her fatherless sons.

At this time the city of Cape Town was struggling to adjust to the changes brought about by the war. Over twenty-five thousand people flooded into Cape Town after the outbreak of war. The insanitary conditions in which refugees lived, plus the movement of wartime supplies into Cape Town, provided ideal conditions for the outbreak of bubonic plague which afflicted the city in 1902.

Black and coloured Cape Town residents had become politicised during the war and, like the unemployed, were growing more strident in their protests. To the settled white population of Cape Town, the white skin of new arrivals such as my widowed grandmother and her sons – like all Lithuanian Jews, scathingly called 'Peruvians' – was the only feature which set them apart from the scorned black population.

In this volatile, hostile climate my grandmother opened a small shop selling fruit, sweets and vegetables in the southern suburbs of the city. The shop later moved to Gabriel Road, Plumstead – then a quiet but rapidly growing suburb – ending up, by the strangest coincidence, on *exactly* the site of my first real store in Cape Town after I bought Pick 'n Pay more than half a century later.

My grandmother's enterprise, sole support for herself and her two sons, gradually grew into a small grocery shop. Both boys, Gus and Mick, were expected to help their mother after school. I, too, remember going up there as a little boy and being told that I could have one sweet if I served three people, another one if I served so many others. Helping out in my grandmother's shop, as my father and uncle had done before me, was my first experience in retailing. Beyond question, my father's love of retailing also came from his experiences in that shop.

So, my father grew up without a father, and he grew up working very hard. He left school in Standard Seven at the age of 15, and went to work as a salesman cum agent for a wholesale company. He sold soft goods – haberdashery, towels and such like – up and down the Western Cape. Nearly every penny he earned went towards family commitments, especially on educating his young brother Mick.

This tough and uncompromising upbringing caused my father to grow up conscious of every penny. He remained always deeply aware of what money *meant*, what it cost in terms of hard work to make it. He also developed a whole belief that in order to sleep well at night you couldn't owe a penny to anyone. When retaining ownership of his business later came down to deciding whether or not to borrow money, my father could not overcome his aversion to debt, from which he only once wavered to get started in business. Ultimately, he chose to sell rather than borrow money.

The tight financial constraints my brother, sister and I encountered at home were also direct results of my father's early struggles growing up without money. These were the hard facts at the core of his unforgiving and unbending attitude about money. When my Uncle Mick, for instance, opted for a career in retailing, turning his back on the college education my father had funded, he was never really forgiven. The clash carried on all their lives and adversely affected my relationship with my uncle.

Meanwhile, across the world in America, events in another vibrant new industry, one which would dominate activity in the Ackerman family into the next millennium, were accelerating. In 1912 Clarence Saunders had come up with the idea of displaying his farmer father's crops in a warehouse, where customers would serve themselves and pay at the door. This revolutionary merchandising method reduced overheads, allowing for lower commodity prices, a factor of great importance to the people for whom there was no American Dream because they were too poor. In this way, the basic blueprint for modern-day supermarkets – low overheads equals lower commodity prices – came about. Clarence Saunders went on to develop the quaintly named Piggly Wiggly chain, the world's first real supermarkets as we know them today.

South Africa, a Union since 1910, entered the First World War in 1914 when Prime Minister Louis Botha acceded to a British government request to send troops into German South West Africa. My father immediately joined the army and became a company cook, which almost certainly saved his life. In 1916, when his company was about to ship out for France, one of the meals he cooked poisoned a lot of the soldiers. As a consequence, he was behind bars in detention barracks and not among the thousands of South African soldiers, including most from his company, who fell at the Battle of Delville Wood.

After the war my father and two fellow soldiers who had become friends, Leon Segal and Sam Kirsch, cast around for a way to utilise their savings to get into business for themselves. While he was on the road trading soft goods before the war, my father had met Morris Mauerberger, a complex character. Socially, he could be charming and entertaining and he had a good sense of humour. Yet he was given to violent outbursts of temper. Although this volatility caused him to be generally disliked, there was grudging admiration for his undoubted abilities in business. Morris Mauerberger had started off trading from door to door in the Sea Point area of Cape Town, working on a commission basis. He later admitted that he hated having to call at the back doors of houses, selling to the servants and collecting their weekly instalments.

I remember Morris Mauerberger as an aloof but not unpleasant man who lived a few doors away from us when we were growing up. He had four daughters and we were often invited to their parties. When my father and his two friends needed money to set up in business after the war they knew that their friend Morrie had funds available because the Mauerbergers had prospered and become shippers and traders of stature. Mauerberger, who liked and trusted my father, decided that for him he would put up finance in the form of two shops which my father could rent at £20 per month. In addition, Mauerberger agreed to finance stock to the extent of £1 250.

But Morrie Mauerberger – clever man, shrewd man – also wanted 10 percent of sales from my father's new stores. The agreement my father signed with Mauerberger, a document just over four pages long, incubated the germ of a disaster. Ultimately it altered the course of chain-store trading in South Africa.

Significantly, the agreement between Mauerberger and my father referred to goods and conditions in the *'business or businesses'*, which suggests with the use of the plural that the two had already talked over the possibility of opening multiple stores. Morris Mauerberger signed similar agreements with Sam Kirsch and Leon Segal, who opened independent stores of their own. Before long, however, the three Mauerberger-funded men went into partnership to launch South Africa's first chain-store group. After much debate, and clearly because anti-Semitism remained a feature of their lives, they decided to call their group Ackermans – a name that could be Afrikaans, coloured or white as easily as it could be Jewish.

The main idea my father and his partners devised was the system of pricing at 1/11 – one shilling and eleven pence – because it sounded cheaper than 2/- and also because such a price obliged sales assistants to ring up the sale and open the till to extract change, lessening the likelihood of the proceeds of the sale being pocketed. In so far as merchandise was concerned, the idea was to have so many yards of calico for 1/11, six pairs of socks, six pairs of shoelaces, etc. They became a household name on the strength of the 1/11 concept. In bars people asked for 'an Ackermans' when they wanted a popular mixed drink of the day which cost 1/11.

In spite of the constraints imposed by Mauerberger's commission, there is no doubt that Ackermans was successful. By the end of the first four years, 15 stores had been opened. On the occasion of the group's twenty-first birthday there were 28 branches, rising to an eventual tally of 35 stores countrywide. My father and his partners took turns travelling overseas to do the buying for Ackermans.

In 1922 my father married Rachel Margolis, whose family had migrated from Lithuania to settle in Dublin, Ireland, before Rachel was brought to Cape Town. Early in their marriage there was a flaming row between Morris Mauerberger and my father, after Rachel persuaded her husband to take her father into the business against the wishes of Mauerberger. Although Mauerberger fought furiously, all the partners sided against him.

I have read suggestions that from then onwards the relationship between Morrie Mauerberger and my father soured, but up to the time of the split between them that I witnessed as a boy, I cannot remember my father ever speaking badly of the man who had, after all, given him his start in business. As the family-spirited person he was, I can only think that Morrie Mauerberger opposed the employment of Rachel's father on the grounds that he was already an old man.

At any rate, what is certain is that while the relationship between Mauerberger and my father remained affable, the same cannot be said for his marriage to Rachel, my mother.

* * *

When I think back to my early childhood, the noises I remember most are shouting – and the sound of slamming doors. There were some happy times – I think on the whole I *was* a happy child – but the warfare within my parents' marriage ultimately overwhelmed everything.

Although my parents' relationship soured soon after their marriage, my sister Moyra was born in 1922, my brother Kenneth in 1928, and I myself on 10 March 1931 in Claremont, Cape Town. I gather that my parents had me in an attempt to shore up their crumbling relationship but, if so, it did not work. When I was quite small, and as my father's business prospered, our family moved to Bishopscourt to a lovely house named Le Rêve – 'The Dream' – for the majestic outlook from the grounds of the property.

In retrospect, our childhood was very strange: sometimes happy, but often very, very sad. I don't remember anything of a real home life, mainly because my father and mother were always fighting. We had a nurse and a governess looking after us. Sometimes we wouldn't see my mother for a month at a time; she would stay locked in her room. I am sure that today she would be diagnosed and treated as a depressive, but things were different then.

I know that the austerity which characterised my father had been fashioned by the hardships of his own upbringing, but in his determination not to spoil his children he sometimes overdid it. When Ken and I were on holiday from school – prep school and high school – he would tell us, 'Right boys, you can't be lazy now.' He would put the housekeeper in charge of us and we had to do three hours' work in the garden every day. I resented that, wanting to go off and have some leisure time but, under the scrutiny of our overseer, this was not possible.

Most of the happy times which I remember revolved around sharing sport with my father. Sport always formed a strong bond between us. He used to be a soccer goalie and was a very keen player in his youth until a bad accident to his arm ended his footballing activities. Later, we played a lot of golf together. Conversely, as sport bonded my father and me, so it complicated the difficult relationship between my father and Ken who, as an asthmatic, was not able to play sport competitively.

During my early childhood my father was away for long periods on buying trips overseas. When he came back he would put me on his shoulders and walk with me around the house and garden. I valued those times very much. One day, I remember, he bathed my brother and me. As we were brushing our teeth he told us we must always push the tube from the bottom upwards so as not to waste toothpaste. Whenever I squeeze a tube of toothpaste today, I push it from the bottom. I remember that bath so clearly because we had so little contact with my mother and father.

On his travels overseas, buying goods for Ackermans, my father picked up marketing ideas which he recognised, to his great credit, as winning strategies with the potential to work in South Africa. So it was that local consumers were introduced to house brands with catchy names such as Ackra, Ackersley and Ackersown, some of which are still in use fifty years on. As well as the trademark 1/11 Ackermans price tag, my father introduced the concept of in-store sales held on a basis so regular that stores were on sale more often than not. The purpose of this – then a daringly

different device – was to create a sense of excitement, a carnival atmosphere to heighten customer expectations and draw them in.

Mass marketing techniques introduced into South African retailing by
my father were soon widely copied by other chain-store traders. Many of
his innovations remain an important part of modern retail marketing to
this day. Without doubt, my father – the most adventurous and dynamic
member of the original Ackermans trio – was South Africa's first mass
marketer. He certainly taught me the importance of keeping retail trading
exciting for consumers.

The Great Depression of the 1930s created a chill trading climate for
South African business. Even though Ackermans succeeded in attracting
new cash customers into the stores during that testing time, the
Depression was actually only one of their problems. My father's avowed
intent never to borrow money placed his business under enormous con-
straint. Without borrowing, Ackermans could not compete with new
enterprises playing on the retail stage, among them OK Bazaars and
Woolworths. These lively new chains traded unfettered by the crippling
commission on sales that still hobbled Ackermans. They also borrowed
freely to buy stock ahead.

The Great Depression, the commission paid to Mauerberger, competition and outdated financial constraints conspired among them to put
Ackermans under severe stress. Around this time my father did persuade
Mauerberger to reduce the vexed 10 percent commission to 7,5 percent,
and it ultimately went as low as 5 percent. Even so, it remained an enormous impediment. To see it in context, in my company today we are lucky
to make 3 percent on sales, pre-tax. Imagine what giving away 10, 7 or
even 5 percent to someone else would do to our prices.

In 1938, the year before the outbreak of the Second World War – the
event which finally drove Ackermans to the wall – tensions within my parents' marriage built up beyond any chance of reconciliation and my father
started divorce proceedings. He left the family home in Bishopscourt and
moved into a little rented house in Claremont.

I was seven years old when I suddenly found myself in the centre of a
bitter child custody battle between my parents. Unusually for the time, my

father had decided to sue for custody because, so he told me, he thought that he was the right person to bring us up; that we would have very unhappy lives in the custody of Rachel, our mother. The divorce attracted plenty of unwelcome publicity and was extensively written up in law books because it was so unusual for a father to seek custody of children at that time.

But my father was convinced that my mother was the wrong person to bring us up. Over the years she had become very isolated and the divorce merely deepened an already thoroughly depressed state. The custody fight became a very vicious one. One day, I remember, we were told to attend a meeting with my father's lawyer in Kirstenbosch Gardens. We had to ensure that this meeting was kept secret from my mother. In the serene setting of the beautiful botanical gardens beneath Table Mountain's Skeleton Gorge, my brother, sister and I were coached by the lawyer to say in court that we didn't like our mother and didn't want to live with her.

Coaching was also carried on by our governess with whom we'd grown up. She had no time for my mother and had, besides, been told that if she looked after us children during the divorce she could come and live with us afterwards and keep her position as family governess.

Just before the divorce proceedings started, as part of the process of building up a case for my father, my sister Moyra was told to plan for us children to run away from the Bishopscourt house where we still lived with my mother. We ran away at about 6.30 p.m. one evening, just before supper. Our governess made sandwiches for us and we rode off on our bicycles, each carrying a little school bag.

When we reached our father's house we refused to go back to Bishopscourt, just as we'd been told. My father's lawyers were then able to say that we had run away from our mother to our father on our own initiative, had left our mother and gone to our father of our own free will. It was all part of the legal game played in my father's bid to win custody, but it was very, very cruel to my mother.

Rachel did try to fight the legal onslaught against her but she lacked resources and was anyway in a terrible state. As the 'baby' of the family I had been specially coached to cry and scream in the courtroom. When I was called before the court during the divorce proceedings I did as I was told and screamed, 'I don't want to stay with my mother.' I was the key witness and was told afterwards that my performance secured custody for my father.

It was a terrible burden for a seven-year-old to bear and it had a huge effect on my life. I still wake up in the middle of the night with that scene in the court echoing in my head. My mother was so angry and embittered, she was never really able to forgive me for the role I was taught to play in the custody battle. She never remarried and remained all her life a very unhappy woman. It took the warmth, wisdom and kindness of my future wife, Wendy, to bring some sort of peace and reconciliation between Rachel and me – but in 1938, the year of the divorce, bitter reproach predictably reigned supreme.

In the same year that the OK Bazaars chain was founded – 1927 – Harry Herber, who had arrived in South Africa from Lithuania in 1902, set about founding another important South African drapery and clothing chain with his half-brother Somah. It seems likely that the surname *Herber* should have been *Gerber*, but was misheard and wrongly registered by immigration authorities, as so many immigrant names were. As Herbers, Harry and Somah adopted the same carnival approach to retailing as their innovative rivals, Ackermans, opening 15 new stores up to 1934. The stores went under various names – Bettermans, Brightermans and Cheapermans among them.

Sometime in the 1930s Harry Herber had a brilliant idea. According to his son Norman, he woke up one day and said 'Greatermans'. He was so excited and pleased. He suddenly knew that what he wanted to do was build a chain that was *greater* than Ackermans, and now he had the perfect name for it.

So Greatermans, the group destined to play such a pivotal role in my life, came into being in a bid to out-trade Ackermans, which, unfortunately for my family, is precisely what they did.

CHAPTER 3

Adieu Ackermans

Freda Feinstein and her five-year-old son, Peter, came into our lives unexpectedly when, shortly after his divorce, my father married her. In 1939 Germany and Russia invaded Poland; the Smuts Government took office in the Union of South Africa and, along with the governments of Britain and France, declared war on Germany; and we got a stepmother.

Meeting Freda Feinstein a couple of years earlier had galvanised my father into the realisation that he could not continue to live within the miserable confines of his marriage to Rachel. He decided on divorce and so did Freda, who was married to a much older man with whom she had one son – Peter.

In a curious twist, when Freda divorced her husband he was awarded custody of their son because she was divorcing to marry another man – my father. As Rachel had attempted to do, Freda tried fighting for custody of her child, but ended up instead as custodian by marriage to Moyra, Ken and myself. She and my father had a son together, my half-brother Bruce, born in 1944 in my father's fiftieth year.

After the marriage my father bought a big house in Tennant Road, Wynberg, which he and Freda remodelled and called Oakleigh. Here my stepmother tried to make a home for us and from that time on, in many ways, we did have a much happier home life. Freda suffered an enormous amount of social ostracism. Being divorced placed her beyond the pale of polite Cape Town society. She and my father mostly lived in a cocoon of isolation, receiving only occasional visits from less judgemental Johannesburg friends.

Politically, my father was very pro-Smuts and his United Party, and during the Second World War he did a lot of fund-raising for charities. He was one of the founders of the Red Cross Children's Hospital, which remains to this day Africa's only specialist children's hospital south of the Sahara. I remember watching him sign many piles of appeals and saying, 'But Dad, no one can read that signature.'

Today I have a very similar signature.

But the halcyon days, for me, after Freda married my father, happened when Freda's son Peter came down from Johannesburg in the June and December holidays to be with us. Although I got on very well with my stepmother it was only during Peter's visits that I felt I really had a mother. When Peter was with us Freda read to us at bedtime, took us to the beach every day in the summer holidays and gave us a real family life.

The moment Peter went away she didn't do those things for me and my siblings. They all stopped. It wasn't that she was unkind. It was more that she felt awful about having left Peter and tried very hard to make it up to him. But she couldn't invent maternal instincts when she looked after us. Still, she ran a good home and she made my father happy.

Moyra's relationship with Freda was more complicated than mine because she was seven years older than me and going through the dual difficulties of coping with puberty and a new stepmother. She and Freda used to have deep conversations but it was never a really close relationship. During the time of my parents' divorce Moyra had been very good to me, had mothered and taken care of me. We remained close right up to her sad death from cancer in 1991.

As an adult Moyra did wonderful work for the Space Theatre in Cape Town. Here she was at her happiest, involved with the amazing pioneering work that went into putting on fearlessly outspoken productions in the abnormal conditions apartheid imposed on the arts. The Space launched the careers of many illustrious theatre personalities

– Pieter-Dirk Uys, Yvonne Bryceland, Athol Fugard, Paul Slabolepszy and Bill Flynn among them. For Moyra the Space Theatre was a reason to live.

While we were growing up at home my father never talked about his business and never had any social contact with his two partners and their wives. For recreation he pursued the solitary hobby of stamp collecting, communicating with fellow collectors only by letter. The major extramural love of his life, however, was golf, a passion passed on to me in equal measure. I was encouraged to play from a very young age, joining my father and stepmother on the Clovelly Club course.

My father's connection to the Clovelly Golf Club was another chapter in our family history that grew out of anti-Semitism. In the early 1930s my Uncle Mick was blackballed from joining the Mowbray Golf Club on the grounds that the club had filled its 'quota' of Jewish members. After this incident my father and a friend of his, Michael Pevsner, decided to look for a piece of land suitable for founding a club with more palatable membership criteria.

Their plan was put on track when an estate in a beautiful valley bordering the Silvermine River in the Fish Hoek area of Cape Town was put up for sale. The asking price in the early 1930s was £3 000. There was an established 9-hole golf course on part of the estate, mainly used by naval personnel based in nearby Simon's Town. This club was not a very prosperous one, and was run very much on a hand-to-mouth basis. The hundred-odd golfers who made up the membership could not raise the money to buy their course when the land came on to the market.

The extent of the land up for sale turned out to be greater than initially offered. My father and his partner found they could buy the entire lovely valley, right up to the river, for £5 000 and this is what they did.

The new owners, Michael and my father, planned a country club complex incorporating an 18-hole golf course, club house, bowling greens and tennis courts with facilities for other amenities too, which they called Clovelly Country Club. They also offered to donate the land on which the new club and facilities would be positioned so that the original members could continue playing golf there.

Most of these original members, however, weren't very happy about this because they had been told that while they could carry on with their golf, the club would henceforth be open to everybody – which at that time meant open to all religions. Much further down the line I got that changed to all races. Clovelly, I have always been proud to say, became the first multi-racial club in South Africa, but that's another story.

The navy people were particularly disgruntled with the new dispensation at their golf club. Donation or no donation, they did not want Jewish members. Consequently, most decided to pull up their stakes. They went off and established the Westlake Golf Club on another old farm, Raapkraal, near Lakeside. So, my father's purchase of the valley on which Clovelly Country Club would stand actually spawned two golf clubs in the area, both of which still thrive.

During school holidays, I used to play golf at Clovelly with a 15-year-old golfing wizard called Rita Levetan. As Rita Easton she went on to be named best South African lady golfer of the twentieth century. The hours of our boyhood that Ken and I spent playing rounds at Clovelly acted as a safety valve, separating us from tensions at home while bonding us as brothers.

Apart from a passion for playing golf my father was a naturally austere man not given to any overt shows of affection. He was also a very tough father, demanding that Ken and I put in a stipulated amount of work – at home, at our grandmother's shop, at his business – before we could lay our hands on the paltry pocket money we received.

Later, when I was in my last year at school, a prefect running a study, I received the princely sum of one shilling a week pocket money. Other boys were getting at least £1, so I used to run to my grandmother and she would give me an extra half a crown – two shillings and sixpence.

It wasn't that my father was mean, it was simply that his background had been so tough, so uncompromising, that he didn't know how to behave differently, how to bend a little in his disciplinarian mould. I do know now that I was afraid of this tough man who didn't talk to us as children. I loved him but I was afraid of him.

The only time I remember him hitting us was when Ken and I pulled away the chair our grandmother was about to sit on. She sat down on the floor, which we thought very funny and clever until our father took his belt to us.

Ken and I used to fight a lot when we were boys because we were so different. Also my father tended to favour my pursuits, especially sport, so Ken saw me as the favoured son, which I wasn't. It was more that there was a natural affinity between me and my father, and he didn't understand Ken. For his part, Ken objected to what he saw as my father's Victorian interventions in the lives of his children. It was such a pity that they could never understand each other's sensitivities.

When it was time for me to graduate from preparatory school my father called a family meeting. Always conscious of his own very tough background and of having given up his schooling for his brother, he wanted his sons to have the very best education, which is so much of a Jewish tradition. He chose to send first Ken and then me to Bishops, the Anglican Diocesan Cape Town school, which is the Eton of the Western Cape.

As the only Jewish boy at Bishops before I joined him there, Ken had been in solitary combat on several fronts. As I have said, he was a sensitive boy who did not fit snugly into the Bishops mould. Because of his asthma he wasn't keen on sport and he had been refused leave to absent himself from school on Jewish high holidays, which was hurtful.

Prior to packing me off to join Ken at Bishops, my father gave us a pep talk in which he lauded the full and rounded education Bishops was famed for. To his mind, academically, sports-wise and in extracurricular activities, there was no beating Bishops for quality education. I know that he later felt guilty because our schooling set us apart from other young Jewish people, but I have never forgotten how, as a Jew, he justified sending his sons to a Christian school. I remember how he told me that as long as I knew who I was, nothing could ever change me, that he wanted his sons to be at Bishops even though it meant having to attend chapel services. He believed his decision to put us into an Anglican school was justified because we did not live in a Jewish society but a Christian one. Our schooling at Bishops would make us insiders, so to speak. We would have first-hand knowledge on our side, said my father, no doubt remembering how ostracised he had felt in the past.

So off I went to Bishops to boost the school's Jewish pupil population to two. I have to say of my school career that on the whole my father's judgement proved sound. I thrived in the sports-orientated atmosphere of Bishops, becoming an especially passionate rugby player. And I did get a well-rounded, wonderful education which taught me to respect Christian society, even as I clung, sometimes desperately, on to my Jewish heritage. I became a prefect and rose quite high in the school hierarchy. I also have my participation in Bishops' Night Schools project, which taught literacy skills to underprivileged Africans, to thank for converting a boy's inkling that something is owed in recompense for privilege, into the conviction of a lifetime.

I wish I could say that everything I extracted from my education was that positive, that constructive. Unfortunately I can't, because at Bishops, as elsewhere, I learned something else too: how it feels to be a victim of prejudice.

* * *

Throughout the Second World War there had been strong pro-Nazi elements at work within South Africa. Towards the end of the war I had the opportunity to witness at first hand how effective the whipping up of anti-Jewish sentiments had been. Employees of Jewish-owned chains such as CTC Bazaars, OK Bazaars and Ackermans embarked on acrimonious strike action organised by unions setting out specifically to target Jewish firms. Chains not owned by Jews – such as Stuttafords and Garlicks – were not targeted.

One day, during the strike, I went with my father to the main branch of Ackermans in Cape Town. As we approached his office we found that the way was barred by a furious mob of pickets, who screamed and yelled abuse. Suddenly, some people in the crowd started to spit. They spat on my father, who was, as always, immaculately and elegantly dressed in a pressed grey suit, wearing his familiar Homburg hat.

Despite the terrible troubles he had running Ackermans profitably at that time, my father had never deviated from basic principles of caring for people who worked for him. Although there is no doubt that the unions were specifically targeting Jewish-owned companies at that time, my father was deeply shocked by the behaviour of people in his company who he had always thought were loyal to him, whose hands he had shaken.

I had cause to remember that day with my father during the war-time Ackermans strike when I later had to contend with ugly strike actions of my own. I remembered how my father had behaved and was able to draw on that and deal with industrial action against Pick 'n Pay in 1994 in a dignified but very tough way.

Strikes and union action against Ackermans were unfortunately far from being the only concern my father was grappling with at this time. With his original partners now dead or out of the management picture, keeping Ackermans viable during the difficult war years had been a terrible battle. The chain had been kept operational but the problems of war-time trading had been compounded by having to keep up with paying the commission to Mauerberger and by the fact that my father's chronic aversion to borrowing had put his chain at a competitive disadvantage.

Whenever I was out of school at this time I was very aware of the tension at home. One memorable night Morrie Mauerberger, back in Cape Town after spending the war years with his daughters in America, came to our house for dinner. During the meal my father, who normally never discussed business at home, suddenly raised the issue of the Mauerberger contract. 'Morrie,' he said, 'can't we cancel this deal? It's killing Ackermans. I've gone right through the war years with this percentage, but I've managed to hold Ackermans together, threadbare as it is. But we can't go on paying this. We've got to get out of it.'

Mauerberger banged the table, shouting that a deal was a deal, to which my father replied, 'Well, we can't go on. I'll have to sell out.' This comment further antagonised Mauerberger, who angrily pointed out that the deal between them disallowed any sell-out without joint consultation. Battle was fully joined then and I was hastily sent off to bed. As I left the room, I heard my father, who never normally raised his voice, fling back at Mauerberger: 'No, if I can't go on I'll have to sell out – and I don't have to discuss it with you.' Later, when the combatants had moved into my father's study, I crept downstairs and listened to the thunderous voices through the keyhole.

My father must have succeeded in establishing his right to negotiate a sell-out without Mauerberger's participation because a few days later the people who had founded the OK Bazaars – Sam Cohen and Michael Miller – arrived at our house. That meeting didn't go well either. I believe this was mainly because Sam, Michael and my father never really got on.

It must have been about a week later that Harry Herber and his half-brother Somah, co-founders of the Greatermans Group, arrived on our doorstep. This was the Harry Herber whose avowed intent was to build a chain of stores greater than Ackermans.

Again, as discussions went on in the study, I crept downstairs and in this way heard that Ackermans was going to sell to Greatermans. The conversation certainly sounded more agreeable than the one with Sam Cohen and Michael Miller. I heard Harry Herber say, 'Gus, if you don't sell to OK Bazaars, but sell to me, you'll be Vice-Chairman and run Ackermans and I'll be Chairman and run Greatermans. And our sons will do the same, it will be a family combination.'

It was all agreed and Greatermans bought Ackermans lock, stock and barrel. By floating Ackermans as a public company, the Herber family was able to make Mauerberger a very good offer for his contract, which also offered an honourable exit from a situation that had become an impasse. Ackermans Holdings Limited was floated at the end of 1946, after which an exchange of stock finally terminated Mauerberger's contract.

Future events and later exchanges between my father and me, I now know, can be traced back to his embarrassment about having sold out our birthright – frankly, to get rid of a problem. Before 1946, before the difficulties of trading during the Second World War brought Ackermans' financial woes to a head, the problem could have been surmounted with a change in my father's philosophy.

In the end, all the innovative business acumen that had allowed my father to build South Africa's first real chain-store group, to become indisputably the country's first mass marketer, came to nothing before his simple inability to borrow money.

CHAPTER 4

Hard Lessons

On Adderley Street, the main thoroughfare of Cape Town, relentless waves of heat rose off the pavements on which we had been standing attentively for three and a half boiling hours, decked out in our cadet clothes. It was Monday 7 February 1947 and our cadet corps from Bishops had been pressed into service to help line the streets of Cape Town for the State Visit of King George VI, Queen Elizabeth and the Princesses Elizabeth and Margaret.

People were fainting in the heat all over the place but we stood there stoically doing our duty, standing in front of part of the crowd of thousands waiting to see the royal visitors. At precisely 10.20 a.m., twenty horsemen formed into a guard of honour, preceding the King, Queen and Princesses in procession along Adderley Street. For a brief few minutes I could have almost reached out to touch the royal family, they passed so close to where we boy cadets stood. I found it all absolutely thrilling and it became a day I have never forgotten.

During the first half of 1947 I kept a daily diary, a habit that revived in adulthood when I started making daily entries in diaries I have kept for nearly forty years. Lining Adderley Street for the 1947 royal visit is one of that first diary's highlights although the schooldays' effort only lasted six months, after which a final, cryptic entry records that I am 'too lazy' to carry on. The short diary is peppered with comments about teachers making 'weak cracks' and 'talking silly tripe'. Fellow pupils are 'sporting', outings are 'good fun'. Life in summer-time Cape Town for this 16-year-old sounds idyllic: surfing at the beach, watching cricket at Newlands, playing billiards, darts and golf at Clovelly.

There is mention of having gone down to the beach to bring back two sacks of white sand for baby brother Bruce's sandpit. By this time I had obviously got over being so embarrassed by having a baby in the family. For a time, I used to tell visitors who heard Bruce crying that it must be the neighbour's baby.

Measured against what a 16-year-old today would be saying and doing, my 1947 diary sounds incredibly gauche, naïve and innocent. Ken and I spent evenings at home listening to quizz programmes on the radio. There are enthusiastic descriptions of cinema outings with a special mention for Crackerjack Popcorn – obviously relished. Although this early diary of mine often mentions meeting friends randomly at this or that beach, this or that cinema, it is clear that actually I always went with either my brother Ken or stepbrother Peter.

Above all else, there is not the merest hint of unhappiness, no suggestion of how difficult I was finding the last two years of my schooling at Bishops. Although I never lost my awareness or appreciation of the rich life of the school, it wasn't always an easy environment for me to live in. I was very alone.

From 1945 there was a build-up of difficulties for me at school around world events as they affected Jews. Indeed, from 1945, an anti-Semitic impulse around the world saw the bewildered survivors of the concentration camps treated with thinly disguised loathing rather than sympathy. There were pockets of people all around the world who thought that the trouble with the Final Solution was that it wasn't final enough.

Because of events around the issue of Palestine and the declaration of the State of Israel, I got into some vicious fights over accusations that the Jews were anti-British. Every day we read the newspapers in the common room at school. I remember what an awful time I had over the bombing of the King David Hotel in Jerusalem in July 1946. The hotel was blown up because it housed part of the British Administration in Jerusalem and the explosion killed 28 British, 41 Arabs and 17 Jews.

These and subsequent British deaths, notably the gruesome murders of two British sergeants, Clifford Martin and Mervyn Price, unleashed a wave of anti-Jewish riots – in England, the first since the thirteenth century. Many of my colleagues at school were of British stock and I had to endure a steady stream of vituperative anti-Semitic sentiment which sometimes made me feel as though I was living under siege.

I was very proud of my brother Ken at this time. He was then at university and had joined a group of very enthusiastic Zionists, though he wasn't a Zionist himself, who were training to go and fight for Israel. In the end he didn't go because of his asthma. My father wasn't very pleased about all this, but I remember being proud of Ken for being a person of principles.

In 1948, my last year at Bishops, against every expectation D. F. Malan's Reunited National Party and Afrikaner Party coalition narrowly defeated Smuts's United Party. When all the returns were in, Malan and his ally had an overall majority of a mere five seats in the House of Assembly. Slim as the new governing party's majority was, the unexpected victory provided Malan with the mandate he needed to introduce apartheid policies to South Africa.

At school I remember having a prefects' meeting with the house master on a Sunday night when we talked about the Nationalists' policy aimed at entrenching white supremacy. Many of my fellow prefects were in favour of the new regime. But to me, as a result of my upbringing and roots and because I was now involved through Bishops in teaching literacy classes to Africans three times a week at Night Schools, the politics of the new governors of South Africa were absolutely abhorrent.

The Bishops' Night Schools were held in the school's science laboratories. My 1947 diary records how rapidly numbers of learners increased. African waiters, gardeners and domestics working in the area flocked to the classes. Teaching in the Night Schools project gave me a feel for the work which would prove directional in the future.

When it came to surviving at Bishops I was a lot luckier than Ken had been because when I got close to boiling point I had an outlet. I could get rid of my frustrations on the rugby field, an avenue not open to my asthmatic brother. I loved participating in sport of any kind – athletics, swimming, football, cricket, golf, snooker – but rugby was my sporting passion. I had played my way through all the junior teams until in my Matric year I was Bishops' first-team rugby fullback.

One day, the rugby coach sent word that I should go to see him. At that time the first team had been practising long and hard for a rugby tour to Rhodesia, which I presumed was what the coach wanted to see me about. This indeed proved the case, only in an utterly unexpected way. Without ceremony the coach informed me I'd been dropped from the touring team. Imagine the effect this had on me, coming like a bolt out of the blue. It turned out that the coach had decided I must stay behind because he did not see how he could have a Jewish player in a team touring church schools in Rhodesia. It was not fitting, he thought.

No amount of frantic recitation of the hours I'd spent practising, the team game-plan or fair play prevailed on the coach. I was bitter, angry and desperately miserable when the rest of the team left. That tour turned out to be a great success for the Bishops' team. When they returned I set about playing like mad to show the coach he'd made a mistake. Still, it was very sad to be taken back into the team, on merit, they said, when no lack of merit had kept me out in the first place.

On another occasion during my time at Bishops, nominations for Head of House were about to be made. A young supposed friend of mine went around telling everyone that a Jew couldn't be made Head of House at Bishops. As a result, I lost out on the nomination although I was made a prefect. I was really upset, mainly because he had been a friend but also because he showed me just how tough life could be.

But despite the difficulties, I loved Bishops. I loved my school work, loved sport and loved being a boarder although life at home had also been happier since my father's marriage to Freda. Once in a while I would bring friends home but we were not really encouraged to do so. Occasionally I went out with friends. I particularly remember a three-day holiday at St James with a friend of mine, which I loved. I recall it so clearly because it happened so rarely. Until I was 18 I don't remember going away with my parents for any holidays. We just didn't, we had to make our own enter-tainment – playing rugby and golf and riding bicycles.

In my last year at school I decided not to go to chapel on one of the high holidays at the time of the Jewish New Year. By now I had matured sufficiently to find a chapel service too incongruous on a Jewish high holiday. As a result of this minor insurrection, the school's Vice-Principal summoned me to his study to say that the misdemeanour was sufficient to have me thrown out of school. Since I was on the eve of writing my final Matric exams, this was a substantial threat. I still remember how angry and insensitive the powerful Vice-Principal was but I decided to brazen it out and said I had no regrets, whatever he decided to do, which turned out to be nothing.

In my last few months at Bishops, I was one of three boys nominated as a candidate Rhodes Scholar. Rhodes Scholars are nominated by the boys each year in terms of the conditions that Rhodes himself set down when bequeathing the scholarships that bore his name. I considered myself very fortunate to have been nominated until I heard that one of my 'friends' was going around telling the other boys 'not to vote for Ackerman' because Rhodes didn't like Jews. Amazingly enough, the spreader of that schoolboy anti-Semitic propaganda surfaced again when I was riding high on success (as did various other 'friends' from my past), asking for business favours based on our past acquaintance.

Despite the battles that went with being Jewish at a Christian school at a particularly sensitive time, I now see that those troubles were also responsible for developing my character. Although I have never been able to forget the hurtful incidents, in later years it was the very good things about being at Bishops that dominated, so much so that I sent my own sons there. Now, decisions are being made about schools for grandchildren, and some, indeed, have already joined their fathers and grandfather as Bishops boys.

The way attitudes have changed was brought home to me when a grandson of ours, Nicholas, had his bar mitzvah not long ago. All his Christian friends from school came to watch the Rabbi bar mitzvah him, which I thought was wonderful. I would never have been able to do that because I would have been embarrassed, at 13, to have Christian friends around. Being Jewish back then was something you didn't hide but it did set you very much apart.

When I look back at my school days there were some sad times, some difficult times, but also some happy and beautiful times. Although I was really very alone, especially in the last year, and although my father's teaching – that you don't ever discuss your private affairs anywhere with anyone – sealed my isolation, I also learned to stand up for myself and what seemed right; to respect Christian people; to give something of my privilege back to the underprivileged; and, above all else, I learned how it really *felt* to be discriminated against.

CHAPTER 5

New Experiences

The year I went to the University of Cape Town – 1949 – was also the year the Voortrekker Monument, that granite symbol of Afrikaner domination, was inaugurated. At the time there didn't seem to be any particular symbolism about those two events coming in the same year but, in retrospect, I see that there was.

With the coming to power of D. F. Malan's National Party in 1948, a mere two and a half million descendants of the Boers whose deeds the Voortrekker Monument commemorates began a 46-year-period of domination over the lives of ten times that number of other South Africans – white as well as black.

As the new Nationalist government began to assemble the apparatus of apartheid, education was seen as a key to re-regulating society into one in which members of each race group would have a designated place. The racial superiority of whites could never be debated; people of colour were never to question the positions assigned to them.

Of the places where people of colour could most easily absorb dangerous liberal ideas, seats of education were soon singled out for special attention. A government commission set up by the Nats in 1948, for instance, had already launched an attack on the mission schools, crucial shapers of opinion since they trained almost all black teachers. The commission concluded that the missions had done nothing but destroy black culture. From then on, the relentless pursuit of racial separation dealt blow after blow to the aspirations of young black people in search of a higher education according to their choices until, in 1959, the government sought to put an end to integrated education at university level. When I went to the University of Cape Town, terribly tough questions were being asked about which way the country would go, which created an atmosphere of uncertainty and underlying tension.

But as well as being tense, it was also a fascinating time for me. I soon got very involved with my work – with my Bachelor of Commerce – which I thoroughly enjoyed. I loved working under Professor W. H. Hutt, who taught me an enormous amount. He gave me a passionate belief in the career I was to follow. At the time he was often vilified as an egghead, a failed businessman sitting in some university, when he spoke out against monopolistic practices, cartels and collusion working against the interests of ordinary people.

After I left university he wrote some wonderful books and was hailed as one of the leading economists of our time, indeed as the 'economist of the century' according to the *Wall Street Journal*. Writing when Professor Hutt was 84 years old and Professor Emeritus at the University of Dallas, Texas, the *Wall Street Journal* further said that it was only Professor Hutt's relative obscurity in South Africa that had enabled the Keynesian theories, on which the West's economic policies had been based for the past four decades, to become accepted as economic gospel over those of the former University of Cape Town professor.

Professor Hutt taught me the importance of fighting for the rights of ordinary people. I found his lectures and theories absolutely riveting. Far, far in advance of his time, he used to tell us that if, when we ran our own businesses, we *cared* for our people and society, the businesses would succeed. That has stayed with me and had a huge influence on my life.

Over the years of building Pick 'n Pay I have often been challenged on the motivation behind our policy of caring for our people and operating on principles of consumer sovereignty. The cynical observation is that such philosophies in business are little more than window-dressing disguising the real motive for trading – making bigger and better profits. On the contrary, I've always said that following the principles of consumer sovereignty and caring for people is precisely the way to make money and to be successful. It is an absolute fact that the more we ploughed into staff benefits, the more we gave to charity, the more profits rose. But, I've never shied away from saying that I *like* profits very much. They are the bloodstream, and I couldn't live without them, but they are not my life. The bloodstream of profits keeps me alive but my mind gives me the energy to do what I know should be done.

At university Professor Hutt taught me that a division between caring and making profits does not exist, because if profit-making becomes your whole being, firstly you won't be a very nice person, and secondly you won't *make* profits. Profits flow from having a mission and a goal – that is the way to succeed. If your mission is just to make money, you'll probably end up being a pauper. But if you say 'I want to be a great doctor or lawyer or whatever to help people', it doesn't mean that you don't send out your fees and you don't make a lot of money from them. You can't be too theoretical; to be able to achieve you must be able to dream.

I listened and listened and listened to Professor Hutt and took it all in, developing a habit that would serve me well for the rest of my life – always listening to what people have to say. As my future mentor Bernardo Trujillo later said, no matter how elevated you get, if you can still listen it means you are not getting too big-headed to learn.

Professor Hutt was fiercely opposed to the policies of the newly installed Nationalist government, not only from a moral abhorrence of a doctrine based on racial superiority but also because he thought the Nats were doing everything wrong to build the economy. He believed you could not build an economy on apartheid because the system worked against releasing economic energies, dictating that whites should be productive and non-whites non-productive.

Professor Hutt and I had deep discussions on the inequalities the system was feeding and on lost opportunities. Those discussions helped to form the views which later fuelled my part in campaigns by the business community to purge the South African economy of the apartheid policies that were drowning it.

I also particularly remember Professor Hutt's thinking on the role of labour unions in economies, which was way ahead of his time. He wrote extensively about the positive potential if unions would work within the economy rather than destructively from without. At that time in my student career I thought that if you ran a decent company you wouldn't really need a union, any more than the country would need unions if the government ran a decent economy. If businessmen were not rapacious, unions were superfluous. Now I've come to think differently. I believe that even in the best-run company unions *do* have a role to play, and that both company and union can learn good lessons from one another.

Professor Hutt's futuristic thinking and teaching, the lessons my father taught me about courtesy and avoiding debt, and the practical applications later suggested by marketing genius Bernardo Trujillo became the triple-layered bedrock on which I built Pick 'n Pay. When I was able to form the teachings and theories of these three massive influences in my life into a practical core, I had the foundation for my own business philosophies – from which I've hardly since had cause to swerve.

Another lecturer in the Commerce Department whose teaching and intellect I admired was Owen Horwood. He was a wonderful lecturer to us in the 1950s and was in those days, like Professor Hutt, *very* opposed to the National Party. Later, as Principal and Vice-Chancellor of the University of Natal, he became embroiled in serious student unrest. By that time his opinions had changed, which surprised me in view of the involved conversations we had during his days at the University of Cape Town. Then, his lectures were often laced with the theme of apartheid killing the economy and the wrongs of Nationalist policy.

As Minister of Finance in the 1970s, Senator Horwood, as he became, featured prominently in the Information Scandal which ultimately led to the fall of Prime Minister B. J. Vorster. This major political crisis had its origin in 1969 when Vorster set up a security services special account to cope with the perceived needs of the country's external security. Gradually the practice developed under which these funds could be channelled through individual government departments. Ultimately the issue that brought down Vorster and others, and saw Owen Horwood labelled as a liar, turned on who had or had not known to what uses the secret funds were put. I too was to find myself unwittingly embroiled in repercussions of the Information Scandal.

After university, despite fundamental differences in our thinking, I maintained a good relationship with Owen Horwood up to the time of his death.

During my first year at university, as well as working hard and absorbing prodigiously, I played a lot of rugby for the Under-19 first team. Some fellow sportsmen among my contemporaries became sporting celebrities. The four famous Fry brothers were prominent personalities. Dennis Fry has been written up in rugby's hall of fame as the best catcher and passer of a rugby ball of all time. He went to Europe on the 1951–52 Springbok tour, in the team captained by his brother Stephen.

Paul Johnstone, a wing in the Under-19 team, went on to wear a Springbok jersey. Brian Pfaff, another famous South African sportsman, suffered from epilepsy, so no one thought he would get his Springbok colours. He did, however, and toured New Zealand where he suffered the knee injury that forced his retirement from rugby, although he went on to captain a Western Province cricket team with distinction.

As for myself, I definitely wasn't good enough to have got into Springbok rugby, as another team-mate of mine, hooker Albertus 'Bertus' van der Merwe, ultimately did. In my second year at university I got severely hurt playing in a curtain raiser match at Newlands, which very sadly blew the final whistle on my rugby career.

At university, I also became deeply involved with student politics, particularly after I was elected to the Students Representative Council. I was also a member of the Students' Liberal Association, through which I got to know Zach de Beer very well. When I arrived at university, Zach, who was older than me and in Medical School, was very involved with student politics. With a confident bearing born of having spoken in public since his schooldays, Zach was already being mentioned as a possible future South African Prime Minister.

As Dr Zach de Beer there was a long, honourable political career ahead of that erudite student leader. He worked for years with Helen Suzman, forming first the Progressive Party, then the Democratic Party, which in

1999, sadly the year of Zach's death, made impressive gains in South Africa's second democratic election.

In my second year at university the increasingly vice-like grip of the Nationalists secured the banning of the Communist Party, which had hitherto maintained a presence on the university campus. With their party banned and outlawed there was a flurry among the student communists to join us liberals, which we interpreted as a take-over bid. Urgent emergency meetings were called. One I remember, under the leadership of Zach de Beer, was held beneath Rhodes Memorial above the university. Because of what we saw as a Communist Party take-over, we resolved to resign from the Liberal Party to form a new party – the Students' Democratic Association. Our supporters, however, viewed the change of party as defection, insisting that as elected representatives of the Liberal Party we had got into those positions on a liberal ticket and could not change allegiance. But we insisted that as we stood for the same principles as before, we merely needed to adopt the new name 'Students' Democratic Association' to counter the communist take-over.

In all the debates reverberating through the university, we were forming both our personal and political characters. At the conferences of the National Union of South African Students (NUSAS) which I attended as an elected member of UCT's Students Representative Council, fundamental questions were being asked about where apartheid was taking the country, about educational segregation and interference with academic freedom. Countrywide, seats of higher learning and their students squared up to the National Party, but the battle against their interventionist bullying had long years to run.

The issue of apartheid meddling in education was of special interest to me. Together with other students I had helped develop the first SHAWCO (Students' Health and Welfare Organisation) Night Schools, which had grown into a chain of schools. I taught at one, as I had done in my senior year at Bishops. After leaving UCT, I became principal of them all – my first experience of running a chain, though of schools, not stores. My involvement with Night Schools, as I have mentioned before, had a distinct bearing on important directions in my life, although the legislation of the Bantu Education Act that ultimately terminated this independent education initiative was already being assembled.

By 1951 a commission had been set up, under the chairmanship of a confirmed segregationist, Dr Werner Eiselen, to look into means of controlling African education, and further curtailing the influence of mission and independent schools. Such independent influence was viewed as extremely dangerous. The Nats fretted over liberal and subversive ideas of all kinds, which they believed were being fed into untrained black minds by malicious outsiders and left-wing subversives, who ought to know better.

The upshot of the Eiselen report was the implementation of the Bantu Education Act of 1953. The Bill was introduced by Dr H. F. Verwoerd. Significantly, it was not the Department of Education that then assumed responsibility for African education but the Department of Native Affairs, a twist with profound implications for future generations of black youths.

While I have mentioned the study side, the sports side and the political side of my life as a UCT student, what is obviously missing is the social side. Although I did take out various girls while at university, I know that I was too serious, still too much of a loner. I was too stiff and would certainly have had a much better time if I'd relaxed. But all the years of being discouraged from taking friends home, the trauma of my parents' divorce, battling anti-Semitism at Bishops, and isolation from the young Jewish community imposed by my Christian schooling combined to set me in a solitary mould. There was also the matter of being continuously underfunded by my father, who was still compulsive in his resolve not to over-indulge his children.

There were many changes at home during my last year at university. Ken had settled in England, where he was to remain permanently, and Peter, Freda's son, had moved in. I had also begun to talk my father into sending me on one of the recently revived NUSAS tours to Europe after my graduation. Amazingly he agreed to fund this unprecedented extravagance – although I would naturally have to travel on a shoestring – and I looked forward to the adventure all through my final undergraduate year.

My parents didn't come to my graduation, which was very sad. Staying away would have happened, I know, at my father's insistence. His inability to offer his children any encouragement, ever to praise or applaud, was based on a strange inverted belief that to do so would distract us from further effort. All the years I played rugby, I knew he would never be in the spectator stands. 'I'll come and watch you when you're a Springbok, Raymond,' he used to say. He would have justified staying away from my graduation with something like 'I always knew you'd get your degree, Raymond, I'm not surprised', but he did later congratulate me warmly for having done so well. This is the only time I ever remember being praised by him.

It is important for me to say, however strange it may sound, that my father was not a cold man; he was simply reserved. He thought that if he revealed himself it would make him weak, and he wanted to be strong. He had had such a very tough life and he was always scared that I was too nice, too susceptible to being taken for a ride. He didn't recognise the steel in me. While I may sound critical of my father, I am not, because I always recognised that his character had been formed through leading such a tough life himself. Once he had taken an attitude he found it impossible to bend or change his mind, however persuasive the argument that he should. For example, he never reversed his objection to my brother Ken's marriage, simply because Ken had chosen his own wife without consulting my father. When my sister Moyra was being courted by several hopeful suitors my father simply called in Issy Fine, his choice of husband for his daughter, and told him he wanted him to marry Moyra.

My father and Freda also disapproved of my marriage to Wendy. They thought I should have taken a wife selected by them, one who accorded with their strict criteria for social and financial standing. Many, many years into my marriage with Wendy, Freda told her she could not believe how unkind she had been for so many unforgiving years.

On the credit side of my father's personality, I must also say that he was a man of terrific integrity. If he said something, then that was it. But if he said he wouldn't help, he would never bend or waver from that stand. In his determination that his children should grow up knowing that the world was a tough and competitive place, he could seem cold, because he thought that by being warm it would make him soft. As an adult I do see that he felt bad about selling out our birthright, but he was right about so much, such as sending me to Johannesburg after Greatermans bought his business. I owe him a great deal.

Perhaps this better explains why I received my B.Com. degree unsupported by anyone in the audience. At any rate, the major part of my attention at the graduation ceremony was focused on the eagerly anticipated NUSAS tour. Immediately after graduating I handed back my gown and headed down to the docks.

* * *

Aboard the Union-Castle mail ship after graduating, I found many students I knew from the Cape Town branch of NUSAS. By far the majority of students on board ship, however, came from the Universities of Natal and the Witwatersrand. Because there were so many students travelling in the NUSAS group, people tended to gravitate towards forming smaller groups among themselves. I had been pleased to find a girl I knew from the Night Schools – Denise Rocke from Rhodesia – among the Cape Town contingent on board. Denise and I formed a foursome with another couple, Val Kilpin and her partner, Ian Newman. It was fantastic to have these friends because without them the trip would have been too transitory.

The relationship which developed between Denise and me was the only serious relationship I'd ever had, and it was wonderful. The NUSAS holiday tour took us to England, France, Holland and Switzerland. It should have been an entirely carefree time, but I had to devote far too much attention to wondering whether the frugal £100 spending money my father had allowed me would stretch to last through the trip. Most of my fellow travellers had three, four or even five times what I had to spend.

At the end of the tour my journey back to Cape Town was a miserable one. Denise had stayed behind in London and I was ill on the ship travelling home. When I got back to Cape Town I talked to my stepmother about my feelings for Denise. She reacted with predictable dismay to the news that Denise was not Jewish, warning that if I persisted with the relationship, it would kill my father. I was 21 at the time and utterly convinced that Denise was, at last, the right woman for me.

Six months later, when Denise came back to Cape Town, I took her home to dinner and decided there and then to break off the relationship. It was very hard and traumatic but the opposition was overpowering. Denise later married happily and she lived in Zimbabwe. In spite of how hard it had been to end our relationship, I know now that I would never have been truly happy married outside the faith. Thankfully, when I had the experience of my eldest son wanting to marry someone who was not Jewish, I was able to draw on a different perspective that made me approach the issue more sensitively. One thing is certain, I would never have excommunicated any of my children for marrying outside the faith, which is what happens in orthodox Jewish families. Because of my parents' bitter divorce, family is terribly important to me and I'll do anything in the world to sort out a family problem.

In 1952, with the one serious relationship of my life ended, I started work as a trainee manager at Ackermans, now of course part of the Greatermans Group. I went to work there partly out of loyalty to my father but largely because Professor Hutt's teaching had convinced me that retailing could be among the most exciting of careers. Fired up by theories I was desperate to put into practice, I was nevertheless obliged to accept that my business beginnings at Ackermans had to be of the humblest. 'You', said my father, 'are going straight into learning retail from the bottom.' The first thing he did was to put me into the Ackermans Corner House store in a blue suit and stiff white collar and made me greet people, offer chairs and show them the way as Courtesy Officer.

And that is all I did for six months.

My friends at that time all thought I was mad. They were all going into professions or getting great jobs while I was running around retail stores offering chairs. My father kept saying, 'If you don't learn courtesy, you don't know anything about retailing.' After spending six trying months offering chairs I was moved to the distribution warehouse for Ackermans – and kept *there* for two years.

Ackermans was principally a clothing chain, and my working life was now parcelled into six-month stints dealing with the distribution of merchandise from the warehouse. So it was that I spent six months sorting ladies' panties into various sizes and colours, making them out into different store parcels and packing them into trunks for sealing and sending out to the stores.

I then went on to do the same thing in haberdashery, men's wear, ladies' fashion and on and on and on. The idea was for me to learn merchandising from the warehousing side. It was a very good training but it went on for too long. I remember often thinking that I was wasting my life. Twice I wrote letters of resignation but both times changed my mind before handing them in, thinking that I owed it to my father to stick it out and see it through.

When I was finally deemed competent to take on a managerial position I was sent to manage a little store in Long Street, central Cape Town. The entire store was smaller than my office is today but I was so proud to be its manager. One day while I was working there, Wendy Marcus walked in. She was 19 (I was 23), and she had come to get my signature on a list of books the Night Schools project needed to buy.

At that time I was still principal of the chain of Night Schools initiated during my years at university and, as such, planning was part of my portfolio. When the name Wendy – a name I particularly liked – came up on a list of volunteer teachers supplied by the university, I listed her on the same nights that I worked, and before long had started taking her out.

There was an instant, strong attraction between Wendy and me even though we both carried on going out with other people for a while, and despite the fact that culture and the arts were closest to Wendy's heart, while sports made mine beat faster. She had grown up in a family in which relationships were complicated by sadness and loss. A small brother died of meningitis and the only other surviving child, Pamela, was handicapped from birth following a difficult delivery.

If I thought *my* schooling had been difficult at times because I was a Jew in a Christian boys' boarding school, Wendy was sent during the war, as a young Jewish girl, to a *convent* in the conservative mining town of Welkom to be tutored by Catholic nuns. As young adults working together at the Night Schools, shared values and a mutual commitment to the ideals of social responsibility formed a huge part of the attraction between us.

* * *

At the end of 1953 Harry Herber, who had heard that the learn-from-the-bottom apprenticeship being served by Gus Ackerman's son was so tough it could 'ruin the boy', offered me the chance to join Greatermans in Johannesburg. Somewhat to my surprise, my father was in favour. In fact, he urged me to accept. 'Don't stay in Ackermans', he said, 'although we're part of the Greatermans empire. This is the third team now. Go to the first team, Raymond; show them you can grow with the leaders away from my influence.'

I found out later that although my father had encouraged me to move to Greatermans in Johannesburg, he expressed the fear that I would be eaten up in the tougher world of up-country retailing because I was too kind, too theoretical in my approach. Or so he thought.

By this time Wendy and I knew that things were serious between us. I had overcome obstacles put in the way of our relationship, insisting that my family's attitude to misfortunes in Wendy's family were unfounded. My family liked Wendy, but they were petrified because of the little brother who had died of meningitis and her brain-damaged sister. Although my father knew Wendy's father, Dr Marcus, a well-respected dentist, he tried very hard to get me away from Wendy, having convinced himself that she must have inherited 'troublesome' genes – a ridiculous idea. But this time I insisted.

Little did he know that the independence with which I fought for the right to stay with Wendy I had learned from fights over principles at school. Facing up to my father's opposition was a harsh lesson but it did teach me to cope and to fight my own battles. If I had been under my father's control, without the independent spirit, I would probably have gone along with what he wanted and said that Wendy was the wrong girl.

I've thanked God ever since that I didn't.

CHAPTER 6

Marilyn Monroe Marketing

I moved up to Johannesburg to start working for Greatermans in 1954, the year Prime Minister D. F. Malan retired and was succeeded by J. G. Strijdom. I began my training in Greatermans at various small department stores in the surrounding towns – Boksburg, Springs, Krugersdorp. I sold fashion, fabrics, furnishings, moving from department to department. I even went out to houses to fumble my way through on-site curtain-measuring exercises.

Supermarketing had started in South Africa in about 1951 when the OK Bazaars chain put the first food department into their flagship Eloff Street store in downtown Johannesburg. Following that, Harry Herber decided to put a supermarket into his Springs store, which was where I was sent to work as an assistant manager with another young trainee from England. We were placed under a wonderful retailer from Greatermans – Martin Fonn. Greatermans was experimenting with food for the first time and it was, to me, an infectious game. Suddenly I began to get a feel for food.

It's strange, but I've never really spoken before about how I came to understand *the* fundamental in food retailing, which is this: even though the margins in food are lower – you make much more gross percentage on clothing and hardware – with a low gross margin you can make a much better *profit* in food. Selling food in supermarkets with their lower expenses means that profits can be better. Food did not have to be a poor relation in the profit stakes at all. My father had always taught me his belief – shared by all his retailer contemporaries – that food was just a loss leader. To be profitable you had to have departments making 30–40 percent, because expenses were in that region.

Martin Fonn, however, worked out that if you had a fast-moving food department on an 11 or 12 percent gross margin, expenses for that could be kept as low as 9 percent. For me, with that calculation, the penny dropped. Night after night Martin and I argued out the profit scenario relating to food. This was a time of crucial importance when I formulated the very basics I have ever since applied to the marketing of food.

As I worked out in my own mind the precise reasons why food could equal profit, I thought with increasing excitement about how I could relate Bernardo Trujillo's conclusion that *'you don't bank percentages – you can't have percentages for breakfast – you bank money'*, to supermarket sales. Therefore, if you sell a thousand tins of peas and make just one cent on each tin, that's one thousand cents in the bank. Although the *percentage* may be lower, the contribution to profits is higher. And that is really when my life in food started, when I came to that central point about trading profitably in food.

In December 1954 Harry Herber died, pitching his son Norman into the challenging role of Chairman and Managing Director of Greatermans. At the time Norman was only 31 years old and, by his own admission, had no idea what he was doing when he assumed his father's mantle. This was a very traumatic time for the new man at the top. He had very little training or experience but he was wise enough to realise that he would not be able to emulate his father's unique management style, which had been based on tremendous character and total self-confidence in the absence of formal education or training.

The empire Norman Herber inherited was doing well, but not very well. There were constant crises over money, stock, organisation. The Board was made up of much older men who controlled a great number of capital-intensive, low-profit small stores. They played the young Norman Herber like a fish on the end of a line. Every aspect of their management was imbued with politics. As a result of the unlovely intrigues I saw at that early stage in my career, I vowed that if I ever ran my own business in-house politics would be outlawed wherever possible.

Once Norman had found out, as he put it, what and where and which existed in the sprawling enterprise he had inherited, he went to America to study retailing in the land of the industry's leaders. His intention was to research how Greatermans could be revamped for greater profitability and operational efficiency. The concept he decided upon, to his credit, was to open free-standing, cash-transaction supermarkets like those he saw in America.

It was even New York's chequered cabs which provided the inspiration for the fresh name and look needed to separate the envisaged new stores from existing Greatermans outlets. Checkers, Norman decided, was what the supermarkets would be called and, like the cabs, the corporate colours would be a bold combination of bright yellow and black.

Norman Herber returned with a blueprint for Checkers in his briefcase. He decided to bring in an overseas expert to manage the chain he planned because no one in South Africa knew nearly enough about food to take on the task. I was delegated to assist the English expert because it was thought that my background in the cash business environment of Ackermans would prove useful to the new venture. When the imported manager I was understudying had to leave due to ill health, I persuaded the sceptical Greatermans Board that I was best suited to succeed him.

The first Checkers store opened in 1955, followed by another three within the first year. They were not an instant success. Early trading patterns showed that the public were trying the new shopping experience, coming back once or twice more, but then staying away. While there were plenty of pessimists around who believed that South African shoppers were just not ready to take to supermarket shopping, I was sure that pricing was the real problem in those early Checkers stores. We had taken away consumers' credit facilities, we had taken away deliveries and we had taken away personal service too. But we had given nothing in return.

What we needed to offer in return, I was absolutely convinced, was lower prices. My passion for the concept of consumer sovereignty edged into gear and I began a two-year battle to convince Norman Herber and the conservative, non-food-orientated hierarchy on the Greatermans Board that I knew where we were going wrong.

While I had been working in Johannesburg, Wendy and I had kept in touch, although I had been seeing someone else and so had she. Now, however, I decided that I wanted Wendy as my wife and, luckily for me, she agreed. We were married in Cape Town on 4 September 1956, auspiciously on a Tuesday, which has always been my lucky day. My father and stepmother were not gracious in their defeat over my marriage and for many years largely ignored us. When we also found ourselves on the wrong side of Wendy's parents over who ought to care for her sister Pamela, we wondered what was wrong with us that we found favour with neither family. Still, we settled down to married life in Johannesburg very happy with each other and soon Wendy was expecting the first of our four children.

One day in 1957 when I was working in an office on the Chairman's floor at Greatermans, a representative from the American company National Cash Registers, suppliers of Greatermans' equipment, came to tell me about courses National Cash sponsored for MMM – Modern Merchandising Methods – in Dayton, Ohio. National Cash clients from all over the world were invited to send delegates. I had been chafing to get to America to study supermarkets there and find out what we were doing wrong in South Africa ever since I got involved with food at Checkers. I knew they were light years ahead of us in marketing and merchandising techniques and I desperately wanted to learn what they had to teach.

When I passed on the proposal that I should go to America to Norman he turned me down flat. But I continued to yearn to go. I kept on avidly reading supermarketing magazines from overseas, which only served to confirm my suspicions that Checkers was not going anywhere in its present guise.

In 1957, when Wendy had just delivered our son Gareth, Norman Herber suddenly decided, over the heads of dissenting Greatermans Board members, that I could go to America if I went immediately. This presented Wendy and me with a terrible dilemma. We had no wish to be apart for six months so soon after our marriage and the birth of the baby, but

Norman had told me I went either then or not at all. Wendy bravely decided to leave the six-week-old baby with her parents, a decision which proved life-changing for both of us. It directed our future by establishing our marriage as a partnership in which we were joint decision-makers. Gareth didn't suffer from any sense of loss because he was just too young, but what he gained was an especially close relationship with his grandmother which lasted all her life.

Once the question of where to leave the baby had been settled, the next practical problem was how we were going to afford to travel together. Norman Herber had agreed to give me £10 a day for expenses, so this had to be divided by two. For the most part we funded our first trip together to the USA on our wedding money – another shoestring excursion for me.

First stop in the USA was the MMM seminar run by National Cash Registers. The seminar we attended was the second to be held and was made up of only ten delegates. Later, the same seminars attracted thousands of delegates including the founders of Coles Supermarkets in Australia and Sainsburys in England.

It was at the first MMM conference which Wendy and I attended that I made contact with American marketing genius Bernardo Trujillo, the man whose dynamic thinking exerted the strongest single influence over my life after the teachings of Professor Hutt. I was thrilled, excited and buoyed up beyond belief by Bernardo's dynamism. Listening to him, I could see how Professor Hutt's theories could be put into practice. Bernardo told us, 'Remember Modern Marketing Methods as Marilyn Monroe Miller – desirable goods, openly displayed and readily accessible.' I could hardly contain my enthusiasm, hearing as well how retailing could translate practically into the cause of consumer sovereignty, which I began to see was a very intelligent form of enlightened self-interest.

The reason to be in business is to interpret what the consumer wants. Fight like hell for her, and she'll fight for you. Treat the consumer as queen, and she'll make you king. Rich people love low prices, poor people need them.

It was thrilling, absorbing, as though pieces of a puzzle fell perfectly into place. For the first time, unconsciously, I heard the heartbeat of Pick 'n

Pay, although I thought I was hearing solutions to the ills of Checkers. I began to know what we needed to do to fix things.

After the seminar Wendy and I set off on a six-month tour of the southern United States. Bernardo Trujillo had told us to go and see how this group and that group, emergent supermarkets of the early 1950s, worked. We travelled on Greyhound buses and stayed in dingy motels because our meagre funds wouldn't run to anything better. We went and introduced ourselves to supermarket owners as a husband and wife team. We used to get off the bus in some small town and say to the store owners, 'We're South Africans, can we come and work with you?'

There we would be, working away in some bustling supermarket, with Wendy on the deli side and me on the meat counter; or I'd be at the fresh produce and she'd be serving bread. We worked behind tills, swept floors and packed shelves. It was a wonderful, wonderful experience. Strangely enough, lessons I learned from the warm-hearted supermarket people we met in the USA, so willing to share their knowledge and show us around, stood me in unexpectedly good stead when later I was similarly able to share expertise with someone who played a key role in my future.

In the evenings Wendy and I bounced ideas off one another and I wrote reams of notes which went into detailed reports that I sent home to Norman Herber and the Greatermans Board. Because I was simply bursting with enthusiasm for all I was seeing and experiencing, it didn't cross my mind to wonder how my report-backs were being received. Surely such a deluge of enthusiasm could be nothing but infectious, especially as I was translating admiration of what I saw into practical suggestions for reviving Checkers.

On that first trip to the USA, I saw how serious a retailer could be about the rights of the consumer, and how serious grateful consumers could be in response. A New Orleans storekeeper, Mr Schwegman, for whom we worked for a few weeks, went to jail for selling milk below regulation price. While he was in jail, Schwegman's company ran advertisements telling the public where he was in jail and why. Within two days the public outcry was so great that the authorities had no option but to release him. Soon afterwards Schwegman was elected mayor of the city, an office he held for about ten years.

This same Schwegman also taught me how simple but unconventional marketing techniques could work wonders for sales. During the time we worked for him I noticed that he had a chronically bruised elbow. When I commented on this he demonstrated why it was so. When he came across a line that was not moving on display in the store, he would elbow it so that the cans came clattering down into the aisle. Customers coming across the dislodged cans tended to bend down and drop a couple into their trolley. Whether people were prompted to do so to reduce the haphazard heap or whether the fallen cans simply attracted their notice, I was not sure. I was convinced, however, that being lively, daring and unconventional kept customers interested and maintained the carnival atmosphere retail outlets had to have to succeed.

Drawing on another strategy I learned in the USA, I still remember the sheer excitement a '1 cent Watermelon Day' generated during my days in charge of Checkers. I bought watermelons direct from farmers – just as American retailers did – and set up a great mountain of watermelons in the parking lot outside a Johannesburg branch of Checkers. Juices from cut fruits ran all over the ground – it was quite a messy promotion – but people came along in droves to buy the 1 cent watermelons and talked about the event for years.

Unconventional, adventurous, exciting, vibrant – that was supermarketing American-style. By the end of our six-month trip I was bursting to get back to South Africa to start applying all I had learned to Checkers. I also thought that the origins of the supermarket movement in America, which had gained momentum during the Great Depression when poverty made ordinary people desperate for low prices, accorded well with present conditions in South Africa. Thousands of poor black South Africans desperately needed basic food at low prices and I began to think seriously about marketing to this silent majority, hitherto largely ignored.

When Wendy and I boarded the plane to fly home from the USA I was anticipating a warm welcome in South Africa. Norman and his Board would surely have caught the glow of enthusiasm radiating from my reports. As it turned out, I was soon to discover that most of what I had written – including ideas for expanding the profitability and reach of Checkers – had ended up as crumpled pieces of paper in rubbish bins. My great excitement and enthusiasm had been interpreted as a young man losing his head, going over the top, becoming too extreme to warrant serious attention.

* * *

Robert Herber, the leader of the delegation from Greatermans who stepped forward to meet us when Wendy and I landed in Johannesburg, looked embarrassed. I was fuelled up like a rocket set for launching, with all the ideas and excitements of American retailing buzzing around in my head. I could hardly wait for Monday when I would put everything I'd learned into making the Checkers stores really work. Imagine my amazement when the designated bearer of bad news drily informed me that during my absence I had been moved out of Checkers altogether and was to report on Monday morning to the jewellery and gents department in one of the group's Belfast stores.

Out of Checkers – my career path, my road with a destination now clearly defined because of all I had absorbed in America? I now *knew* how supermarkets should be run, where we at Checkers had gone wrong and how we could put it right. But, unbelievable as it seemed, there was no mistake. My removal from Checkers was so much a done deed that a replacement had already been appointed. He, I soon learned, was an older, more temperate man, one who would work obediently within the dictates of the Greatermans hierarchy, undisturbed by anything as troublesome as vision. To the Greatermans Board, who had shaken their heads over the extensive reports I had been sending back from America, my absence had provided the ideal opportunity to oust me.

In my new position at Belfast I fretted about all the marvellous examples of innovative retail thinking I had seen working in America, which I could not, after all, introduce into Checkers. But I never lost sight of the importance of the USA trip in my development. I kept the knowledge close and never stopped working towards getting back into Checkers.

Meanwhile, Wendy and I settled down to the changed circumstances of our lives in Johannesburg. In 1959 our first daughter, Kathy, a sister for two-year-old Gareth, was born. I went off to work each day, every bit the loyal, if constrained and champing, Greatermans employee, with 2/6d in my pocket, doled out daily by Wendy, keeper of the purse strings, for lunch and pocket money.

In company with so many of our generation in the 1950s, Wendy and I talked and talked and talked: politics, policies, realities and outcomes; round and round for hours with friends at home. We did have some friends from the sporting fraternity but most tended to be in the political field, with Michael O'Dowd the bright light on the scene for me, because his theories accorded so closely with the vision I had for South Africa.

Michael had written an amazingly prophetic treatise on how he saw the future of South Africa. His was a very positive and realistic take on how Nationalist policy would evolve in South Africa. He wrote that the powers of the world would force apartheid to weaken, but that integration of blacks and whites would actually force its collapse. He based his premise on the fact that white segregation could not be upheld in the face of economic integration. It was so interesting, so far in advance of most contemporary thinking in the late 1950s, which held interventionist military incursion to be the greatest threat facing apartheid South Africa. Events did, of course, eventually evolve in the way Michael O'Dowd predicted; the process just took considerably longer than anticipated.

At this time Wendy was teaching disadvantaged black pupils in Soweto as well as looking after the children and giving me moral support on all fronts. She had already determined never to succumb to merely staying at home operating as wife and mother. Society still decreed, as it had for her mother's generation, that no matter how intelligent, able, educated or talented a woman was, her place remained at home, with all her energies channelled into her role as wife and mother. A wife who worked did so because her husband could not provide satisfactorily. So it was that in the early part of our marriage Wendy concentrated on her teaching programme, mainly in Soweto. To this day what she remembers most about that time is driving down broad, *empty*, sun-splashed Soweto streets, a rare image in view of what Soweto became and what happened there.

Nevertheless, the underlying, seething unease in relations between black and white South Africans always lay just beneath the surface – actually on the surface. However, you didn't sense it if you were an ordinary white living in Johannesburg or Cape Town because there was always the separation and the natural courtesy of the Africans. But underneath, if you got to know people of other races, you knew there was seething, seething discontent. The propaganda the Nats pumped out all the time, telling whites that everything was under control, that whites were firmly in charge and all that, couldn't disguise the underlying certainty of what we knew had to be coming.

Meanwhile, my career path with Greatermans continued on its mercurial course. After endless pleading and negotiation Norman Herber gave me one Checkers store to 'experiment with'. The store I was given was the worst of the four Checkers outlets, an ugly, dingy little shop in Boksburg, east of Johannesburg. Apart from the unprepossessing appearance of the shop, it was also the one with the lowest turnover. But I wasn't deterred. I was back where I wanted to be.

I poured all the information learned in the USA into rejuvenating that Boksburg shop. In spite of the inevitable grumbling from the Greatermans Board, it was patently clear to me that a first move had to be the lowering of prices. When I was prevented from reducing the prices of certain branded goods, I got the staff to take the labels off cans and replace them with handwritten labels. Candles were removed from packaging and tied together in anonymous bundles. So started an entire retail phenomenon that would reach maturity as the no-name and own-brand-name movements, hugely important developments in future trading.

When shoppers at the Boksburg store were introduced to sales incentives they reacted with such enthusiasm that an entire stock could sell out on the first day of a promotion. Such devices, so familiar to today's supermarket shoppers, were brand new then and people were *excited*. The carnival atmosphere I wanted to create was in the air and the goodwill translated into sparkling turnover. The tatty little store that had been scraping in R3 000 a month suddenly took R9 000 on one day alone.

The experiment was terrifically successful but instead of building on this success I was, unbelievably, again pushed out of Checkers and sent back to the department stores. I should have walked out then and left them to their own mistaken devices, but it was lucky I didn't because before much longer, fortune finally dealt me a winning card. In 1960, when the man who had taken over Checkers failed, I replaced him as General Manager controlling the four existing supermarkets. My appointment marked the beginning of the halcyon years for Checkers, during which a chapter of remarkable expansion unfolded against a backdrop of unprecedented turbulence in the troubled history of modern South Africa.

On 3 February 1960, English-speaking white South Africans, for once in accord with Afrikaners, were shocked to hear in British Prime Minister Harold Macmillan's 'Wind of Change' speech that the growth of African national political consciousness was a fact which, whether it was liked or not, had to be accepted. Since the Nationalists' policy of apartheid ran counter to the aims Britain held as a colonial power, apartheid South Africa could expect no aid and comfort from the United Kingdom. White South Africans interpreted Macmillan's speech as an affront: Britain was getting out of Africa to suit her own interests and white people who remained could expect no help from the British government. The British position, which seemed to accord whites no place of their own in Africa, was used by Dr Verwoerd to brilliant effect in his government's campaign to have South Africa declared a Republic a few months later. From now on, South Africa had to stand on her own feet, he was to say. At this time, Prime Minister Verwoerd was taking on the mantle of father figure in whom all whites could have confidence, which was, I thought, a very worrying situation.

A little over a month later, on 21 March, while South Africa was still mulling over the implications of Macmillan's speech, police in Sharpeville, a township outside Vereeniging, south of Johannesburg, opened fire on a crowd protesting against the pass laws, the hated legislation which dominated the lives of black people and led to thousands of them being fined continuously, arrested and imprisoned. One of the policemen started firing without orders and his colleagues took it as a command that they should do the same. When the shooting was over, 69 Africans were dead and 180 injured.

News of the Sharpeville shootings flashed onto radio bulletins – South Africa had no television then – that afternoon. I was out playing a round of golf, and when we returned to the clubhouse an agitated buzz filled the air. There was a palpable feeling of panic, with people wondering if this was the start of the black uprising against whites that many had feared and, if so, whether the government could contain it. I was still following the O'Dowd thesis – that the powers of the world would force apartheid to weaken – and, although shaken, I still said and believed that things would work out.

These were dark days. At the end of March 1960 the government declared a State of Emergency and instigated the Unlawful Organisations Bill, outlawing both the Pan-Africanist Congress (PAC) and the African National Congress (ANC). In April, Dr Verwoerd survived the first assassination attempt on his life when he was attacked by a deranged white man at the Rand Easter Show, an annual Johannesburg event.

The Sharpeville shootings scandalised the outside world. Condemnation was universal. The American government publicly regretted the tragic loss of life and a protest meeting called in London drew over ten thousand people. The United Nations demanded that apartheid be abolished and foreign investors hastily began to withdraw their money. Gold shares, the lifeblood of the South African economy, slumped.

It was in this climate of panic and despair that Norman Herber had what I have always applauded as his finest hour. He had the courage to see that this was a time to boldly expand rather than quietly retract along with the rest of South African business. Norman chose this period to vigorously implement the idea of building shopping centres (which both he and I had seen in America) with Checkers as the anchor tenant. By the early 1960s Sanlam, South Africa's insurance giant, had already decided that they wished to build shopping centres on American lines. The deal Norman Herber struck with Sanlam was notable not only for the climate in which it was negotiated but also because it broke down the barrier that had hitherto existed between Afrikaans-speaking South African investors and Jewish businessmen.

I recall this as a most exciting time when Norman and I got on extremely well. I was working night and day travelling around the country, building a chain, and he was supplying the money. We were a winning combination all the way. Growth was phenomenal: in our best year we opened 23 stores and on average we opened 15 to 20 stores a year.

* * *

During 1963 I took some time off to make another trip to America, bound for a conference in McAllen, Texas, and another meeting with marketing wizard Bernardo Trujillo. This time I left behind my family, now grown to three children since the birth of Suzanne in 1962. When the conference ended I travelled down to the border with Mexico, on the Rio Grande, close to Dallas. I planned to cross the border to take pictures of America from Mexico as I had promised Wendy and the children I would.

It was 22 November 1963 when I showed the amiable American border official my passport and asked if I could go across to the customs on the other side to take my pictures of America from Mexico. While I was clicking away with my camera, terrible news reached the American border post. President John Kennedy had been assassinated in Dallas. Unaware of this dramatic turn of events, I ambled back to the American customs post to go back into America, only to be met by a very different atmosphere. There was a feeling of dreadful shock, bewilderment and panic. Suddenly, the American officials didn't want to allow me back, saying that my American visa did not permit more than one entry. Of course they had been put on full alert, not then knowing all the circumstances of the Kennedy shooting, and the border had been closed. I had to do some of the most persuasive talking of my life to get the Americans to let me cross back into the USA.

The incident at the Mexican border on the afternoon of John Kennedy's assassination was not my last brush with that extraordinary event. Two days later, on 24 November, I was back in Dallas and found myself among a crowd milling around the main square, gathered to catch a glimpse of John Kennedy's assassin being taken to his arraignment. Suddenly I was propelled towards a spot from where I could see into the building from which Lee Harvey Oswald was being moved. If you can picture that amazing *Life* magazine photograph which captured the precise moment when Jack Ruby stepped up to Oswald, manacled between two FBI agents, to shoot him, you will be able to visualise how close I was. I was standing immediately behind one of the armed guards at the moment Ruby shot Oswald dead. Pandemonium ensued with people shouting and screaming and crying.

Apart from the dramatic events surrounding John Kennedy's death, the 1963 McAllen conference introduced me to Bernardo Trujillo's towering concept – deceptively simple like all brilliant ideas – on which I built Pick 'n Pay and continue to run it to this day: the four legs of the table, with the consumer perched on top. Trujillo's model made such perfect sense. The four legs of the table relate to the four parts, or legs, supporting a healthy business, the table. One leg, the most important by far, is people, one is merchandise, one promotion incorporating social responsibility while the fourth is administration. Each leg is vital to maintaining a healthy balance in the business but the consumer atop the table and the principles of consumer sovereignty are always paramount, always providing the *reason* for the existence of the structure below.

I seized on Bernardo's shining model and subsequently adapted it as the core principle on which Pick 'n Pay was built. Through all my years of expansion those same four legs have remained rock-solid foundations, reinforced over the years with added aspects, greater refinements in each category, but always *there*. It is almost impossible for me to express adequately how crucial the concept has been to the overall development of Pick 'n Pay. Balanced on the four legs we have become more than just another successful company. We have developed a business culture which balances profits with investments in our people and social responsibilities. Over all these years of expansion I have never ceased to acknowledge the huge debt of gratitude I owe to the thinking of Bernardo Trujillo, as I do to Professor Hutt and to my father for his teaching.

CHAPTER 7

Fired

With Pick 'n Pay still a hidden factor in the future, on my return from America in 1963 I set about applying the 'four legs of the table' concept to the running of Checkers. Growth continued to proceed apace but there was always an undercurrent of friction in the company. At this time the myth that I was 'difficult and unmanageable' was gaining currency, when in fact all I was trying to do was to get the Greatermans hierarchy to develop supermarkets the way I knew they should be developed.

Norman Herber's attitude towards me at this time can best be described as ambivalent: one moment he would be heaping praise on my head as a brilliant go-getter, the next trying furiously to rein me in.

Since I had been heading up Checkers in Johannesburg, Wendy and I had got to know Arthur Goldreich and his wife very well. Arthur worked for Greatermans as an architect, so we were closely connected planning new Checkers stores in the era of rapid expansion. Arthur was very erudite, very witty and a great conversationalist. He was keenly interested in art and culture and was a great sportsman too.

Alongside his social attributes there was also a serious side to Arthur. In the 1940s he had fought with the military wing of the Jewish National Movement in Palestine, becoming knowledgeable about guerrilla warfare. At home in South Africa he was a member of the Congress of Democrats and one of the first members of Umkhonto weSizwe (MK), the military wing of the ANC.

The ANC had secretly purchased a farmhouse and property – Lilliesleaf Farm in the northern Johannesburg suburb of Rivonia – as a safe house for their members working underground. Nelson Mandela had stayed at the Rivonia property, posing as the caretaker, before leaving South Africa surreptitiously, on the run from a warrant of arrest issued against him for inciting black workers to strike. Arthur and his family moved into Lilliesleaf Farm as official tenants, an opportune arrangement as Arthur had managed to keep his political activities concealed from the usually all-seeing authorities.

One day, when Arthur and I were sitting together having lunch, the conversation took an unexpected turn. We had been arguing companionably about whether a new building should have yellow walls – my choice – or his choice of white, when he suddenly asked me straight out whether I was playing any political role. I replied that while I had been passionately interested in politics since university days, I still believed that economic forces rather than violence would ultimately undo apartheid.

I was entirely taken aback when he started to tell me about the group assembled at Rivonia, a group who were forming a shadow government ready to take over running the country when the ANC assumed power in two or three years' time – which they anticipated would happen. He told me about the role Nelson Mandela had played, about Oliver Tambo and other stalwarts of the cause. I was made party to these revelations because the Rivonia group were having a recruitment drive. They were looking, said Arthur, for bright, intelligent people who cared and who had skills to join them. The suggestion was that my economic training and experience in commerce would be welcomed. After thinking it over, I declined to become involved. Some people, myself included, still believed that a non-violent solution to South Africa's problems was possible.

On 11 July 1963 the farm at Rivonia was raided by dozens of armed policemen. The main building and outbuildings were surrounded and everyone found was arrested, including Arthur Goldreich, who had driven into the farm while the police raid was in progress. The police confiscated hundreds of documents and papers, although they did not find any weapons. Ironically, a plan for guerrilla warfare in South Africa stayed undetected right where it had been left lying on a table. At one stroke the security forces had captured the entire high command of MK, all of whom were marched into detention under the new ninety-day detention law, precursor of the infamous Terrorism Act of 1967, which allowed for indefinite detention without trial.

Next morning, news of the Rivonia raid blazed from banner headlines. As soon as I got to work I went to the Planning Office on the fifth floor where Arthur worked. Everyone there was very quiet, white-faced. Then I saw two policemen standing on either side of an equally white-faced Arthur. They had come to search Arthur's office and go through all his papers. When I went to speak to him, one of the policemen warned me not to because anything I said could be taken down and used in evidence against him. I was very worried, shocked and upset, thinking how recently Arthur had asked me to join the Rivonia group.

At the time of the Rivonia raid Nelson Mandela was on Robben Island serving a five-year jail sentence for inciting black workers to strike. He was brought to Pretoria Central prison after the raid and says in his autobiography that as soon as he saw that Thomas Mashifane, the foreman at Rivonia, was detained there, he knew the security police must have discovered Rivonia and, consequently, his connection to the farm.

A few weeks before the Rivonia accused stood trial on charges of treason, Arthur Goldreich, his friend Harold Wolpe and another two accused bribed a young guard and escaped from jail. Arthur and Harold made their way to Swaziland disguised as priests, then flew to what was then Tanganyika. Nelson Mandela and the others were tried and sentenced to life imprisonment.

The daring escape of Arthur Goldreich and his accomplices severely embarrassed Dr Verwoerd's government in 1963 although the Rivonia arrests added credence to rightist assertions that communism threatened to overwhelm us. Paradoxically, as internal tensions and external pressures on the apartheid state nudged South Africa deeper into isolation, the defiant country at the southern tip of Africa was about to experience the greatest economic boom in its history.

While Dr Verwoerd's government continued to insist that the rest of the world simply did not understand South Africa, the implementation of restrictions on trade, sport and travel and the exclusion of South Africa from participation in all spheres of the international community sealed our national solitude. Save for a tiny club of 'friendly' nations and bordering countries which had little option but to tacitly go along with their powerful neighbour, South Africa stood alone, creating a need for considerable ingenuity on the part of organisations whose business was reliant on access to wider world markets.

Although capital continued to flee the country, the condemnation and retaliatory restrictions imposed by the international community were little more than frustrations for South Africa. Despite the worst the world could do, the economy was flourishing. In the two decades following the 'Wind of Change' speech, South Africa's immense mineral wealth and her role as the world's largest producer of gold resulted in the windfall revenues which underwrote apartheid. South Africans experienced the irony of watching the incomes of their most vocal enemies fall, while theirs rose.

In business, the years from 1960 through to 1966 were halcyon for me, embodying all I had hoped to achieve in my mission to build the Checkers chain, even while the political situation remained desperately worrying.

In addition, my relationship with Norman Herber and the Greatermans Board remained tense. Every working day involved some element of battle as they kept insisting that I couldn't do this and couldn't do that, that I was acting 'illegally' and contrary to the interests of suppliers, as though this took precedence over the interests of consumers. No one, however, could deny that my efforts on behalf of the chain were incredibly successful.

Of the endless disagreements between the Greatermans hierarchy, Norman and myself, one that erupted over an issue of cut-price toiletries – health and beauty aids – illustrates perfectly how deeply battle lines were drawn between people who were supposed to be on the same side. We had been cutting the price of food for years, but toiletries remained on high, sacred ground, unsullied by price cuts. I failed to see why these commodities should be treated differently from food and persuaded Norman that Checkers should embark on a first-ever cut-price toiletry campaign. He agreed with me, not an unusual occurrence when we were alone, and we went storming ahead, creating huge public interest through massive advertising and press coverage.

As the campaign broke, alarm bells shrilled in the competitors' boardrooms. Norman began to receive frantic protests from the OK and Woolworths, who complained bitterly that he was starting a price war. They demanded that he stop the promotion and put prices back to where they were: he agreed, to my utter amazement. I was summoned and told to adjust prices back up. However, this time, I plainly refused. I pointed out, incredulous at his short-sightedness, that the entire credibility of Checkers was on the line. How could we advertise one set of prices, yet charge another? I was deeply upset, but determined to stand by the campaign and not put the prices up even, as I told Norman, if it meant being fired. I left the office and went off to relieve my tension by playing 18 solitary holes on the City Deep golf links.

Next day I went to work convinced that I would be called in and fired for my insubordination, but instead, and again to my complete surprise, it was Norman who decided to back down. I had won through. We didn't put the prices of toiletries back up that time, which I took as a triumph for consumers over suppliers.

By 1966, the countrywide network of Checkers stores had grown to 85, a phenomenally successful and profitable chain. Turning Checkers into a household name had taken a huge amount of dedication and hard work but, as I have said, I saw this as my life's business mission. Meanwhile, not everyone who watched the Checkers experiment was as delighted as they should have been, although I remained blithely unaware of this fact. I led a tremendously hard-working life, underpinned always by the degree of worry and uncertainty that went with living in South Africa in the 1960s. Since Sharpeville the exodus of white skill and capital had continued and, like most couples with young families, Wendy and I wondered whether we too would be wiser to leave.

It was at this time that we sat down to draw up a balance sheet weighing the pros and cons of leaving South Africa or staying here. We listed under 'credits' reasons for staying and under 'debits' reasons for leaving.

The final greater tally of credits showed that in our hearts we not only wanted to stay but believed we could make a worthwhile contribution. We had decided that if our balance sheet came out in favour of staying, we would choose actual goals to work towards, mapping what we wanted to achieve. Wendy's choice was to continue channelling her energies into the teaching programme in Soweto. I committed to creating employment and improving conditions, in so far as was possible, according to how I believed responsible commerce should behave.

An interesting thing, which Wendy reminded me of not so long ago, was that neither the original balance sheet which we drew up reflecting our goals, nor any since, featured 'making money' among our aspirations. No list of short-term goals or long-term objectives we devised has ever mentioned the accumulation of wealth. When we say now that we feel we have achieved our goals, we speak of achieving what we saw as the real, important, meaningful elements of our lives.

At the time of drawing up our first balance sheet, which confirmed on paper the feelings that we belonged *here*, we continued to cling to the conviction that some variation on Michael O'Dowd's theory of economic integration breaking down apartheid *would* eventually happen. As the theory applied to ourselves, we thought that creating employment opportunities for as many people as possible would ultimately have a greater impact than our leaving the country to make a point although, like everyone else, we feared for the future.

Random acts of terror, such as the 1965 bomb explosion in the passenger concourse at Johannesburg station, set by John Harris, who was ultimately executed, affected urban nerves badly. To the north, the last bastions of colonialism were crumbling. After 1965 the civil war in Rhodesia threatened to remove the last friendly buffer between South Africa and the 'hostile' north. All businesses adjusted to having numbers of their white male workforce conscripted into the Defence Force for tours of military duty at any one time.

I still erroneously imagined that my position within the Greatermans Group was being strengthened by the sparkling performance of Checkers. In reality, the buzz in the Greatermans boardroom orchestrated to label me as unmanageable and difficult, even something of a liability, was building to a climax. After my break-up with Greatermans, a lot was said and written about my supposedly 'difficult' personality during the Checkers expansion period, but I know I *wasn't* unmanageable. I do admit that I can be difficult, that I have very firm ideas when I want something, but over and above everything else, I am a team player.

The Greatermans old guard, still old-style department-store men at heart, fretted about food assuming too much importance in the group's merchandise mix. Not only did I see this as wrong, I said it was wrong and refused to follow their misguided judgements. This they could not countenance.

Set down in sequence, it looks as though I should have picked up ominous signs from the attitudes of the Greatermans Board and Norman Herber. This, however, was not so easy to do because I continued to receive as much approval as criticism. In 1965 Norman backed my nomination for the Junior Chamber of Commerce (JAYCEE) 'Outstanding Young Man of the Year' award. He thought that if I won it would boost me personally and attract applications from bright young men leaving universities and looking for a career in retailing.

I wrote my speech for the competition around the 'four legs of the table' theory as I was applying it within Checkers. I was one of four candidates, the young Gary Player was another, and I thought it was a really great day for the *company*, more than myself, when I won. As Norman had hoped, the award did attract new recruits for the Greatermans Group but, again, not everyone was pleased by my success. The undercurrent of envy and friction, tugging at my feet on a daily basis, quickened after the JAYCEE award.

One usual working day during 1965 I picked up the phone to find Jack Goldin on the line. Predating his days as king of the Clicks empire, Jack was interested at that time in developing Cape Town grocery stores in a modern way. Strictly speaking he was the opposition but I remembered how kind and accommodating the Americans had been to me when I wanted to inspect their stores. I told him that he was most welcome to have a look around. I met him at the airport and personally gave him a

tour. Afterwards he said he had been amazed at the courtesy and friendship I had shown him. This event had an unexpected repercussion a little
later, when I ended up acquiring as my own a store into which he had
incorporated all of my best ideas.

Up until 1966 my father had remained on the Board of the Greater-
mans Group, but towards the end of that year his health failed. He died in
Cape Town, soon after the nation had received the shocking news of
Dr Verwoerd's assassination.

I went to Cape Town to arrange my father's funeral and wind up his
affairs, leaving Wendy and the children behind in Johannesburg because
she was very ill in the last stages of her fourth pregnancy. One day, shortly
before I was due to return to Johannesburg, I decided to go for a walk in
Kirstenbosch Gardens, a place of many memories – some good and others
not so good. As I walked around the gardens the day after the funeral, it
suddenly seemed as though I could hear my father's voice echoing off the
mountains saying, 'Come back to Cape Town ... You belong in Cape
Town.' I'll never forget how clear his voice was, and although I'm not a
psychic or anything like that, I do take cognisance of inner feelings, gut
feelings.

When I got back to Johannesburg I told Wendy about my father's voice
seeming to echo from the mountains, telling me to come back to Cape
Town, but at that stage we could make no sense of it.

A couple of weeks later, on Monday 6 October, I was called in to
Norman Herber's office and unceremoniously fired. As I have already
described, it was unbelievably shocking to hear this man, whom I counted
as a friend as well as a colleague, shouting furiously that I was difficult,
unmanageable, out of control and would have to go.

In later, calmer times I could clearly see that there had been a concerted campaign to get leadership of Greatermans exclusively into Herber
hands. I thought there had been honour between our two families since
the original take-over of my father's company in 1946, but Norman had
been fighting a subversive war of succession.

If Norman could have succeeded in welding the Ackerman and Herber
families together, we would have had a wonder business – Checkers was

poised to take the lion's share of the food market. As it was, the chain soon started going down after Norman axed me. Although it was sad to see the thriving chain of Checkers stores wavering under what I saw as mismanagement, if Norman hadn't fired me there would never have been a nationwide Pick 'n Pay.

On that fateful Monday in October 1966 I went downstairs and cleared my desk as instructed, entrusting important papers to Keith Blumgart, who was later to enjoy a long and fruitful career, up to retirement, with me in Pick 'n Pay. Keith was able to deliver my precious papers to my home later. Greatermans did subsequently try to retrieve my personal documents under threat of court action but decided ultimately not to proceed with that line of attack.

With the mocking thought that I had lost Checkers as my father had lost Ackermans chasing round in my head, I said goodbye to my stunned, tearful staff and left the Greatermans building and the career that had been my life, with no more ceremony than if I had been caught and evicted as a common thief.

Marinus Daling, head of insurance giant Sanlam, which would own Checkers at the end of 1985, subsequently described my dismissal from Greatermans as 'the single greatest error in South African business'. To me, on the afternoon of 6 October 1966, it merely seemed like the single greatest blow in my life.

PART TWO

Setting the Table

'You can dream, create, design and build the most wonderful place in the world, but it requires people to make the dream a reality.'
– Walt Disney

CHAPTER 8

90 Percent Guts, 10 Percent Capital

'This', said Wendy, 'is the *best* day of your life, Raymond!'

Wendy was wonderful when I told her that I had been fired. She immediately jumped out of bed, which she wasn't supposed to do since she was so ill, and flung her arms around me. My assets comprised a small inheritance from my late father, minor savings and two weeks' salary from Greatermans – not much to support a wife and family of nearly four children. Even so, Wendy told me that this was just the push I needed to do what I should have done years ago – go out on my own.

Next evening Wendy insisted we should go out to a pre-planned function because it was certain that we would meet some of the Greatermans friends who were part of our social circle. She was similarly insistent, a few days later, that we should attend a dinner marking the first anniversary of the Outstanding Young Men of the Year awards, the first of which I had jointly won after being nominated by Norman Herber, so as not to seem petty. Wendy's insistence that we should appear in public immediately after I had been fired was based on a determination to demonstrate our solidarity and to refute untrue rumours circulating about the circumstances of my dismissal.

But I felt very embarrassed and distressed. The reality of the situation was that I had just about enough in savings and salary to tide us over for three months without drawing on the small inheritance I had from my father. I knew I could use the experience I had gained from building Checkers to start a chain of my own but I lacked sufficient capital. While I brooded about the injustice of my dismissal and the immorality of kicking out a married man with a family, Wendy and some of my friends continued to insist that I should see this setback as an opportunity custommade to turn my entrepreneurial skills to my own account.

My American mentor, Bernardo Trujillo, who had died a short while before, had often sent messages in the past encouraging me to start my own enterprise. Now, as I wondered which way to turn, I was reminded of his tenet – that founding a business takes 90 percent guts and 10 percent capital – a truth I have since seen proven over and over again.

I finally decided that I would give myself three months to cool down and think things through. I had to sort out a future for my family in Johannesburg and take care of my Cape Town family's affairs. Although I wasn't the eldest son, the family had looked to me for leadership since my father's death because my older brother Ken still lived in England.

After Jonathan, our second son and fourth child, was born, Wendy got me a cabinet for filing and we turned the study at home into an office. Here, I spent three frustrating months suspended in a kind of business limbo. True, lots of people did phone wanting me to join them – the Cohen family wanted to talk about me going into their Foodtown chain of stores; someone suggested I go into a handbag factory. I had endless propositions but none of the opportunities sounded right. We even wondered whether this was the right time to emigrate and sent my résumé off to an American-based head-hunter.

One day I took a call from journalist Stephen Mulholland. There had been plenty of press coverage about my dismissal from Greatermans because building the Checkers chain had attracted considerable interest at various times. I had been seen as a young Titan in retailing – at the time of the dismissal I was only 35 years old. Speculation around the reasons for my untimely axing was rife. For their part, the management of Greatermans insisted on propagating the fiction that I had resigned. Stephen wanted my version of events. Was there any truth in rumours of a disagreement between Greatermans and myself over stock? Had my supposedly 'difficult' demeanour been at the root of my ousting?

When we met I gave a perfectly honest account of events. I told him that I had been unceremoniously fired and that the Herber family had become impatient to conclude a long, concerted campaign to rid themselves of Ackerman influence. I was the last obstacle after my father's death and therefore had to go. Those were the plain facts. Towards the end of the interview the topic turned to my future plans. It was then, to my own surprise, that I found myself telling Mulholland that I was going to open my own chain, that this was the beginning of a whole new era.

What can have made me say that, other than bravado? I certainly didn't have anything like enough capital to put into building a chain of my own. But once the words were out of my mouth, it was too late to take them back, particularly as my declaration soon appeared in the national press under a banner headline – 'Ackerman to Open Own Chain'.

Businessmen who read the news started phoning me, offering stores here and stores there. I was surprised and gratified to find that public interest intensified, while the financial press watched and waited. Just as I was beginning to regret my impulsive statement, I received a phone call from my brother-in-law, Issy Fine, in Cape Town, who at least offered some opportunity for action. 'Get on a plane, Raymond,' Issy enthused, 'and come and see a wonderful little chain called Standard Provisions that's going very cheaply.' If Standard Provisions didn't fit the bill, Jack Goldin had three little stores called Pick 'n Pay with a fourth cash store, Suburban Provisions, on the market although at an asking price way out of my league.

As I put the phone down, surprised by the surge of intuitive excitement I felt, a recent conversation flashed into my mind. I had been mulling over my future business options with my friend Ivan Lazarus, wondering whether I really should start a new retail chain, when Ivan suddenly said, 'Look out for a business where the tea's already being made, Raymond.' He meant that I should look out for an existing business that was already trading, where I wouldn't have to start from scratch.

A few days later I flew into Cape Town to look over Issy's finds. It was a Tuesday – always my lucky day – and I had my baby son Jonathan –

always my lucky charm – with me. I handed the baby over to his grand-mother and set off with Issy to look at his first-choice chain, Standard Provisions, on offer at R150 000. Before leaving Johannesburg, I had arranged a facility for that amount with my bank in case I found I shared Issy's enthusiasm. But after we had toured the little chain I had to tell Issy, bargain or not, it wasn't for me. I did want to start a chain of my own, but not with these stores, which were too general. I really wanted to concen-trate on food, start from scratch with a proper supermarket, not take over department stores with small after-thought food sections – the problem at the core of many battles I had fought with Greatermans.

Issy, meanwhile, was treading the path of prudence. He kept reminding me that the price ticket on the remaining purchase option – the three Pick 'n Pay stores and cash store making up Suburban Provisions – was way out of range at an asking price of R620 000. But I was strangely drawn and still anxious to look them over. The fact that these were Jack Goldin's stores struck me as an omen. Jack, you might recall, had contacted me in Johannesburg while I was still in charge of the Checkers chain, to ask if he could tour our stores as he was looking for ideas to incorporate into this very chain of his in Cape Town. I had gone out of my way to make him welcome, to show him around and to share expertise just as my American mentors had done with me.

Now, in an ironic twist, I found myself looking over shops organised precisely according to my own ideas. Jack had put what he had learned from my Checkers stores into practice in the very stores I was now hoping – tremendously – to buy. When I spoke to Jack Goldin that Tuesday in 1966, he told me he wanted to sell because the pressures were too great. He knew his asking price was high but this was what he intended to hold out for. He also suggested a joint partnership as an alternative, but I was still far too bitter after my experiences in Greatermans to want anything other than complete control.

However, I also wanted Jack's business – badly. Once Issy saw that my mind was made up, he took me off to meet with his brilliant young accoun-tant, Harold Gorvy. Harold saw my steely resolve and immediately started working on ways and means. He told me I would have to go back to my bank in Johannesburg to raise extra funds, but that it should also be possible, with my reputation, to enlist the participation of vendors from Johannesburg and Cape Town, to raise loan capital. We arranged to meet with Jack Goldin later that day at Issy's house. All settled down there to plan how we could raise loan capital in such a way as to allow me to keep the control that was so close to my heart.

The hours flew past. It seemed we had only just started talking when Jack Goldin arrived with his advisers. We all sat down around a green baize card table and negotiations started in earnest. Just as he had said he would, Jack held out for his R620 000. Issy and Harold advised me to go in at R580 000, maximum R600 000. Arguments went back and forth, but all the time, with all my being, I could feel how badly I wanted this deal. In the end I said to Jack that I would give him his R620 000, whereupon Issy kicked me so hard on the ankle under the table that it took me a year to get my ankle right.

I offered to settle the asking price as R600 000 cash with R20 000 provided to Jack in the Raymond Ackerman shares I was going to issue. The shares were offered as compensation for Jack helping me in the hand-over of the business. He would work with me for six months while I assembled a team. Jack's advisers were very against allowing him to accept my offer, but he finally decided to follow his own counsel and agreed to my terms of payment. By 1.00 a.m. on the Wednesday morning the deal was done.

This ushered in a period of frenetic activity on our part because now we had to find the money that Jack Goldin and his advisers assumed we had had all along. I was required to transfer the funds on the Friday, so we had only three days.

I hobbled back to Johannesburg on my bruised ankle while Issy swung into action in Cape Town. He took time off from his office to visit thirty different people in the quest to interest potential vendors. In Johannesburg, Ivan Lazarus set about the same exercise, while I drew up a balance sheet reflecting every asset Wendy and I could muster, including the entire R100 000 bequeathed by my father. I presented this to my bank manager and pleaded for backing. I pointed out that even though I wasn't much of a big deal then, I did have a reputation and felt I had a huge opportunity here if I could only fund it. The three little Pick 'n Pay stores in Cape Town formed a great base. I just knew they had to belong to me.

We set about raising stakes of R3 000, made up of R1 500 in capital and R1 500 in loan, from each of 53 original vendors. We said that the interest on the loan would not be paid for the first two years. In other words, loans were interest-free but, as only half the loans were capital, I could keep control. Of the 53 original vendors – 25 from Johannesburg and 28 from Cape Town – Issy directly introduced 23 of the Cape Town contingent.

Organising the funds for Jack Goldin blurred into a few nail-biting days of enormous nervous intensity. When the necessary funds were to hand and I was able to breathe freely again, I suddenly remembered the strange incident in Kirstenbosch Gardens when I had heard the voice of my deceased father telling me to return to Cape Town. As an utmost sceptic when it comes to matters psychic or paranormal, I now knew I had received guidance. I *was* returning to Cape Town.

CHAPTER 9

Into Battle

First thing on the morning of 1 March 1967, I set off from my temporary lodgings at my in-laws' southern suburbs house in Campground Road, and headed for Belvedere Road, Claremont, and my first day at work in the little business I had acquired. I was now the owner of a tiny operation, but one which nevertheless presented me with a tremendous challenge as I had to learn to do everything myself. I had been able to take care of the big, overall picture while I was with Checkers because competent people were taking care of peripheral matters such as property, advertising and, most important, buying.

When I acquired Pick 'n Pay, I didn't know a great deal about buying – *the* crucial component in retailing. I was therefore very pleased that Jack Goldin had agreed to stay for six months to help me with the company, particularly as he was an absolute, if unconventional, master at the art of buying. Jack's buying skills were to tide me over until John Lawley, a big, vibrant, personality-plus Scotsman I had hired from Greatermans for his wonderful, aggressive buying skills, could join me in Cape Town.

In those early days I learned an enormous amount just watching Jack outmanoeuvre the big chains. His real forte was in chicken buying, where he would play intricate games with suppliers, negotiating tough deals when they were at a disadvantage. I didn't always agree with all the tactics, in fact I very often disagreed, but I loved to listen to it all. Jack had an especially wily way of dealing with Des Lurie, supplier of County Fair chickens. Knowing that Des played golf every Wednesday afternoon, Jack would make a point of opening up tough negotiations with the County Fair people at those times. As arguments flew back and forth, frantic County Fair people would keep contacting Des, who was vainly trying to get through his match. In the end, Des would always come on the line, fuming, and tell Jack out of sheer exasperation that he could have his price if Jack would just leave him alone to finish his round in peace.

I had the utmost respect for Jack's talents as a buyer and as a merchant.

If I think back to how I felt right at the beginning of owning Pick 'n Pay, I recall an overwhelming sense of freedom, a sense so exhilarating that negatives simply melted into insignificance. It was such a happy time because I could operate without continuously looking over my shoulder and I could put all my training into practice – especially my ideas on consumer sovereignty. There were plenty of worries but generally it was a tremendously exciting time.

When Wendy had finished tidying up our affairs in Johannesburg, she joined me in Cape Town with the children and we moved into a house which my sister Moyra had persuaded me to buy. The house, Norwood, was situated off Edinburgh Drive, part of the freeway linking Cape Town's southern suburbs with the city. I had voiced my misgivings about living so close to a major thoroughfare – surely it would be terribly noisy? Definitely not, Moyra responded firmly, because noise only travelled *upwards*. While lying awake on our first night at Norwood we discovered that the noise of all the cars roaring up and down the main road, punctuated by screeching tyres and not infrequent crashes, didn't travel upwards – it travelled straight into our bedroom. We were soon on the lookout for somewhere quieter, although we remained at noisy Norwood for just over two years.

At work I was occupied with assembling a team. I had to go through the existing top Pick 'n Pay people to see which of them I wanted to retain – I didn't just want to take over all Jack Goldin's people. Don Cobb, who had a long career with me, becoming one of my directors, was someone I took on from Jack's staff. Otherwise, Keith Blumgart, my staunch friend and ally from Greatermans, came down to the Cape to join me, bringing his great operational and organisational skills and loyalty. I had personally discovered the financial expertise of Mel Jacobson through the unlikely avenue of taking his advice on fund-raising while I was Chairman of my children's nursery school. He now joined me as Financial Director at just about the same time as John Lawley arrived to make his dynamic impact on my company and my life.

The time between Jack Goldin's leaving, after fulfilling his six-month obligation to me, and John Lawley's arrival was a very crucial period for me. After six months of paying close attention to the art of buying according to Jack Goldin, I took on the buying for Pick 'n Pay as an interim measure until John Lawley joined me. Then, he and I set about laying the foundations for Pick 'n Pay's buying strategies. We devised the system of buying forward on a rising market. When prices were rising we would buy forward into warehouses – sometimes purchasing enormous stocks. This meant that when prices went up we could continue to offer goods at the old price. Sometimes we bought such vast quantities that we were able to hold a price for six or even nine months. Customers and our competitors were astonished. The other chains soon came to the conclusion that we were getting special deals, but we weren't.

Once I started navigating the twisted highways and byways of buying on a day-to-day basis, I came to understand how rampant collusion among suppliers, fixed prices and market manipulation were impacting adversely on consumers' pockets, while lining those of the manufacturers and suppliers. Early confrontations we had with supplier organisations, control boards and loose cartels were merely opening skirmishes in the long battle that has been waged on many fronts over decades. Some struggles have taken on epic proportions extending, as in the case of petrol, to the present day.

In the early days we cut our fighting teeth on the issue of Resale Price Maintenance (RPM) regulations, because the practices of fixing prices and regulating supplies under the guise of RPM did not accord with our obligation to offer consumers quality merchandise at affordable prices. If the laws of the retail land, spoken or unspoken, got in the way, they had to be challenged. While I was still so excited and happy with my independence, I decided to tackle issues of price control and regulation, with the admirable back-up of John Lawley, as a priority.

The methods we used to challenge RPM in South Africa were much the same as those that the feisty, mercurial Jack Cohen – maverick, rags-to-riches founder of the British Tesco chain – had used. Tesco took on British lawmakers, who decreed that retailers were not allowed to cut prices, while suppliers were allowed to set prices: precisely the situation here in South Africa. Jack Cohen's Tesco was hauled before courts on numerous occasions during the 1960s, when they defied laws they knew were unfair to consumers. Ultimately they were instrumental in getting RPM taken off the British statute books. Squaring up to tackle RPM in the late 1960s on our own retail turf, I felt like David facing Goliath. The opponent was a giant of formidable stature and considerable resource, while my only weapon was conviction.

Prominent among the giants were the Rembrandt Group and the United Tobacco Company, which between them fixed the price of cigarettes in South Africa and regulated supply. Retailers could only buy through a wholesaler. Insurrection was dealt with conclusively: cut the price of cigarettes, retailers were told, and we will cut off your supplies – for which we have the full support of the law. Retailers muttered and fumed over this blatant form of bullying but mostly took the fixed cigarette price as a fact of retail trading life.

Meanwhile, John Lawley and I planned an upset. We quietly bought up all the cigarettes we possibly could, without telling the suppliers, so as not to alert their interest. This massive buy-in obliged us to take an additional warehouse, into which we packed pile upon pile of cigarette boxes, tying up by far the largest slice of our capital resources at the time. I was petrified of losing the cigarettes, imagining ruin in a pall of smoke unrelated to the purpose of the products. John and I spent two nights guarding the warehouse ourselves, armed with guns like a couple of gangsters. Eventually I persuaded Lloyd's of London to insure our warehouse of cigarettes – no South African insurers were willing to do so – and we were ready to launch our cut-price campaign.

As soon as we did, in November 1967, all hell broke loose. Tobacco companies demanded to know where we had got the cigarettes. They announced ominously that price maintenance was the recognised structure of the cigarette trade and warned that supplies would be cut off if price cutting continued. Our large stockholding neatly disabled that threat.

Manufacturers were enraged. They encouraged national retail chain stores to undercut our reduced prices in an attempt to rein in our rebellion. By July 1968 cigarette manufacturers had resorted to using spies to seek out wholesalers and suppliers suspected of helping us to keep our retail prices down. Some manufacturers even began marking their stock before release in an attempt to trace under-the-counter suppliers. Once our initial stockholding was exhausted, we had to resort to getting cigarette supplies from all sorts of unlikely sources.

In the thick of the first cut-price cigarette campaign, I appealed widely to everybody concerned through the press. I asked the obvious question. If I, as a retailer, could supply the public with cheaper cigarettes, which I was happy to do, why shouldn't I be allowed to? Why should the public be penalised to perpetuate the powers of a monopoly? I also made representations to the government of the day on the cigarette issue. Eventually we triumphed and RPM was withdrawn from cigarettes.

Soon after this success we decided to tackle price control on bread – a product that was the staple food for millions of South Africans. Government had a fixed price for bread which retailers were not permitted to cut. The price fixing was in place to protect the bakers, who all worked together with the government to obtain various subsidies and to set the bread price. As retailers, we believed that we were getting too big a margin as our slice of the profits.

Government response was swift and uncompromising. 'Cut the price', they said, 'and you will be fined R10 for every loaf of bread you sell, because you are challenging government control.' It was a dilemma but we remained convinced that controls over bread prices worked entirely against the interests of consumers. We went ahead and cut the price of bread, and government duly imposed the fine. At that time we sold an enormous amount of bread because the cheaper price was so gratefully accepted by consumers. The amount we 'owed' in fines leaped higher and higher, until paying the fine would have made us go broke.

When I told the press this, they printed headline stories day after day. This was the beginning of the extensive press coverage that was to follow our fortunes as a company for decades. That early media interest also laid the foundations for one of the most common criticisms levelled against me – that I am a publicity seeker. It is true that I have always used media opportunities to promote our principles as a company and my principles as an individual. For the most part, though, my policy for dealing with the media has never deviated since early trading days. I am always available and I always make a point of knowing the facts.

In the late 1960s headlines such as 'Ackerman Against the Minister' reinforced our position as champions of consumer rights and gave us a foretaste of a long fighting future ahead. The press backing we received was tremendously helpful but, of course, we were giving them a good story too. In the first bread price war, the publicity went on for such a long time that the issue was eventually taken up in Parliament. There, members agreed that retailers ought to be allowed to lower the price of bread if they wanted to and, in the end, the Minister responsible was removed.

We certainly notched up some significant successes in early battles over price fixing and controls. Although some of the fights with suppliers were awful – and would remain so – I believe that our stand made those suppliers more efficient. After all, if I didn't have competition with other supermarket chains, I too could have become very comfortable. So we continued to challenge the monopolies and we were instrumental in gradually getting RPM removed on all products except newspapers, which we tried to tackle in the 1970s, and petrol, an ongoing crusade.

As I sat in my little office at the end of 1967 I thought about the world's first heart transplant that had recently been successfully performed by Dr Christiaan Barnard at Groote Schuur Hospital in Cape Town. I felt that the timing was symbolic. For a few months I had been thinking that if little Pick 'n Pay was to stay in healthy circulation, we were going to need a new boost too.

The following year I discovered what that boost was.

CHAPTER 10

Down Diagonal Street

We gathered in the foyer of the President Hotel in Johannesburg and walked together down to the Johannesburg Stock Exchange. Flanked by my lawyers, advisers, various interested friends and family, we were off in a high state of exultation to witness one of the most exciting events of my life. This was the day in September 1968 when my little upstart chain of Pick 'n Pay went public.

Some months earlier, my half-brother Bruce, a University of Cape Town undergraduate, had come to me and asked if he could do a treatise for his degree modelled, hypothetically, on Pick 'n Pay going public. I told him by all means to do it, just as an exercise, because at that time we were far too small a company to consider listing. However, when Bruce brought me his treatise, I read it again and again. It made so much sense. I looked over that model and I thought, *Why not go public?*

Once the seed of the idea was planted, I could see both enormous advantages and practical difficulties. On the one hand, I knew that sooner or later Pick 'n Pay would have to expand, although I had every intention of limiting expansion to the Western Cape for the foreseeable future. When the time for national growth came, I was going to need capital and a flotation was a wonderful way to get it. On the other hand, there was my familiar paranoia – and yes, that's what it amounted to – about losing control. I didn't want to have a public company if it meant that I had to lose control, as both my father and I had done at the hands of Greatermans.

I put the problem to my lawyer, Arnold Galombik, and my accountant, Harold Gorvy. They were both enthusiastic and suggested we should bring their senior partner, Barney Hoffmann, into the discussions so he could devise a scheme to get a greater allocation of shares for the founder – me – enabling me to keep control. Barney advised me to call all my prospective shareholders together, put my cards straight on the table, and tell them that they could buy so many shares, but I would hold a majority.

That done, I couldn't wait to start working on the flotation. I still retained a high profile as a result of my success in building up Checkers. There had been endless articles and photographs in the press and so, even though Pick 'n Pay was still small and only had a presence in the Western Cape, there was a lot of confidence in my potential. Not everyone championed my cause to take the company public but I had a deep-down conviction. Now I had a base, I would build on that. I had no intention of letting the public down.

The economic upswing experienced in South Africa in the 1960s and 1970s accounts for the fact that a company as small as Pick 'n Pay could be listed on the Johannesburg Stock Exchange. After the political insecurities of the early 1960s, foreign investors gradually relaxed and capital that had fled South Africa in panicked haste after Sharpeville, started flowing back. The relative absence of major outbreaks of violence after the early 1960s convinced investors abroad that South Africa was a good risk, despite apartheid. It was something of a paradox that apartheid-governed South Africa was perceived as being stable, because so much of black-ruled Africa was just the opposite.

That same perception allowed the government of South Africa to attract new immigrants – definitely white and preferably Protestant according to government immigration policy – to alleviate the critical shortage of skilled labour that all business and industry were experiencing during the 1960s. Immigrants, mainly from Britain and Europe, were undaunted by prophecies of doom for the apartheid state. They saw opportunity and arrived in their hundreds of thousands.

A 'feel good' factor permeated the entire South African economy at the time Pick 'n Pay went public and the actual day of the flotation was simply breathtaking. We arrived at the Johannesburg Stock Exchange that morning expecting that the share – due to come out at R1,00 – might go up to R2,00 or so. Instead, it shot up, reaching as high as R6,50 at one time. One of my friends sold the shares he had got and bought a house, which he called Pick 'n Pay, with the proceeds. Another friend sold his shares at R6,50, bought a car and then bought his shares back again at R4,50. In a period marked by high-voltage happenings, the September 1968 flotation of Pick 'n Pay on the Johannesburg Stock Exchange was among the most exciting.

Suddenly, Pick 'n Pay was the toast of the country. News of the flotation buzzed along financial wires, generating incredible excitement. For myself, besides having more capital, the most important gain was that I could get myself off the hook of personal guarantees on which I had been uncomfortably hanging. I had signed a number of personal guarantees but my father's dictates and training still exerted a huge influence over my financial attitudes. Now it was a terrific relief to be able to say goodbye to sleepless nights spent worrying about what would happen if I put a financial foot wrong.

Since my acquisition of Pick 'n Pay in 1967, opposition chains had contented themselves with circling lazily at a distance, remaining studiously unfazed and uninterested in my activities. Greatermans *couldn't* show any concern about my endeavours, because that would have indicated that their judgement over firing me had been poor. And while Greatermans ignored me, the OK Bazaars could afford to do the same.

Actually, the first hurdle in the field of opposition that I faced came from Jack Goldin after he had fulfilled the obligation we had agreed upon when I bought the business from him, which was to help me through my first six months in control of Pick 'n Pay. About a year after I had bought Pick 'n Pay, he came to see me, mooting the idea of setting up a chain selling toiletries – health and beauty products – and gifts. While his proposed new venture did not breach the agreement between us that he would not sell food, it would bring us into competition on other lines – and I had paid him a goodwill factor of R20 000 worth of shares and more, to prevent this from happening.

Jack and his family had already hit on a name for their new enterprise, the catchy Clicks – like Pick 'n Pay, a name with nice alliteration. We met at his accountant's office, where he asked me if I would delete the clause in our agreement which said we couldn't compete. I told him that while I had no wish to hold him back or make an enemy of him, there was the matter of the R20 000 worth of shares I had paid him as extra goodwill. It took some close negotiation and concessions on both our parts to reach agreement, but once we did, Jack Goldin's Clicks empire was born. After building Clicks in South Africa, Jack, great merchant that he was, moved to Australia, where he started yet another chain.

While all this was going on, John Lawley and I continued working hard and well together on the building of Pick 'n Pay. By now Wendy had joined us, handling human resources and the social responsibility side of the business. She juggled time dextrously between the growing demands of the business and our children at home. I wrote in a diary entry at the end of 1968 about my plans for Pick 'n Pay: 'I want us to be the leaders in courtesy as well as the leaders in price and efficiency.' I also put down our aims for the coming year as the promotion of black people (so-called non-Europeans in the parlance of the day) to managerial positions, and the doubling of our outlets, but still only in the Western Cape.

The former aim fell under the 'people' leg of the business philosophy on which I was building Pick 'n Pay. Unfortunately, such decisions soon began falling behind an increasingly blurred line dividing business from politics. From that time to this, I've had to accept a great deal of criticism, from outside and within, for getting the company mixed up with issues of political policy. But I have always held that since the political dispensation in South Africa continually impacts on the lives of our people, politics could not but be part of our responsibility towards them.

The first black manager we appointed at Pick 'n Pay was put in charge of our store in Rondebosch, the same southern suburb of Cape Town where, according to one of the uncomfortable compromises of the Group Areas Act, the black Malawian ambassador was 'allowed' to live. Freddy

Overmeyer was efficient, hardworking, charming and committed. He had been promoted to managerial status purely on merit, but his appointment at the Rondebosch store was illegal because a black person was not permitted to be employed at managerial level. The main point about the particular white area in which Freddy Overmeyer worked – Rondebosch – was that many politicians lived there. The wives of Cabinet members or Members of Parliament popped in and out of Freddy's Rondebosch store to do their shopping. As a diligent manager he came to know these ladies well and before long I started to receive letters from wives of The Honourable This or That telling me what a pleasure it was to shop at Freddy's Rondebosch store and how much they liked the cheerful, obliging manager.

Receiving those glowing letters gave me an idea. One day I made an appointment to see Prime Minister John Vorster at his parliamentary offices and I set off with a big batch of the complimentary letters in my briefcase. I told Mr Vorster that we wished to continue employing Freddy as manager at Rondebosch, not least of all because he made so many of our customers happy. I put the pile of letters down in front of the Prime Minister and watched his eyebrows rise as he riffled through them, taking in the signatures of wives of his colleagues. In the end he took off his glasses, fixed me with a shrewd look and said, 'Alright, Mr Ackerman. You can keep your manager at Rondebosch. I won't send in the police, as I should do, but I'm not going to change any laws either.'

Taking stands as a businessman in South Africa has always been complicated. It is impossible to please everyone given the diverse range of race, language, religious and political groupings which comprise the South African public. Issues of politics and business could get inextricably intertwined, such as the time when Islamic fundamentalists issued a confusing pamphlet linking me with Jonas Savimbi of Angola, South African President P. W. Botha, Chief Mangosuthu Buthelezi and American President Ronald Reagan on the grounds that we were all controllers of public taste for the sake of profits.

Still, the policy I put in place from the earliest days went according to the principles of the four legs of the table – the four pillars of retail wisdom

– and caring for people both within the company and in society as a whole fell naturally under the all-important 'people' leg. I could justify a wider involvement because, diverse as they were, the majority of our customers wanted to live in a peaceful country, wanted to avoid bloodshed. I became involved with many issues for the same fundamental reason: I wanted to help steer South Africa away from violent confrontation.

I have always thought that the policy of caring is, in itself, a good one. From the beginning I did not believe in isolation, saw no virtue in being free from mundane matters in order to plan big things like company strategy. Strategy should not be done outside day-to-day business. I made a vow on the first day of owning Pick 'n Pay that I would never be above the ordinary concerns of people. This has advantages just as great for me as for them. Showing concern over the marriage problems of an employee, or the health of someone's child, or the plight of any section of society, is also enlightened self-interest, because the people you have cared for will, in turn, care better for you. I have always fostered this philosophy within Pick 'n Pay, although there were to be times when goodwill seemed decidedly thin on the ground.

In February 1969 I was delighted by a pre-tax profit declaration of R310 000 for Pick 'n Pay in our Western Cape base. I still had no plans to make my chain national and wanted to consolidate our Cape base. But the honeymoon – the first two years when the opposition had left me mostly alone to get peacefully on with consolidating Pick 'n Pay – came to a decisive end later in 1969.

Opposition chains had noted, but chosen not to respond to, the attention that our well-publicised fights over cigarette and bread prices had stirred, but when our listing created such huge excitement, they awoke with a sudden start. When their attack was finally launched it was fought with incredible ferocity. Given that we were still minor league players, operating solely in the Western Cape, the intensity of the pincer attack which national giants Checkers and OK Bazaars launched against us was breathtaking. Between them they instigated a vicious price war, cutting items across the board in their Western Cape outlets to well below cost. It was an orchestrated attempt to push us to the wall and make us go broke.

Their concerted drive to wipe us off the retail map swung into top gear, paying no heed to such niceties as advertising decorum. When Checkers published a newspaper advert showing our Pick 'n Pay name being blasted from a gun, letters flying in different directions as we were shot to smithereens, I took extreme exception and met them in court, winning a judgment in our favour.

The most worrying aspect of the onslaught was the magnitude of the resources ranged against us. Greatermans, through Checkers, and the OK Bazaars could sustain losses in the Western Cape for as long as it took to strangle me, because this was just one area of operation for them. The dilemma for us in our solitary location was that we couldn't lose our image as the Western Cape's discount kings, but if we met their prices we would go broke. As the situation grew ever more desperately worrying I cast about frantically for solutions. The only certainty at that time was the fact that we faced ruination in a war my adversaries could wage as long as it took to destroy us.

CHAPTER 11

Ironic Expansions

'As far as I can see,' said my military strategist friend solemnly, 'your back is right against the wall, and you have only one chance. You've got to make them fight you on two fronts. Just go out and buy something, anything vaguely suitable to get you trading somewhere outside the Western Cape.'

This piece of advice was not easy to accept at first, mainly because I was sticking doggedly to my resolve to consolidate in the Western Cape before expanding elsewhere. But the situation had become increasingly desperate.

As I mulled it all over I remembered receiving a letter from someone named Billy Ryan, saying that he had heard of me and thought I might be interested in a little supermarket in Port Elizabeth he wanted to sell. At the time I had thought the store he offered was far too small to be of any interest but I had replied immediately, thanking him for the offer and telling him I would file his letter away for future reference. Now, I retrieved Billy Ryan's letter, phoned him up and arranged to fly to Port Elizabeth first thing next morning – once again, a Tuesday.

Billy's store in the Walmer district of Port Elizabeth really was tiny, surely too small to be of any use. But my intuition told me not to simply ignore this unprepossessing piece of real estate. When I arrived I had noticed a church hall adjacent to the premises. Could that make a storeroom, which would immediately more than double available space? In no time at all, it seemed, I was talking with the church authorities, who readily agreed to lease the hall. Billy and I met with the Port Elizabeth City Council, which was wonderfully helpful and cooperative. Then I went back to the Walmer store and talked to Sam Miller, owner of the centre where the store was located. Everything fell neatly into place, every part of the negotiations ticked along like clockwork.

I went home to Cape Town that night having closed the deal in one day, exactly as I had bought the first stores in Cape Town. From then onwards I have always savoured the delicious irony that I was pushed unwillingly out into new territory, which in turn set in motion a huge programme of expansion, simply because the opposition wanted to wipe us off the retail map.

If students of business practice need to study an example of how an ill-conceived policy born of bad intentions can backfire, there can be few better examples than the price war instigated by Checkers and the OK Bazaars against Pick 'n Pay in 1969. There was not the slightest intention on their part to cut prices to the bone for the benefit of consumers. Their sole purpose was to break Pick 'n Pay. After I had expanded nationally I made a firm decision never to engage in regional price wars simply to score points against opposition traders. In our stores we would have nation-wide price *promotions*, not wars, and if we could drastically cut a price in Johannesburg we would do the same in Cape Town, Durban and all around the country. Consumers had to benefit from low prices, not us in opposition to other chains.

At the time I opened the Port Elizabeth store, there was already speculation in financial circles that saturation point was approaching in supermarket turnovers – a mistaken premise to say the least. Individual amounts that consumers were spending seem incredibly low by today's standards. In 1969 I made a special diary entry recording a customer's record buy for R159,00.

As soon as I acquired the Walmer store in coastal Port Elizabeth, we started trading with opening special prices cut to the bone. As a result, Checkers and the OK Bazaars were obliged to lower their prices too but, just as in the Western Cape, they had to offer the same cut prices in each and every one of their Eastern Cape outlets. Heavy losses had to be shouldered, all because the one little store we owned was on the local scene and doing well.

Now they were losing money in the Eastern *and* the Western Cape and such losses were too high to sustain. Quietly, the war began to ease up. My military friend's words of wisdom had worked, and I had once again confirmed for myself the importance of listening and learning from other people – 'keeping one's ear so close to the ground that the grasshoppers can jump in' – as Bernardo Trujillo sagely put it. For the time being, the opposition decided to lick their wounds and leave me alone.

As to our overall position at the end of the volatile 1960s, we had been voted forty-second out of the top one hundred companies in a newspaper poll, right in the thick of the price onslaught against us. The price war had hurt us, and hurt us badly, but we never dropped profit, nor indeed ever would until, for a short time, we were overtaken by purely extraneous events in 1994. In the early 1970s resources from the flotation also helped to keep us bobbing along fairly buoyantly while the price attack persisted.

Not all events in the early years after I took over Pick 'n Pay were quite so serious as the commodity and price wars. Some were pure fun. Early in 1969, I decided to have what we called a Mad Chicken Day in the Cape Town stores. I bought tens of thousands of chickens for the stores and put them on sale at 8½ cents a pound for a 3½ pound chicken. Previously, the lowest price ever charged for frozen chicken had been 15 cents a pound. It turned out to be an absolutely amazing day. The public just went mad. The newspapers reported on Cape Town's frantic chicken rush, picturing crowds queuing for blocks, holding up traffic. Queues outside one store even stretched into the next suburb. Clamouring consumers formed lines outside our stores hours before opening time. As soon as the doors opened, people stampeded to chicken counters to snap up the bargains that Wendy and I, John Lawley and colleagues had spent most of the night marking, cursing as we tried to deal with the slippery, frozen birds in our numb hands.

By the end of the Mad Chicken event, noses among other retailers and chicken suppliers were severely out of joint. No one was happy – except, of course, Cape Town consumers. The Mad Chicken Day really caught their imagination. I was particularly pleased about the event because I had been able to conceive an exciting idea and put it into practice according to my own intuition and initiative without a disapproving Board crying caution in the background.

On the night of 29 September 1969 the Western Cape town of Tulbagh was shaken by an earthquake, which destroyed a large part of it. The tremors that shook Tulbagh were sufficiently severe to send shockwaves clear across 130 kilometres to Cape Town, where our 12-year-old son Gareth felt the vibrations and picked up the news of the earthquake. He burst into our bedroom, vivid with excitement, calling, 'Dad, Dad, quick, let's rush into town to get the wording of tomorrow's ad changed to something to do with the earthquake.'

We rushed to the St George's Street offices of the *Cape Times*, where we begged the Foreman to make changes before the morning print run on the newspaper started. It was by then late at night and the Foreman was not easily persuaded. Our insistence, and perhaps the promise of a bottle of whisky, finally did the trick. That's how, the very next morning, the newspaper appeared with our adverts headed 'Earth Quake Prices' and such like.

The adverts caused something of a sensation, but after it became known that nine people had died and a large part of Tulbagh was destroyed, we were heavily criticised for cashing in on a disaster. Still, it was quite a brainwave coming from my 12-year-old son.

Early in 1970 we moved to a new house on a beautiful estate in the Constantia Valley, where we still live thirty years later. I had first looked at the property early in the 1960s on one of my trips to Cape Town for Checkers. Although I didn't have any money, or much time at that stage, I did phone an agent and finally bought the land for R12 000 in borrowed money. It turned out to be a significant purchase, because two years later I had lost my job at Greatermans, precipitating our move to Cape Town.

* * *

Once the family had settled into our new home I turned my attention to further territorial expansion for Pick 'n Pay. The move to Port Elizabeth had convinced me that in order to protect ourselves from future opposition attacks, we had to become much more of a national presence. Rubbing a lamp to conjure up the means to outmanoeuvre my adversaries had loosed the genie of expansion and, once out, he wouldn't go back in. I decided that it was time to tackle Johannesburg.

I flew up there and immediately got together with architects Len Bentel and Dennis Abramson, who ran an independent architectural practice. I had first met this talented pair while we were all working for Greatermans. After I acquired Pick 'n Pay, I asked Len and Dennis if they would do architectural work for me, although I realised this was asking them to take a huge gamble on an unknown future. Working with me would obviously rule out further work with Greatermans, a rich source of commissions. Still, they thought they would take the chance and agreed to join me. Over the years we achieved some great things between us and they were our company architects through huge phases of expansion.

In 1970 we set about securing the site for our first Johannesburg store. We had to have the perfect location for our thrust into South Africa's eco-nomic powerhouse city. As it happened, we secured a site I had first identified as one with potential while I still worked for Greatermans. It was called Darras Market Gardens in the Kensington area of Johannes-burg. I went to see the owner and told him that although we were a relatively new company, we were going places. I had to talk long and hard to get him to agree and not wait for responses from OK Bazaars and Checkers, to whom he had also been talking about the site.

We built a lovely centre deep in the heart of opposition territory. The Johannesburg venture was crucial from numerous points of view, so it was essential that I had the best possible team running it. I had made a few mistakes with staffing Port Elizabeth, which persuaded me to put my top man – John Lawley – in control. Opening in Johannesburg, I needed a sea-soned campaigner like him, and I thought it would be possible to split our operation successfully between Cape Town and Johannesburg.

The opening of the Darras store was a hugely exciting event. John Lawley and I had to throw our net wide to attract enough quality people to staff the important new outlet. Among them, we had picked people for our deli, meat and fish sections who came from behind the genteel counters of the select grocery store Thrupps, as well as some from the food ranks of Greatermans. The day the doors opened at Darras in May 1970, crowds just poured in. The public remembered me from my Checkers days and were curious to see my new Johannesburg store and snap up the bargain buys. The poor former Thrupps and Greatermans people simply couldn't cope with the crush, unheard of in the dignified foodhalls they hailed from. Their response was to walk out; mine was to send an SOS to my secretary in Cape Town, telling her to hire a plane from South African Airways, pack it full of all the deli, fish and meat people she could muster, and fly them up to Johannesburg.

Next to fall by the wayside was the man I had chosen to head the Darras store. I had clearly hired the wrong person again, just as I had done in Port Elizabeth, in both cases choosing men who could not handle the intense pressure that went with opening a new store. When it seemed the staff situation couldn't worsen, John Lawley collapsed on opening day with a back problem caused by lugging great bags of cut-price sugar around. Then the accountant I had brought up from Cape Town went down with hepatitis.

In the middle of all this, with the public streaming through the doors, I received a terse phone call from a customs official at the airport. As one of our Darras opening specials I had advertised live crayfish, fortunately with the forethought to arrange for a second batch to arrive on the afternoon of opening day. It was this second batch of crayfish which formed the subject of the irate official's call: the crate containing them had burst open, releasing dozens of the crawling crustaceans onto the airport floor. I jumped into my car and rushed out there. I found everything in a terrible mess, with women standing stranded on tables, while the crayfish walked all over the floor. Now, I'm quite a squeamish guy myself, but there was nothing for it – I had to go round systematically picking up and repacking the squirming crayfish before rushing back with them to the store, flinging profuse apologies over my shoulder to the ladies as I left.

The plane-load of relief staff arrived that night, so luckily no one but we knew that we had suffered a collapse on our opening day at Darras. A brighter story to emerge from this opening concerned the young son of a Greatermans director who had been recruited to work for us. The Roumanoffs were related to the Russian Imperial family. More important from our point of view, Mike brought his mother along to help us on opening day at Darras, so we had the son and wife of a Greatermans director in our camp, so to speak. Mike told us that when the Greatermans staff heard about our opening, they poured into the store to bargain-hunt. As a result, the floor of the Greatermans directors' office suite disappeared beneath a vast assembly of Pick 'n Pay bags containing staff purchases. The sight of such sacrilege apparently sent Norman Herber into a state of apoplectic rage, fuelled by the stubborn insistence of his staff that Pick 'n Pay's prices beat those of Checkers.

Because of the many staff problems, for the next few days I had to take charge of the Darras store. As it turned out, having to take control of the first Johannesburg store proved to be prophetic, because I was to find myself in exactly the same position four years later at the opening of our first hypermarket.

When I bought Darras I knew that putting in a buying team and an accounting team could only be cost-effective if I opened more stores, thereby creating a chain. So with Darras up and running and new outlets opening in the Western and Eastern Cape, I moved to set up a second Johannesburg store in a little-known, out-of-town location called Blackheath. At that time too, copy-cat stores whose owners traded under the name Pick 'n Pay opened up every so often. It was still too soon for me to be able to prove, as I could later, that the imitators were 'passing themselves off' as my original. If you were a small chain in Cape Town you could open up in Johannesburg and call yourself Pick 'n Pay and I could not stop you unless I had enough publicity to prove that you were using my name because people knew the name. In the early days I couldn't stop businessmen opening up stores with our name because I couldn't *prove* that they knew our name.

I began to get alarmed when stores using our name opened in places where we had no presence. This meant that the impostors were there first and – crazy as it seemed – we would not be able to open under our own name. There was a particular rash of copy-cat openings in Natal, so I had to go down to Durban with my lawyer and pay various Indian traders a sum of money to close down. I really had no choice, because I knew we would want to be in Natal in the near future, as indeed we were. I also had to pay a few people to close down in Johannesburg in the early days, but that soon stopped after we became known nationally.

Our national presence in South Africa didn't stop imitators from trying their luck outside the country. One man opened a Pick 'n Pay store in Zimbabwe – then Rhodesia – complete with an exact replica of our logo. I went rushing up there with my lawyer, but he got away with it because his lawyers insisted that as we were two different countries, 'passing off' could not be proven. Thanks to his actions we were completely blocked and prevented from founding what would have become a whole chain, although we are in Zimbabwe today under another name.

When I took up the site in Blackheath for our second Johannesburg store, everyone thought I was mad to move so far from the centre of town. But sites were simply not available in built-up areas, mostly because they were already taken by other chains. All I could do, really, was to move further out, as they did in America, and hope people would come.

My move to open a second Johannesburg store prompted the OK Bazaars and Greatermans to lobby government about placing a restriction on the number of new supermarkets allowed to open. Once before, while I was in charge of Checkers, Norman Herber had sought to implement an agreement between Greatermans and the OK Bazaars – represented at that time by the respected legal luminary Isie Maisels, who was taking a break from his usual practice of law to 'relax' in retailing – which would have allowed the two groups to put down stores according to pre-arrangement between themselves. The purpose of this arrangement was to protect the profits of the two chains, but of course by so doing they would have formed a cartel. I opposed the plan strongly, although my position did not give me the right to do so, and nothing finally came of that proposal. Legislation to restrict the number of new supermarkets already existed in Europe but there it was aimed at keeping supermarkets below a certain size in order to protect small traders. While the South African lobbyists tried to say that many supermarkets trading in competition went against the interests of consumers, of course the opposite is true. The real aim behind the local lobby was to limit our expansion.

Although the big OK Bazaars and Checkers chains formed my main opposition, they were far from being the only players on the 1970s retail food stage. In Johannesburg, Trevenna, Goldfields and Foodtown were present too. Events in Cape Town – the bitter price war, and now moves to persuade government to place controls on supermarket trading – had tended to concentrate my attention on OK Bazaars and Checkers. But as I was concentrating on the big players, the bit players were concentrating on me.

CHAPTER 12

Stores Do Burn

The scene was surreal. Surely I was imagining this? One moment I was standing on an ordinary street in residential Pretoria, the next I seemed to have strayed into a Hollywood film lot where shooting of a 1930s-style Mafia movie was in progress.

A few days earlier I had been surprised to receive a phone call from one Mimie Kakouris, a member of the Greek family who owned the Trevenna food stores in Johannesburg. I knew that his group had a store near Darras, where I had just opened our first Johannesburg branch, and in Blackheath, where we planned to open our second. Mimie said, not ominously but in a friendly, if forceful, way, that he would like to meet me. I couldn't imagine why he wanted to see me, but arranged nevertheless to meet him outside the Belfast store in downtown Pretoria, from where I would be driven to his home.

'By the way, Raymond,' said Mimie before ringing off, 'make sure you come on your own, will you?' I wondered why this didn't sound like a request.

So, alone as instructed, I made the mysterious rendezvous and was taken off to his house in the suburbs of Pretoria. We entered through the garage, which led directly into an entrance hall, a dimly lit area wreathed in cigarette smoke, with a card table in the centre around which a group of cloned henchmen sat playing cards. Each of them wore a white shirt with wire armbands holding up the sleeves. There were several bottles of whisky in the middle of the table together with their card game stakes. 'Hi Boss,' they intoned in perfect unison as Mimie and I entered.

I was chivvied – probably the best word to describe it – into an adjoining room where Mimie and I were joined by his lawyer. I heard the key being turned from the outside – I was locked in the windowless room with Mimie and his sinister-looking retainer. It was suddenly quite chilling.

Mimie got straight down to business. 'Raymond, you are a Cape Town boy – that is your territory and that is where you should have stayed. But no, you've chosen to come up here and poach on my territory, and I don't like it. But', he went on, 'I'm going to give you an opportunity to make things right. I want you to buy out my business. You take over my stores and I'll leave you alone. I want your answer now, and you're not getting out of this room until I have it.' On cue, the well-trained lawyer produced an agreement with a theatrical flourish, handed me a pen and tapped impatiently at the paper to indicate where I should sign.

I had recovered my wits a bit by this time but I was petrified. However, sounding a lot braver than I felt, I told them I refused to sign the contract, insisting that the door should be opened. I said I had every right to open stores wheresoever I chose. Mimie observed me in silence for a long time while I concentrated on staring back, hoping to communicate a strength of purpose I didn't really feel. In the end, my captor sighed, with the attitude of one who has done his best for an ungrateful charge, only to be spurned. 'Very well,' he said, 'if you refuse to sign I will let you leave, but you must go away knowing that mysterious things do happen to buildings; sometimes they flood, sometimes they burn.' He flicked open the flame of his cigarette lighter and nonchalantly lit up, keeping his eyes unblinkingly on mine. 'Will you remember that, since you've turned down my generous offer?'

I was driven back to the centre of town by one of the clones, through the leafy garden suburbs of Pretoria, through Church Square where Oom Paul Kruger's statue surveyed the city from his granite pedestal. When I told John Lawley and Wendy, among others, about events at Mimie's house I realised how difficult it would be to get people to believe such an unlikely incident. Rumours were already rife that a number of small food-store chains were either in serious trouble or not doing well. This helped to explain Mimie's strategy to off-load his stores onto me. But nothing further happened immediately, and soon more pressing events pushed the chilling incident in Pretoria out of my mind.

Since March 1970 I had been seeing Secretary Joep Steyn, a humourless government official who epitomised the unbending Afrikaner civil servants then running our country according to the Nationalist book. I had been talking to Secretary Steyn about the worst spate of price increases for 16 years in South Africa, which I believed – and proved – were partly caused by manufacturers jumping on the bandwagon of metrication, then being phased in, to up their prices. There were other factors impacting on food price increases too, not the least of which was a terrible drought in the Cape Province. Mostly, however, collusion was to blame.

I had compiled an 82-page report on the culpability of the food manufacturers in price hikes, which Secretary Steyn was studying. The food manufacturers, predictably, reacted to my accusations angrily, but they couldn't refute the accuracy of the case I made. From then on, I was hated by suppliers, because *I* hated the way they colluded together. Lawrence McCrystal was then head of the Grocery Manufacturers' Association and with him I was eternally in conflict. We clashed over issue after issue. There was no umbrella body representing retailers, but when I spoke up I was doing so for consumers and not for fellow traders. It is a fact that the other big food retailers in South Africa – Checkers, OK Bazaars and even Woolworths – did hardly anything at all in battles for the rights of consumers.

But when I went head-to-head – alone – with the authorities over the issue of General Sales Tax, later Value Added Tax (VAT), levied unfairly on basic foodstuffs, over cartels and collusion and unjust controls, I nearly always attracted a lot of publicity for these causes. That, in turn, made people, particularly people from rival chains, mark me out as a publicity seeker, but in my opinion the accusation was not fair.

I didn't get involved in clashes to be a knight in shining armour. I did it because I believed in it, because if consumer sovereignty was to mean anything, we had to fight for consumers. As Professor Hutt taught me, ordinary consumers are virtually powerless against big business and government the world over. Those bodies with vested interests in keeping cartels alive and kicking in South Africa's retail sector felt no constraints about planting their versions of facts into the listening ears of people in high places. Lawrence McCrystal, for instance, was a friend of our later Minister of Finance, Owen Horwood, who, you might recall, had been one of my lecturers in my undergraduate days. When battle was joined over the imposition of VAT on basic foodstuffs, I would give Horwood facts from the point of view of consumers while Lawrence McCrystal would pitch stories from the manufacturers' point of view.

By the time Secretary Steyn and I came to the end of the contacts we had during 1970 over the effect of metrication on food prices, we had become quite friendly and reached agreement on most of the basic points. The main body of the National Party had anyway been more preoccupied with the general election campaign they were fighting that year than with issues of food. The 1970 election resulted in a sixth re-election to government since 1948 for the Nationalists, but this time with a reduced majority.

I settled into a routine of commuting between the Cape and Johannesburg and always seemed to be ruffling some official feathers. We caused great consternation, for instance, among members of the Transvaal Chamber of Commerce by putting our Transvaal female employees on to a five-day week with one afternoon a month off. Unheard-of leniency, they thought, and likely to open all kinds of unwelcome floodgates holding back worker demands. Wendy and her team had been working hard at one of the first schemes to provide houses for black employees in the Cape. As 1970 came to an end, I was delighted by a balance sheet which came out way above anticipation.

During 1970, while the expansion of Pick 'n Pay was steadily gaining momentum, events of enormous future importance were unfolding around us. To the north, Ian Smith declared Rhodesia a republic, following his 1965 Unilateral Declaration of Independence. South Africa, Portugal and Greece were the only countries to maintain relations with the rebel republic on our doorstep.

At home, the Bantu Homelands Citizenship Bill had been introduced which made all black South Africans into citizens of their tribal homelands, whether they lived there or not. This was part of the drive to entrench one of apartheid's main tenets – that all black people should be no more than temporary sojourners in white cities.

Although I didn't recognise it as such when it happened, one event in 1970 had enormous implications for future developments in my life. In May the International Olympic Committee officially withdrew its recognition of the South African National Olympic Committee. Our international isolation as a sporting nation began in earnest after Mr Vorster stopped the black Cape Town-born cricketer Basil D'Oliveira from coming out to play for England against South Africa. Nor would he allow the Maori players in the New Zealand rugby side to compete in South Africa. A few years later Sports Minister Piet Koornhof announced a relaxation of apartheid rules, allowing multi-racial competition at national and international events, while retaining separation at local and provincial levels. The rest of the sporting world treated this with the contempt it deserved, and kept South Africa in sporting quarantine.

While I was preoccupied with the ever-increasing workload that went with the rapid expansion of Pick 'n Pay, someone armed with a pickaxe crept stealthily into a services area of our Darras store in Kensington, Johannesburg, and broke open a water main. When staff arrived the next morning, water was pouring out of the doors. The store was completely flooded by a clear act of sabotage.

'Stores, Raymond, do flood.'

Then, on the night of 26 February 1971, I was woken in the early hours of the morning at our Cape Town home by the insistent shrilling of the telephone. I answered groggily, and heard the voice of John Barry, a Transvaal man of ours, coming breathlessly over the wires. 'Mr Ackerman, Blackheath is burning. I can see it all illuminated by the light of the moon.' I told him I didn't think he needed to be quite so poetic about the disaster, but before he could wax more lyrical, John Lawley came on the phone. He could see, he said, that the store was going to burn to the ground, even though the fire services were at that very moment racing to the scene. 'But listen, Raymond,' he said, 'you are not to worry, because I promise you we'll be open for business tomorrow morning.'

'Stores, Raymond, do burn.'

Next morning I flew up to Johannesburg to survey the wreck of what had been our promising Blackheath store. It was now a smouldering heap of blackened debris. But, to my utter astonishment, John Lawley, that marvellously talented innovator, had been as good as his word. In the dead of the previous night he had arranged for a marquee to be erected next to the burnt-out building. Delivery vans already queued to offload the stock that John had hauled startled suppliers out of their beds to organise during the night. He had already rigged up a check-out near the entrance to the tent. Inside, people worked as though possessed to connect tills and fridges.

By 10.00 a.m. that morning, the Blackheath tent annexe of our burnt-out store was up and running and trading. We had the best Fire Sale Johannesburg had ever seen. John Lawley's achievement has to go down as one of the most remarkable organisational feats in modern retailing. It was sheer genius fuelled by sheer guts and I was filled with admiration for this brilliant friend and colleague of mine.

Wendy has subsequently remarked that it is almost impossible today to comprehend the lengths to which our opposition were prepared to go in the early days to close down Pick 'n Pay. About ten years after the flooding of Darras and the burning of Blackheath I found out, by chance, that there had even been a plan to close *me* down – permanently. I chanced to talk to someone who told me that she had actually been present at a meeting when there was an attempt to take out a 'contract' on my life. The would-be assassin was apparently offered a fee of R10 000, big money in those days, to take me out, but he demanded more. The backers, however, didn't think it was worth paying more than R10 000 for my life – which was fortunate indeed for my future health.

If I escaped the era of serious attacks on my expanding venture with my life, my mother, Rachel, was not so lucky. She had continued to live a reclusive life as a sad and unhappy woman since the divorce from my father, although Wendy's generous efforts had helped her to understand that I had only been a manipulated child in the awful divorce fight between her and my father. But quietly she worried and fretted about me. When I expanded Pick 'n Pay into Johannesburg, my mother worried more because she thought that I was expanding too rapidly, that I was being over-ambitious and that all I had built could go up in flames – her metaphor for the failure she feared I would suffer.

The day after the fire at Blackheath, my mother was found sitting upright in a chair, dead from a heart attack. On her lap was a newspaper, open at a report on the Blackheath fire beneath a graphic picture of the blaze. It must have seemed that what she most feared, my ruin, had happened; her prophecy had come true.

CHAPTER 13

The Boundaries of Loyalty

The Krok twins, Abe and Solly, being product-formulating pharmacists as well as retailers, were equally at home among laboratory test-tubes as they were in the boardroom of their retail chain, Goldfields.

One day the Krok brothers made a twin appearance in my office to sound me out about buying their Goldfields chain. I talked the proposal over with John Lawley and, on the whole, we liked the idea very much. With the stores we had already opened, acquisition of the Goldfields outlets would give us an instant chain. Negotiations began in earnest, with John handling the exploratory work in Johannesburg until a deal was finally struck.

On the morning the take-over was due to come into force, my accountant asked the Krok twins to hand over leases for the stores we planned to buy. A considerable sum for goodwill had been included as part of our deal: in such negotiations, this is what is paid for the take-over of leases. The leases are what you are actually buying – leases for five years, ten years or whatever – when you buy a retail business. But when we asked for the leases we proposed buying, they were not to hand. 'Have you got the leases?' Abe asked Solly. 'No,' replied Solly looking perplexed; 'you must have them, Abe.' Rather than engaging in a long debate as to where the leases might be, we lost patience and left.

In terms of normal business procedure money had not changed hands because my people had not seen the leases we were buying. Therefore, we decided that all we had wasted was time. We decided simply to walk away from the deal and leave it at that.

I got on with the day-to-day business of running my ever-expanding Pick 'n Pay chain, noting in my diary that this was a very pressurised time, with student protests and police attacks. I was dismayed when police raided NUSAS, the National Union of South African Students, an organisation I had represented and worked for while I was at university. The raids on NUSAS and various church organisations were a sign of the times, as was Mr Vorster's announcement, at the first press conference ever given by a South African Prime Minister, that he would be willing to discuss South Africa's separate development policy with black African leaders.

In spite of his reputation as a hard, uncompromising man, I had good dealings on the whole with John Vorster during his tenure as Prime Minister, although along with another minister, Chris Heunis, he often made business a target for stinging criticisms. But at those times, like all politicians, he had one eye on the issue at hand and the other on his constituents, his voters, to see that they were being kept content. Certainly, though, Vorster was not as dour and unsmiling as he's been painted and he recognised the need for change long before it became expedient to do so.

One evening in early August 1972, as we were getting ready to take our children out for a Japanese dinner, Wendy was called to the phone. She was gone for some time and I remember that when she came back she looked preoccupied. She said nothing about the call she had taken but bustled around, chivvying us all out to the car for our dinner outing.

Next morning, a Sunday, a bombshell exploded.

The call Wendy had taken the night before came from a highly distressed John Barry – this time not reporting on a fire. Knowing how devastated I would be by the news he had to give, he had decided to speak to Wendy instead. She chose to keep the news from me until the following morning, but had booked a flight to take me to Johannesburg as soon as I knew.

What had apparently happened was this. After we had walked away from the proposed Goldfields deal, John Lawley had been called to a meeting with the Kroks in the Johannesburg suburb of Hillbrow. There, the Kroks had sat him down and begun mapping out conditions of a highly lucrative employment contract if he would agree to join their Goldfields chain. There is, of course, nothing unusual about the practice of head-hunting in business, and it is usual to offer attractive incentives. However, in the case of John Lawley he had incentives of his own to offer. He could access all the private information relating to confidential discounts, all information on our running systems, our suppliers – everything intrinsic to the operations of Pick 'n Pay. In addition to accessing the entire functional life-blood documentation of my company, John was in a position to initiate a recruitment drive of his own to persuade other colleagues to join his defection to Goldfields. It was just such an approach to another senior member of my staff that resulted in the tip-off which alerted me to the actions of my former friend and closest colleague.

As I have always understood it, John at first refused to be tempted by the fabulous incentives he was offered. He was, after all, not only my friend but a recent beneficiary of a large share allocation, which was already worth a fortune, so successful had our enterprise become. But eventually he succumbed and later came surreptitious into our offices and systematically started making copies of reams of confidential information. Some of the pending deals between Pick 'n Pay and our suppliers, confidential discounts, were still only in John's head – I have previously said what a brilliant negotiator he was.

At this time, the first concerted rumblings against the supposed power that supermarkets wielded over poor suppliers were gaining momentum. I was to engage in many debates – a notable televised one pitting me against Checkers Managing Director, Clive Weil, made broadcasting history in the 1980s – over what were called confidential discounts – a term I have never liked. I prefer to call this type of arrangement between us and suppliers an *incentive*, mainly because it sounds as though a confidential discount goes into your pocket, which it doesn't.

What an incentive does do is go towards bringing prices down for the consumer. These incentives came to be known as *confidential discounts* because big suppliers like Lever Brothers, for example, would obviously not want Checkers to know what they were giving us at Pick 'n Pay, nor us to know what they were giving Checkers. Incentives were, and are, generally structured around an additional percentage being given by the supplier on sales of his product, over and above the normal discounts offered, and they form part of the negotiating process between suppliers and retailers. There is absolutely no doubt that incentives do ultimately benefit the consumer.

At the time of John Lawley's defection a number of incentives were at sensitive stages in the negotiation process. The details of these pending deals were all in John's head. It would have been terribly damaging to Pick 'n Pay's relationships with suppliers, which had to be good and trusting if we were to maintain our core ideal of consumer sovereignty, were sensitive information to have leaked from our offices into the hands of another chain.

Immediately on arrival in Johannesburg that grim Sunday in August 1972, I went to John Lawley's house and confronted him with what I knew. I was astonished to find him brazen and unrepentant; he said he didn't care tuppence for loyalty or friendship or trust; he cared only about himself and his own financial well-being. It was his insistence that he was motivated solely by financial gain that gave me the vital clue I needed to decide on a course of action. Thinking on my feet, I mentioned that it would be perfectly possible for me to arrange the repatriation of the very large, very valuable batch of shares I had recently allocated to him. I caught a speculative gleam in his eye – he knew very well what those shares were worth and had obviously, unbelievable as it was, banked on keeping them in his own coffers after his defection to Goldfields.

To capitalise on my only advantage, I told John that if he would agree to meet with me the next day to give me back all the information he had taken, as well as that in his head, I would consider letting him keep the shares. I also said that I would decide, based on how cooperative he proved to be, whether or not to take him to court for his theft from our offices. He agreed, not having much choice, I suppose, and we arranged a time for the meeting.

Next day, I sat John down in front of a secretary and listened as he spilled what seemed to be all the stolen information, which was in his head, onto a series of tapes. When he finished, I pressed him to rack his brains in case he had overlooked anything or forgotten something vital. Finally, he said he had taped every bit of the information I wanted back as well as all the details of pending negotiations.

'Now,' he said, 'what about my shares?'

I let a good few minutes go silently past. 'I didn't say that you *would* get your shares, I told you that I would consider it,' I said. 'Well, I have considered, and my decision is that you're *not* getting any shares from me. Shares in this company are for loyal people, not traitors like you.' He was still spluttering in protest when I showed him the door and invited him to use it. 'One more thing before you go: I will look forward to seeing you in court.'

I knew that I had hit John where it hurt most, but I suffered no remorse for withdrawing the shares. I had behaved towards him in the only way possible and the whole horrible incident would stand as an example of what I would do, however much of a nice guy I seemed on the surface, if crossed. No matter how sick and sad I was feeling inside, I had to make that show of strength.

We did bring a court action to prevent John Lawley from going to work for Goldfields, which we were able to do in terms of his employment contract. The confrontation attracted considerable press interest until an out-of-court settlement was finally reached. However, all sorts of related dramas unfolded prior to the settlement. At one time, John disappeared and went into hiding to avoid having papers served on him.

I have never felt so sullied as I did by all those ugly events around John Lawley. No single act of treachery or betrayal had, or has since, hit me so hard. At the end of the Lawley saga, with Pick 'n Pay still rapidly expanding, I wrote in my diary, 'nothing comes easily. My major job at this time is to watch attitudes, stress loyalty, to ensure the company is run positively on all fronts.'

Some years later I was shocked to learn that John Lawley was dying of a brain tumour. The big, hearty Scotsman with his booming voice and vibrant personality, a hard-living, hard-drinking dynamo, was struck down in the prime of his life. When I heard what was happening to John, I thought I had at long last found a possible reason for his actions against me. I believe it was the beginnings of the brain tumour that made him act so irrationally, so uncharacteristically. Before he died, the lady John planned to marry contacted me and I made arrangements to visit him. Unfortunately, he died before I got to see him. Although I left the decision to attend up to personal consciences, quite a number of John's ex-colleagues from Pick 'n Pay joined me at his funeral. In his memory, I made provision for the education of his children.

I choose to remember John Lawley for his vibrancy, his incredible energy, talent and verve for trading. His stunning achievement in getting us back in business, trading from an adjacent tent hours after fire destroyed our store in Blackheath, Johannesburg, is his most fitting memorial.

* * *

Loyalty is a massively important issue for me. I see loyalty as a state of mind, a stand, a condition without blurred edges, degrees or room for deviation. I learned hard lessons from the actions of those people who came running to ask favours, expecting loyalty for a shared past, when they had betrayed me as a nobody Jewish schoolboy before I became successful and well-off. Loyal business relationships, like personal relationships, are absolute and unchanging to me, no matter how big my business has become.

When I first acquired Pick 'n Pay, Jack Goldin retained the services of a little company called Hedley Byrne to handle his advertising. They were a small company with Robin Summers as Chairman. Robin is Sean Summers's father – Sean, prime player in the heart-wrenching happenings within my company that are chronicled towards the end of this book.

When I first knew him, Robin Summers was an older man, very English, very polite, very old school. He was the respected partner of David Buirski, a young man who was terrifically adventurous, imaginative and different. Robin and David, chalk and cheese, complemented each other perfectly with their balance of skills. I liked them immediately and told Jack Goldin that even though I had been used to dealing with big, high-profile advertising agencies with Greatermans, I intended retaining the services of the Hedley Byrne team.

David proved especially terrific because he was rare in recognising the excitement of retail advertising. Mostly, retail work is just tolerated for its money-making volume but is looked down upon as an inferior avenue for creative expression. In its present-day guise, the ad agency evolved from the original Hedley Byrne company still handles Pick 'n Pay's advertising, only now they manage an adspend in the multi-millions of rands.

In the business of banking I also established an early, ongoing loyalty. Jack Goldin was with Trust Bank when I bought Pick 'n Pay from him, while my family was with Standard Bank. In those days Trust Bank was being powered by the young, very ambitious Jan Marais. He was doing such exciting things in banking, pioneering a break-away from the hold that old-guard banking cartels had on charges and services. Jan Marais was a maverick. In opposing the powerful banking cartel, the philosophy of Jan Marais's free-spirited enterprise accorded perfectly with my own.

Standard Bank had been very good about helping finance the initial purchase of Pick 'n Pay, and I did not forget that when I thought about keeping Pick 'n Pay's business with Trust Bank. Nevertheless, Standard was a large player in the established banking cartel and just didn't measure up against the offers Jan Marais was making to keep my business. He offered amazing services, revolutionary for those days, such as coming to collect money from our stores, free of charge, without our having to use outside Fidelity Guards. He offered incredibly competitive bank-charge deals – in fact, the more I asked for, the more I got, until I had to tell Standard Bank I would keep them for my personal banking but would put Pick 'n Pay with Trust Bank.

Through his innovative direction, Jan Marais built Trust Bank into a very strong banking organisation. But he was always in the headlines, always challenging the government to change in a very far-sighted manner. He became involved with so many organisations and spent so much time worrying about them that he failed to see how worried he *ought* to have been about the declining affairs of Trust Bank. As a result, the bank got into trouble. Over one weekend in 1972, matters came to a head and Trust Bank hit the headlines.

Rumour was rife that the bank was going broke. Now, in our sort of business, we get the money in, pay suppliers and make interest on the money left in the bank. That's one of the key ways you make a success of our game. We had all our cash assets with Trust Bank – on various call terms. Feeling the first stirrings of fear, I phoned Jan Marais and asked for the truth. How bad, I wanted to know, was it? He confirmed that things were very, very, very bad but implored me not to withdraw Pick 'n Pay's assets. He said that if I left our money with the bank over that weekend it would inspire confidence, which could save the bank. If I pulled out, Trust Bank would simply go down the tubes.

This was where the pull of loyalty tugged me towards taking the chance, keeping our cash with Trust Bank that weekend. Frantic calls from my non-executive directors soon followed. It's all very well being loyal, was their sensible theme, but you've got to look after yourself and your public company. I privately wondered whether I should at least take half the money out of the bank but in the end left it all there – and sweated as I never had or have since. It was a nightmare weekend, an absolute agony of time, before I learned the bank was rescued. Jan Marais had raised money from somewhere, and our assets were safe.

In retrospect, I know I was wrong to allow loyalty to place the total cash assets of Pick 'n Pay in jeopardy. However, I've used that story to great advantage in subsequent dealings with ABSA, the group that took Trust Bank over. They remain our bankers. Whenever I have trouble with them, I always remind them about that nail-biting weekend when their survival and my future hung in the balance. I've got quite a lot out of that early show of loyalty.

* * *

John Lawley's defection clarified a few points of policy, which had far-reaching implications for our company. One of these was my resolution that we would never just accept *any* loss but would always make it up. Thus, even to this day, I tell any manager whose store has lost any money whatsoever through theft, fraud or mistake to set about making up the loss, however small or large it might be. The same rule applies to losses of a more abstract nature – make it up in whatever way possible.

In so far as the company's promotion policy was concerned, at the time of the Lawley incident I had already begun to formulate the philosophy which remains in place to the present time: that is, we grow from within. When Lawley left, I appointed a chief buyer for Cape Town and Johannesburg and René de Wet to be General Manager, all within 24 hours of John's defection. Not only did those appointments put us immediately back on track, they were also excellent morale-boosters.

From then on, we have hardly ever head-hunted, although other companies often try to get our people. I think it is immoral to pass over people within your own company who have given you huge service while waiting for a break, only to get squashed down because some outside guy happened to be good on interview and got the job that should be theirs. I always say, anyway, that an interview is the candidate's best day – the warts come later – whereas with your own people you tend to know the warts as well as you know the haloes, which makes for a much better balance.

One other point with regard to John Lawley's departure: No one within the company could believe at the time that the mighty John Lawley had been replaced by humbler middle-management people. But this was also the start of our policy of growing people into senior positions. Our present CEO, Sean Summers, started with Pick 'n Pay in the 1970s, working his way up through every level and task. I also believe in giving people deals with shares and incentives that mean a lot to them and encourage them to stay and grow with us. During the years when so many enterprising, bright young people were leaving South Africa because of the political situation, our policy of reward for good work paid huge dividends.

In setting all these points of policy down, I am not saying that I never made any mistakes, because I did – I made many. I chose the wrong person to run our first flagship store in Port Elizabeth, for instance. I made a mistake over the first Johannesburg store and another serious error of judgement – not at all in the quality of the person, who had a long and successful career with us, but in the rightness of the role for the man – over the first Pick 'n Pay hypermarket.

When Hugh Herman, then Managing Director of Pick 'n Pay, and a man who had been through trials of fire with me, resigned in 1992, I immediately appointed René de Wet and my son Gareth, with Sean Summers as the deputy. And there, too, I made a mistake. The story of those events and an explanation of what I, not they, did wrong comes later, but the main point is that from the time I lost John Lawley, many years passed before I realised that it sometimes takes an outsider to see things you just can't see yourself. At the moment of the Lawley defection, I was still metaphorically miles away from the time when we, like all forward-looking companies, would hire clear-eyed, outside consultants to point the way forward.

CHAPTER 14

Hatching Hyper Mania

One usual, hectic morning in the early 1970s, when I was working my way through the customary ten or more appointments in my daily diary while taking endless phone calls, our company's next great challenge walked into my office.

I had hardly had time to shake hands with my visitor before he launched into an enthusiastic discourse on the big brothers of supermarkets – the hypermarkets then trading in Europe. The timing of this visit was incredibly opportune because I was beginning to worry about what Pick 'n Pay should do next. Stores had opened in all four provinces of South Africa, making us a thriving national chain, but could we just go on opening stores in the same pattern?

I had heard of hypers, although I had never seen one in operation, but I knew instinctively that the concept sounded *just* right for us. My visitor was particularly enthusiastic about the hypers run by the French chain Carrefour, which was on a big expansion drive at the time. He offered to set up an introduction to the head of Carrefour in Paris. I not only accepted but resolved to fly to France the very next day, driven by a sense of urgency so strong that it had to be heeded.

When I arrived in Paris and met Denis Deforrey, the head of Carrefour, he greeted me with great warmth and friendliness. He took me around for two days, showing me their hypermarkets and those of their main competitor, Euromarche. I was thrilled by the concept but wondered whether hypers could work in South Africa with our relatively small population. Denis Deforrey suggested I should concentrate on Bernardo Trujillo's maxim – that rich people love low prices; poor people need them – rather than on actual population numbers. Hypers, with their massive turnovers, could appeal to all South Africans, rich and poor, which was more important than numbers. South Africans, Monsieur Deforrey assured me prophetically, would *flood* into our hypers.

We discussed the possibility of Carrefour taking an interest in a Pick 'n Pay hyper venture in South Africa before I left for home, once again brimming over with excitement and raring to go. As soon as I got back, I convened a Board meeting at which I had little trouble in convincing members to give me their full backing. Even in the boardroom, enthusiasm is infectious.

The decision to introduce hypers into South Africa ushered in an era of staggering pressure. Apart from the myriad matters needing attention and decisions, commissioning a hyper is an enormously expensive exercise, requiring a massive investment of finance and faith. As a financial investment, you are very, very lucky if you see some profit after a year's trading, but it could take two years or even longer. In the meantime, the investment has to be sustained and supported towards profitability.

Although it would be logical to suppose that the concept of hypermarkets originated in America, the late Sam Walton of Walmart resolved to build hypers in the USA after visiting us in South Africa and touring our stores, as I had toured Carrefour in France. Having won over the doubtful back home, Sam made Walmart the USA's dominant hyper trading group. It's ironic to think an American group of the magnitude of Walmart learning from us in South Africa, but in this instance they did.

In the early 1970s, while planning a hyper network, I worked out that South Africa could ultimately support a total of 20 to 25 mega stores, of which 14 would be ours. I did very careful, detailed calculations around population distribution by radius, population projections and so on, and actually got the sums uncannily right because 14 is the number of hypers we have today.

With the decision to invest in hypers taken, the first hurdle was finding a suitable site. I set out with my architects to secure a location within reach of the prosperous Greater Johannesburg population. Finding the right site for a store the size of a hyper is never easy. You have to identify an area large enough to contain the mega store and peripherals, which will certainly only exist in relatively under-developed, outer-suburban or semi-rural areas. Since the thousands of consumers you have to attract need to drive to the hyper, you require an even greater area around the store complex to accommodate thousands of cars.

The site we finally chose for our first hyper was perfectly positioned, with ample parking space, in the town of Boksburg, a place of special significance for me. The first little store Checkers had given me to manage, the store which launched my career in food, had been located in Boksburg, and now it was to be the location for our first Pick 'n Pay hypermarket.

Once our plans to open the first South African hypermarket went public, other chains soon expressed their intentions to do likewise. I thought this was a healthy sign. Nothing does more for the interests of consumers than fair competition. One of our rivals, the OK chain, announced a huge hyper development programme making use of an overseas architect and an incredibly expensive group of specialists. I decided we would continue to do things our own way – very basic and down-to-earth. Our goal was not to be the biggest but the best, although at times this put special hurdles in our way.

Once, during one of the many times we were in competition with the OK Bazaars over acquisition of one of the rare sites suitable for hypermarket development, I had to interrupt negotiations with an impatient group of architects, planners, owners and builders gathered in my Johannesburg office, to handle an exceptionally long-winded customer complaint over the telephone. Finally, the owners of the prospective hyper site – one I particularly wanted – became exasperated by the long interruption. They gathered up their plans, maps and papers and left, while I remained helplessly hooked up to the long litany of complaint on the end of my telephone. As a result, the deal was lost to OK Bazaars and I ended up opting for a second-best site, one about which I had none of the intuitive good feelings the other had generated.

Oddly enough, the hyper we put on that second-choice site became the only one which did not succeed according to its original specifications. However, I didn't regret the loss, reasoning that if our policy of treating the consumer as queen was to have real validity, then the needs and interests of any one of them took precedence – even over the acquisition of a multi-million-rand site.

While planning for our first hyper was in progress, I kept in touch with the Carrefour people in Paris, who had retained an interest in a joint venture between us. As nought after nought was added to the figures my accountants worriedly presented, I began to be haunted by the magnitude of what I had taken on, and decided to conclude negotiations with Carrefour towards acquiring an interest in our South African hypers.

When agreement was reached and the documents drawn up, my lawyer and I set off together for the Paris offices of Carrefour to close the deal. We were shown into a waiting room outside the Chairman's office, from where we could hear a low murmur of conversation as we sat waiting our turn. Suddenly the door to the Chairman's office opened, revealing a scene so unexpected it took my breath away. Gathered around the Chairman's desk was a delegation from OK Bazaars, engaged in signing, it soon transpired, a financial cooperation deal for *their* hyper developments in South Africa. What an awful moment – I could hardly believe the evidence of my eyes – but it was so; the OK had a deal with Carrefour signed and sealed.

I later discovered that while I was negotiating with Carrefour, they found out that OK Bazaars was bigger than Pick 'n Pay, even though the OK's financial fortunes were already somewhat rocky. The French pragmatists decided to err on the side of numerical strength, but somehow never got around to telling us this before we arrived, just in time to witness them signing up with their chosen partners.

It was some years before I was able to resume cordial relations with Carrefour, but ultimately there was so much more harmony than discord between our two operations that there was no point in perpetuating a distant snub – particularly as in the end I was *delighted* that no foreign company, or anyone else for that matter, owned any part of our thriving hypers.

Throughout 1973 and 1974 I chased endlessly around assembling the army of staff we would need for the Boksburg hyper. Wendy helped me to set up a textile department staffed by some of our best people, but we did have to advertise and go outside for some staff because we needed expertise in areas we hadn't dealt with before. I travelled through Europe extensively and developed a very clear idea of how our stores in South Africa were going to look and how they would be staffed.

During travels to London at this time, I was shocked by the state of tension and anxiety created by a spate of terrorist bombings in that city. But people with special skills to offer who came to see me about joining Pick 'n Pay while I was recruiting in England often stressed that they saw South Africa as just one among any number of countries beset by problems. At home, however, there had been another sharp increase in anxiety among white South Africans as a result of the coup which had ended Portuguese rule in neighbouring Mozambique. White South Africans did not feel so optimistic now that the bastions of white rule in Africa were reduced to two – South Africa and Rhodesia. When I spent time with people prominent in the worlds of finance, banking and politics, they might conclude, after hours of intellectual debate, that the facts if not the omens seemed promising for South Africa. Factors in our favour – such as our ability to evade sanctions, coal reserves important to an energy-strapped world, good crops and high gold prices – boded well for the future, they thought.

But such opinions – sound, well-thought-out and based on solid fact – nevertheless often sounded incredibly detached to me. Listening and contributing to conversation around them was very different from addressing gathering after gathering of staff, as I did at this time, to stress that as a company we were going ahead with store openings and ambitious expansions such as the new hyper. I particularly wanted to hearten the managers so that they could encourage their people, especially the young white men grappling with the demands of carving a career while fulfilling their military obligations.

* * *

With the clock ticking inexorably towards opening day at Boksburg, another issue – the allocation of shelf space in stores – took on a new and unusual twist. Present criticism levelled against all supermarket groups concerns the allocation of shelf space, which is supposedly used as a weapon over those who wish to put their products there. In the first place, the entire layout of supermarkets has been subjected to very intense, scientific scrutiny to make shopping easier for consumers. As an example, although it is true that goods placed near checkouts are calculated to be impulse buys, they may also be memory joggers for customers. While standing in the checkout queue it is very unlikely that someone will remember they have forgotten to buy razor blades, for example, until and unless they see them displayed near the tills.

The art of stocking a supermarket is demanding and dynamic, in that changes are dictated by trends in consumer attitudes and shopping patterns. As well as making shopping easy for customers, you must create visual appeal and you must constantly monitor range control. Do you have twelve brands of tinned peas on your shelves because you want to offer a wide choice, or do you have the six best? Do you pile some bright, attractive produce near the entrance for visual appeal, or do you avoid this because unrelated goods will get put on top of the display?

It is true that suppliers continually fight with us over shelf space. They wave the Neilson Surveys (which show their products' market share) at us. Then they try to get that percentage of shelf space from us. A company will object vociferously to an allocation of 50 percent of shelf space when their product accounts for 70 percent of the market, but we want space to promote our own products too. How such matters are resolved is all part of the negotiation process, in which we are tough but fair. We do get money for giving good space, or for giving an end – always a very good area – but we demand an extra discount for allocation of prime space, which helps to lower prices. We have firm, specified principles of what we consider is fair, and should any of our people overstep the boundaries, it very quickly comes to my notice.

In the cut and thrust of fast-paced retailing – allocating shelf space, dealing with discounts and cash flows – I am not an apologist for profits.

On the contrary, profits are our life-blood. I love profits. We make interest on banking daily takings because that's how our business, and all others like it, work. But our profits are not made at the expense of farmers or suppliers, any more than they are made at the expense of consumers.

The unusual twist – a real reversal, you could say – which we faced over the opening of the first Boksburg hyper was not about what space was allocated to whom, but rather about finding anyone at all to put the goods we wanted to sell on our shelves. What was happening was this: big-name suppliers such as Kenwood, Slazenger, Kodak, Black & Decker and other notables, got together to boycott us. Those who did not want their products to be on sale to the public at the low prices our bulk buying could secure joined forces against us. Privately, many suppliers and manufacturers said that they would love to supply the hyper but had been forced to 'black' us to prevent prices of the goods they supplied – TV sets, clothing, sports goods, electric power tools and toys – from being slashed. They also said that cut-price goods on sale in our hyper would antagonise big 'smaller' suppliers and hardware-store owners, their traditional outlets, because the buying power of the hyper constituted unfair competition.

The battle between us was serious and bitter. Mere weeks before the scheduled opening of the Boksburg hyper, which represented an investment of twelve and a half million rands, it looked as though we were not going to be able to put the disputed lines on our shelves.

As it happened, this issue took on another aspect because in the end the attempted supplier boycott gave us better publicity for the first hyper than any campaign we could have orchestrated. The public were naturally aggrieved by what they saw as the arrogance of suppliers intent on regulating prices. People wanted the better prices we promised, and supported our stand.

The media followed the fight to make suppliers sell their goods into the Boksburg hyper, with keen attention. Extensive coverage heightened public sympathy for our cause, particularly when there was speculation that the boycott might prevent us from opening on schedule. Headlines appeared nearly every day – 'Suppliers Urged to Boycott Hyper', 'Pick 'n Pay Blames Bullies for Boycott', 'Suppliers Deny Ackerman Claims'.

The wrangle went on and on but, no matter how many twists and turns the stand-off took, the public quite correctly identified the basic issue: that certain vested interests stood between them and their right to purchase products such as power tools, TV sets, clothing, sporting goods, furniture and toys at discounted prices.

We held extensive meetings with the government to discuss the issue of the Monopolies Act. Finally they agreed that they had to write to all the suppliers who were boycotting the Boksburg hyper, due to open just 12 days later, because their refusal to supply us was in contravention of the Monopolies Act.

Angry and resentful at having to face up to the inadequacies of that flawed piece of legislation, the irritable government spokesmen suddenly changed tack and began to reprimand me for having made so many press statements. They wanted to know, peevishly, why the government's voice was not being heard in the press. I suggested, reasonably enough, that it might be because they never *issued* any statements on the confrontation between Pick 'n Pay and suppliers, which had, after all, been raging for months.

I only had to point out how strongly the public were feeling on the issue of supplier bullying, how much they wanted to know that someone was fighting on the side of consumers, for the officials to agree instantly to make a statement on behalf of government, asserting their support for the right of ordinary consumers to shop at the lowest prices possible.

It is difficult to believe today how fiercely manufacturers fought in 1975 to prevent hypermarkets from selling protected goods. At the time I told the *Financial Gazette*, which, despite being pro-government, gave us terrific support in editorials and space: 'all we want is the goods to sell at whatever price we want through efficient modern marketing. If they would cut their archaic ideas, there wouldn't be all this hoo-ha at the moment.'

As the scheduled hyper opening day of 19 March rushed towards us, there were never enough hours in any day. A team had been assembled to staff the hyper, but I still had terrible misgivings about the standards of morale and leadership. People with the charisma, the stamina, the flair and experience to coordinate a hypermarket operation and manage some six hundred staff are both very special and very rare. At marathon meetings, sometimes in excess of seven hours, often ending in the early hours of the morning, we tried to set our objectives and clear our minds. There were endless crises, and I became tense and headache-prone – in which I was not alone.

The enormous interest around the country as to whether we would be able to open generated terrific pressures and great publicity. On 12 March I recorded in my diary, 'It's really been a rough, tough time with two speeches on Monday, a press interview on Tuesday and speech on Tuesday night. Interview at the South African Broadcasting Corporation this morning, another speech tonight plus dozens of interviews on the phone, plus all the Pick 'n Pay and Hyper problems.'

And so it went. The boycott issue was just one among numerous problems. Mere hours away from opening we were still finalising agreements for stocking our shelves. I had also not heard from the local police whether we would be allowed to open a restaurant at the hyper for black shoppers, or a liquor outlet.

At the precise time the Boksburg hyper opened its doors to the public, an accumulation of stresses and strains made the store's first General Manager so ill that he had to be sent away to rest and recover his strength. As had happened at the opening of our first Johannesburg store at Darras, there was no alternative other than that I should take over the management of the hyper myself to coordinate matters. The night before opening day, Wendy and all the executive wives pitched in magnificently: stocking shelves, pricing goods, and gearing staff up for the expected influx of shoppers whom we hoped to welcome the next day. I say 'hoped' because hypermarket shopping was still an untried concept in South Africa. We had no way of knowing whether the public would take to it or not, although at heart I trusted the instincts that had brought us this far.

In the early hours of opening day at Boksburg, rain showers smudged the giant calico advertising signs erected around the hyper building, but nothing else about that marvellous day – 19 March 1975 – was blurred. Hours before the doors opened, we began picking up radio reports of traffic congestion as thousands of vehicles converged on the hyper. Queues of cars kilometres long waited to access the parking lot. As we opened the hyper doors to the rush of clamouring customers, they flowed in on a wave of excitement so strong I felt as though I could reach out and touch it. The atmosphere was just magnificent, everyone was so thrilled and enthusiastic. The store was packed and humming, and it was marvellous to see the people in lines at least a mile long, their trolleys packed with cut-price goods.

I am sure that no one who was at Boksburg that day will ever forget it. All my family were with me, including my half-brother Bruce, visiting from overseas, my stepbrother Peter, sister Moyra and her husband Issy as well as Harold Gorvy and Arnold Galombik, my accountant and lawyer. These stalwarts slaved away among the hyper shelves, while other staff worked their hearts out in whatever capacity was called for.

A hoax bomb scare brought squads of security police into the store in the thick of the day's rush. The hoax stopped us from reaching the R200 000 first-day turnover we were heading towards when the incident happened, but nevertheless we did a superlative R176 000. In the following days there were a few more bomb hoaxes, making us wonder whether someone was trying to close us down, to make people afraid for their safety if they chose to shop with us.

We never found out, but intimidation tactics, if that's what they were, didn't work. Nothing kept consumers away from the Boksburg hyper. The public embraced the concept with such enthusiasm that I decided from then on to concentrate on opening hyper stores, which I saw as a natural progression, complementary to the Pick 'n Pay supermarkets. Accordingly I went straight ahead with plans to get one or two more hypers off the ground.

The introduction of hypermarkets into South Africa focused criticism on what were claimed to be the self-serving interests of big business. We were subjected to much vitriol and questioning of motives. I suppose the opening of hypers fuelled the offensive because the bigger the target, the easier it is to hit. Every year at Budget time, newspapers talk about inflation, how prices are going up while supermarkets masquerade as friends of consumers. From the first days of hypermarket trading, vote-seeking politicians stood up periodically to demand sympathy for small shop-keepers doomed to closure by the aggressive expansion of juggernaut enterprises like Pick 'n Pay.

The advent of supermarkets and hypermarkets has changed the face of High Street trading everywhere in the developed world. Small traders have often not survived, but then neither did horses and carts once the combustion engine took over transport. This is the inevitability of trade evolution, an evolution which is now coming round somewhat full-circle, as it happens, to a resurgence of *small* stores. As we have found with our own franchises today, the small stores are doing a terrifically good job against the giant chains. Our franchisees own their businesses but, through linking up with us, as in the case of other franchises, they get the benefit of numbers. These stores are the modern corner cafés, although some of them are as big as the first stores we opened. Hypers continue to thrive but so do efficient convenience stores.

Opening the first hyper taught me many valuable lessons. I resolved that no expansion, however huge, was cause to move people around the country, as though they were pieces on a personnel chessboard, without due consideration for the impact of relocation on the entire family. I also reaffirmed a deep-seated conviction that we needed to cling on to the good things that had formed in the company, and to the good people. It's an old saying, but true – keep what is good for you until it ceases to be good. I knew that there was gold in our midst; now I planned to nurture it.

CHAPTER 15

'Extramural' Activities

During the planning phase for the Boksburg hyper, a wave of illegal strikes, burgeoning from beginnings in the Natal city of Durban early in 1973, intensified nationally until, at one time, militant unionist action resulted in 160 illegal strikes in a three-month period. The writing was on the wall for labour relations in South Africa. A long, hard and bitter period of conflict was grinding into gear in the 1970s. In Pick 'n Pay's case, we were to learn that commitment to political and employment equality and policies of welfare and social commitment offered no protection against union and labour aggression, although we did forge a way forward out of our troubles, which was ultimately a positive outcome.

Far from being able to cut back on what I might call extramural aspects of business while the Boksburg hyper organisation was in progress, I found myself at this time increasingly caught up in clashes with the prescriptive, restrictive food and commodity control boards, those bodies which worked so strongly against the natural ability of a free market to regulate itself. In the case of the food control boards I did accept that farmers needed protection, because their adversaries are the uncontrollable forces of nature. From that point of view controls made sense – but otherwise the South African control boards wielded far too much power, forming their cartels and colluding with suppliers to fix prices.

As well as ongoing disputes with government over bread price subsidies, I had endless fights over price fixing on butter, cheese and eggs. Some of the fights I won and others I lost, but the fact was that no one else was taking on the vested interests that controlled what consumers paid for basic foodstuffs. The present Mbeki administration in South Africa has taken away nearly all the controls and agriculture is actually improving as a result. People are more competitive because they have to be more businesslike.

The accusations which developed, and persist to this day, about powerful supermarket groups like Pick 'n Pay sabotaging growers and suppliers by beating them down to ruinously low selling prices to maximise profits, were doubtless hatched by manufacturers and control boards to counter the awkward questions we were asking right from the early 1960s. Precisely how food chains are supposed to benefit by putting out of business the people who supply what they sell defies logic, but the accusation pops up with monotonous regularity.

According to myth, our buyers too set out to destroy the very people they buy from and poor suppliers have to wait an unconscionable time for payment while we grow fat on the profits gleaned from selling their goods. The facts are rather different. Although I can only speak for ourselves, one of the earliest policies I put in place when I bought Pick 'n Pay was regulated payments to suppliers. To this day we generally pay on thirty days from date of statement, which places us among the best-paying companies in South Africa.

There will, of course, be variations in an organisation as huge as ours has become, and I'm not saying we wear haloes, but it is important to mention that there are many, many cases where really small suppliers, or those experiencing financial difficulties, are paid cash on delivery. Cash payments to small suppliers have given many the initial boost needed to establish healthy businesses.

Regarding power-wielding buyers, those in our organisation are governed by very strict rules. They are known in the industry as tough but fair negotiators. We don't like them to accept invitations to this or that rugby or cricket match, and if a supplier wants a buyer of ours to see his facilities overseas, we always pay for the trip ourselves.

* * *

In the mid-1970s, other gauntlets had been thrown down while my attention was concentrated on opening the Boksburg hyper. Woolworths threatened to require common suppliers to sell their goods exclusively to Woolworths and to stop supplying us. According to their reasoning, it was incumbent on us to avoid buying from any supplier who also did business with Woolworths, on the grounds that we were poaching the technological guidance Woolworths gave suppliers, to our own advantage. They were prepared to put the issue before the Board of Trade, and I was prepared to take the dispute to court, although I finally decided, with reluctance, that there was not enough hard evidence to support a court action. In the end, I came to the conclusion that the whole fuss only showed how much Pick 'n Pay worried Woolworths.

At this time the OK were also engaging us in battle – on this occasion over acquisition of a site in the Cape Town suburb of Milnerton where we planned to put our first Cape Province hyper. The site had gone up for auction, and we had beaten fellow bidders, including the OK group, fair and square. Soon afterwards, the Minister for Community Development, Mr Fanie Kotze, instructed us that I was to be handed an envelope containing a higher offer for the site from the OK, to give me first chance at upping it. I was absolutely amazed, angered and terribly, terribly disappointed by this turn of events. I resolved to take the issue to the highest offices in the land because their tactics left me flabbergasted.

Mr Kotze privately told me that although he was obliged to accept the OK's late offer and present it to his department, he would not entertain something so morally indefensible nor allow their offer to override ours, no matter how much more money was offered. He assured me the deal was ours, but once the OK's team learned of Community Development's moral obligation in our favour, they simply skewed the dispute round to be one based on zoning rights for the site.

Like Woolworths' attempts to limit our access to suppliers, the actions of the OK over the Milnerton site happened because our hyper initiative had been too successful by far. These were their ways of fighting back. I told everyone that it was a rough tough time, but that we would get through it. All we had to do was remain vigilant as a company, always aware of what the opposition was up to, but concentrate our chief energies on running super-efficient stores to satisfy consumers – our reason for being.

Because I was so busy on so many fronts, a stinging attack on chain stores and particularly on Pick 'n Pay, made in a speech by the Constitutional Minister, Chris Heunis, had to be brought to my notice. When I read what he had had to say, I was appalled, particularly as he had taken as allies my old friends the Grocery Manufacturers' Association (GMA). Minister Heunis had somehow got hold of confidential figures of ours, which he used to further accusations of exploitation and manipulation against all big chains, but specifically against us.

Cooperation between government and the GMA was a difficult alliance to understand because, in joining the attack against us, the GMA was biting the hand that fed it. It was astonishing to be pitted against the very people who, when we faced them over negotiating tables, were always telling us how much they valued our business. I was determined not to let either attacker get away with the injustice and accordingly issued repudiations of my own in the press. I said that I couldn't speak for the practices of other chains, but bitterly resented being tarred with one brush when we did not deserve the accusations levelled against us.

Nationalist government ministers at that time were mostly cut from the same cloth – they hated to be challenged, resented being stood up to. Minister Heunis was no exception. As soon as my repudiation of the accusations against us was published, Secretary Joep Steyn phoned, advising me to withdraw my statements and apologise to Minister Heunis 'in my own interests', which I absolutely refused to do.

Instead, I made a phone call of my own – to warn Minister Heunis that more press reports were pending. This exchange, on both our parts, was very cold and acid. He insisted that he had evidence involving the super-market industry in devious practices, but refused to divulge sources and refused to acknowledge that he was tarring the entire industry with one brush. When he, in his turn, refused point-blank to exonerate Pick 'n Pay, I wished him a curt good-day and put the phone down.

This incident, with all its simmering hostility, was happening at just the time we were about to open our Brackenfell hyper. When the time came to choose someone to perform the opening ceremony, I decided to ask Minister Chris Heunis because Brackenfell was in his constituency. His office accepted our invitation with alacrity, which made me think that our conciliatory gesture and his ready acceptance indicated a desire on both our parts to wipe the slate clean and start afresh.

Mistake.

Minister Heunis did not have the slightest intention of putting the past behind us. On the VIP dais at the gala opening of Brackenfell, amid balloons and banners, in an atmosphere of celebration and goodwill, he again launched into an ungracious attack against us.

In reply, I told Minister Heunis that my father had taught me never to insult a guest because to do so was the height of bad manners – a barb that I know hit home.

Running parallel with these issues at this time was what I increasingly saw as the absolute necessity for a broad clean-up of South African business. There were so many iniquities being tolerated or ignored, simply to suit vested interests.

I have spoken of the stranglehold control boards exerted on supplies and prices, but their antiquated interference also entrenched astonishingly inefficient methods of farming, long before products reached supermarket shelves and fridges. While subsidies propped up non-productive farms, the yield per hectare from South African farmland was exactly half that produced in America and Europe. Controls stifled the natural regulation of a free market.

Another component factored into food prices was the take-it-or-leave-it attitude of some food-packaging manufacturers. In 1975, 33 percent of the cost of a can of fruit, for instance, was in the tin, which pointed to handsome profits for supplier monopolies.

Each of these examples, a few among very many, explains why we as a company so often took up the cudgels on behalf of consumers – who were paying dearly, as they still do, for all the inefficiencies and iniquities. However, as far as fleecing the public was concerned, there was – and is – one cartel which reigns supreme, and that is the oil industry.

When I decided to have a go at taking on the oil companies for the first time in 1975, I had never tackled such a large, influential and tough opponent before. But I objected to the arrogance with which oil companies enforced their will, according to an informal agreement among themselves, which cut off any retailer who challenged the prices they set. They touted this commercial tyranny as a means of protecting the interests of six thousand franchised and non-franchised garages trading throughout the country, but it was of course those very garages which collectively provided the petrol distributors with their large profits, so it was their own interests that were being protected at the expense of consumers.

When the 1975 petrol war started, I had been quietly discounting fuel at Boksburg hyper's 18-pump garage, through the device of a simple ruse. During negotiations between the petrol company Trek and ourselves about fuelling the hyper's pumps, a Trek executive had patiently explained the standard agreement between petrol suppliers and retailers which specifically outlawed petrol price cutting. I had already perused the agreement and pointed out that all clauses relating to price cutting were concentrated on a single page of the thirty- or forty-page document. This being so, I suggested, why not simply tear that page out and just sign the rest?

Tear a page out of the agreement? The hallowed agreement? The Trek man wrung his hands in consternation, told me he would get into terrible trouble, but in the end that's exactly what we did – simply tore the offending page out and signed the rest.

It took Trek's legal people ages to notice what we had done, but once the subterfuge was discovered, both Trek and ourselves came into direct confrontation with the other oil moguls and garage owners. I formally announced that we would continue selling discounted petrol from our Trek pumps at the Boksburg hyper. This sparked the biggest row the South African motor industry had ever seen. In a press interview headlined 'Pick

'n Pay Takes on the Oil Giants', I told the *Business Times* that garage owners would do well to question the adverse effects of lack of competition
rather than issuing plaintive cries about needing the 6,8 percent margin on
petrol sales to provide adequate returns.

By enforcing price control at retail level, the oil companies were doing
a disservice to both garage owners and consumers. There was also the small
matter of millions being pocketed every time petrol went up. We could
have pocketed extra millions time and time again if we had upped the
price of previously purchased petrol supplies at our pumps, as the crazy law
in fact obliged retailers to do, but in my book that is called profiteering.

At the time of the 1975 dispute, there was no clarity on whether petrol
price cutting was illegal or not, although some very vague law soon
surfaced which seemed as though it *could* outlaw petrol discounting. The
police were as confused as the rest of us. One day an apologetic police
posse arrived at the hyper, not to close us down but to ask, very cour-
teously, for our help in their investigations into the legality of petrol
discounting.

Joep Steyn, for the government, added to the confusion when he went
on record saying that no law was in place to stop us, but that suppliers were
allowed to cut us off. If that was so, then I believed we could bring a very
strong case against suppliers under the law of contract. When I put this to
the harried Mr Steyn, he was very, very cold, maintaining icily that
government had nothing at all to do with retail petrol prices. I had the
strong feeling his unspoken wish was that they didn't have to have anything to do with me either.

The only certainty in the convoluted case of the first dispute over
petrol prices was that the public loved our cut-price campaign. They kept
the Boksburg hyper pumps busy every minute we had fuel to sell. I decided to stay permanently in Johannesburg for the duration of the petrol
confrontation, although Gareth had started to write his final Matric exams
at home in Cape Town and the Milnerton site saga was ongoing. I wrote
in my diary that it was so difficult living in a fish-bowl, being continually
in the public eye and on one's mettle, although I concluded that I had
chosen to play the game that way.

On the first Monday of December 1975, Trek cut off our supplies. Bigger brothers in the oil industry had prevailed. Rather than capitulating, I decided we would fight the court order against us, and was duly rewarded 12 days later when the presiding judge ruled that as Trek had committed no crime in supplying us, we had committed none in buying.

There was great jubilation in our camp over this judgment and much amongst the public – who celebrated our victory and thanked us for fighting for them. Of course, the ruling in our favour didn't have too long a currency. Soon, Minister Chris Heunis announced new regulations closing existing loopholes, to the great annoyance of the public.

The outcome of that first fight with the oil companies was a fantastic victory but the fight for petrol price deregulation continues. Fighting the government on petrol prices remains a serious matter, because the consequences of making these challenges can be very heavy. There is provision in the law for the imposition of severe fines against retailers selling petrol below the gazetted price, and garages can be closed down. I've spent many worrisome hours waiting to know whether punitive measures would be taken against us.

In 1975 government action was designed to protect the interests of the large petrol companies, precisely as it still is. The only difference now is that emerging black oil entrepreneurs want their slice of the cake too. What remains the same, however, is who pays through the nose for petroleum products.

CHAPTER 16

After Soweto

Soweto, 16 June 1976, a place and a date seared on the psyche of South Africa. On that date, the most serious challenge to white rule in the history of South Africa erupted, ostensibly over a government regulation requiring the use of Afrikaans as a language of instruction in black schools. The trouble started when ten thousand black schoolchildren gathered to protest peacefully against the government language edict, but the protest quickly escalated into a riot. Police opened fire on the densely packed crowd of protesters, igniting a wave of outraged demonstration which spread like wildfire throughout the country.

White South Africa and the government were severely shaken in the aftermath of the 1976 unrest. Although the government pigeon-holed the trouble under the 'total onslaught' being waged against South Africa by subversive elements, they had to make concessions. The inflammatory law enforcing Afrikaans tuition in black schools, which had sparked off the troubles in the first place, was revoked. There were also promises that legislation would be passed enabling blacks to own property in the townships, to grant a degree of municipal urban self-government and to improve the quality of black education.

Meanwhile, the 1976 riots triggered a fresh wave of emigration. White people flooded out, taking their useful skills to England, Australia, New

Zealand, Canada, the USA – wherever they could be admitted. I started to think seriously about the possibility of setting up an overseas operation, partly to provide a diverse investment and partly because I thought young Pick 'n Pay people who were unsettled and unsure, worn down by endless political turmoil and frequent military obligations, would be heartened by the possibility of transferring somewhere out of South Africa if things turned irrevocably bad. Although I could see great practical problems running two companies, the situation in South Africa was so terribly worrying at this time that no one could predict what the future held.

The Soweto riots, and South Africa's involvement in the Angolan War – an involvement about which the South African public had been deliberately misled – unleashed an unprecedented outpouring of criticism in the overseas press. For us, the Angolan conflict took on a human face when, early in 1976, David Smith, one of our young men doing military duty on the Angolan border, stepped on a landmine and had to have his foot amputated. I had spoken immediately with his father to see how we could help to get David back to normal as soon as possible – in fact, he become one of South Africa's top food buyers – but these were the horrible things we were living with on a day-to-day basis.

External pressures; internal pressures.

I wrote at this time how desperately I needed help because I was mentally exhausted. The company was now so big and complex, demands on my time were endless, particularly as regards public relations and property matters. Despite the sterling work Wendy was doing handling the demands of our rapidly expanding staff welfare and social obligations programmes, much still seemed to fall heavily on my shoulders. A perfect example of this was the way we ended up acquiring a site for our third hyper store.

What happened was this. Although we had been winded by the loss of the disputed Milnerton site as a location for our proposed third hyper store, we were determined not to be sidelined in our Cape expansion plans. Accordingly we had been looking at Brackenfell, then a semi-rural area twenty kilometres north of Cape Town, as a possible location for a new hyper. The OK were also looking at Brackenfell land – I have explained how much competition there was over sites suitable for hyper developments, because they were so hard to come by.

One morning, while I was working in my office, I discovered by pure chance that an option we had taken out on a Brackenfell site was due to expire a couple of hours later. I was terribly annoyed, because there were supposed to be people with their fingers on the pulse of such details and now, if we did not sign up for the site in time, the option was to pass to the next interested party.

I was scheduled to attend the opening of a new factory that lunchtime, but sent Wendy in my place and went tearing out to Brackenfell to beat the impending deadline. I met the owner, barely before our option expired, and we soon finalised details for an agreement, jotting them down on the back of my cigarette box, to which we both solemnly affixed scaled-down signatures. Later, when my lawyers drew up the formal agreement, on the basis of notes (which the owner honoured as a gentleman) on the dog-eared cigarette box, I found I had bought virtually the entire town.

Although the day, in that instance, was saved, the near-loss of the Brackenfell site confirmed my worst suspicions – I was up to my ears in unprofessional inefficiency which I just couldn't stand any longer. Problems, and not only on matters of property, that other people were supposed to handle always seemed to be landing up on my desk, putting me under deep, tough pressure all the time. I was having to work at an enormous pace, all day and at home nearly every night, just to keep on top of the company. I pondered deeply about what to do. I knew that much good work was being done by a crowd of very enthusiastic and excellent executives, generally speaking, but were problems arising because the company as a whole was too unwieldy? In spite of South Africa's terrible difficulties, I still saw growth years ahead and asked vital questions about how we should cope.

One crucial decision I took at this time, precipitated by the Brackenfell near-miss, was to persuade lawyer Hugh Herman to leave the Sonnenberg law practice where he then worked, to join Pick 'n Pay permanently, primarily controlling property matters. Hugh was to play a role of the utmost importance in the development of the company, standing with me through more than two tempestuous decades.

On my endless travels around the country on company business at this time, I was often awed by the magnitude of what was going on. Within the space of nine months, four hypers had been built and opened, as well as new supermarkets up and down the entire country. The policy of running the company according to the 'four legs of the table' principle, with consumer sovereignty at the pinnacle, was now a legacy, although sometimes a consumer could take the queenly dispensation a bit too far.

I once took a phone call from an absolutely furious woman – someone Wendy and I knew and often met socially – who told me she had been unpacking groceries prior to lunching at some smart function, when the lid had flown off a bottle of bleach, ruining the imported Parisian outfit she was wearing. Since you're the one who's always going on about consumer sovereignty, she raged, you can demonstrate what that really means and pay me the R3 000 it cost to replace what I'm wearing, in Paris. Was I mistaken, I wondered, in gathering that she was leading up to asking for a trip to Paris to buy a new outfit? This was all a bit much but, then again, I didn't see how I could refuse to compensate her without going against my own policy of holding the rights of the consumer supreme, which she had identified as her best chance with unerring accuracy.

Seeing no alternative, I agreed immediately to cover the cost of the ruined outfit and thought I would mull over making a really grand gesture and giving her a ticket to Paris as well. A few days later I took a call from a very sheepish-sounding gentleman who turned out to be the bleached woman's husband. It transpired that listening to his wife's delight about having duped me had proved too much for him. He had decided to come clean, so to speak. He confessed on his wife's behalf that the dress she had worn on the day of the bleach incident in fact had been purchased from a local chain store for R250. The husband felt terrible that a completely contrived story had been accepted without question, out of loyalty to a principled policy.

As the reach of Pick 'n Pay extended further and further, I found I could mostly adhere to my resolve to keep feeding our senior staff requirements from within, but no matter how many crack senior people we had, the pressures on me remained tremendous. I was finding it incredibly important to be wherever a new venture was starting, to analyse the problems, discuss them with colleagues and get everyone pitching in to make things right. Even top executives sometimes didn't know exactly what was going on, and that was when troubles could begin.

Ever since Pick 'n Pay developed into the thriving chain it was, various interests had suggested that I should put together some consortium or other to buy out Greatermans. But frankly, I foresaw nothing but decline ahead for the group, although I did retain a sentimental interest in what happened to Ackermans, since it had been my father's business when Greatermans swallowed it up in the 1940s, and because it could also have provided a good diversification for Pick 'n Pay. Therefore, when Isaac Kaye later acquired Greatermans I asked him to contact me first if he ever decided to sell off Ackermans, which he agreed to do.

Some time later I was disquieted to hear through the business grapevine that Ackermans was indeed on the market. Clearly, Isaac had entirely forgotten his promise to me, but I phoned him anyway and we arranged to meet the following Friday in Johannesburg to discuss the matter. I remember it all so well: how I addressed a *Financial Mail* symposium, then hurried off to meet Isaac Kaye in his hotel room at 12 noon – high noon, as it turned out, for my wish to acquire Ackermans.

To my disbelief and dismay, Isaac Kaye told me that he had struck a deal with Edgars, and that Ackermans was to be signed over to them two hours later unless, of course, I chose to make a firm offer of my own. I protested mightily, reminding him that he had promised to give me forewarning if he chose to sell Ackermans, to which he replied that that was precisely what he was doing right then. I know I spluttered on angrily about the obvious impossibility of buying a business without having carried out the usual 'due diligence' checks, and that as a public company I couldn't commit to what might well prove to be a pig-in-the-poke purchase. It was all energy expended to no avail. As far as Isaac was concerned, he had kept his promise, and that was that.

Once again, Ackermans had gone.

* * *

In the last years of the 1970s, I found myself facing up to opposition from an unlikely quarter – namely, my own wife. At this time, debate over what should be put on a lovely site our company's property arm had acquired in the Constantia Valley, to the south of Cape Town, was sharply divided into two camps. One camp, to which I belonged, wanted to build a tasteful hypermarket development while the other, to which Wendy belonged, wanted to see a smaller, garden-style supermarket development in the famous semi-rural valley with its farmlands, orchards and South Africa's oldest vineyards.

The anti-hypermarket lobby were fierce in their opposition, even threatening to lie down in front of the bulldozers if the hypermarket plan went ahead, although I don't remember whether Wendy was part of this suicide brigade. I asked my wife how she squared her opposition to the proposed hypermarket with her directorship in the company – Pick 'n Pay – which planned to build it. No matter, she retorted; she did oppose the hypermarket and would continue to fight against it to the bitter end.

Various incidents relating to property matters had caused me to rethink the company's position. I decided we should become masters of our own territory in this regard, owning sites and properties wherever possible. It was thanks to this change in policy that I found myself in conflict with my own wife over the Constantia proposals, a conflict which was to rage on unabated into the 1980s, and which once caused me quite unaccustomed discomfort with the press.

Zoning approval was a cause of equal frustration for each side in the conflict over the Constantia site. Authority was not forthcoming for any development because every application seemed to get becalmed in a vast ocean of contention. One day, two people called at my office, saying they were agents who could help us secure permission to use the site for whichever type of store development we eventually chose. They asked to be paid a commission for their services, which would have been perfectly in order in such circumstances, but then began to mention another, altogether separate sum of money to be used, apparently, to bribe officials. I told them we did not pay bribes – never had and never would – which I thought ended the debate. A few nights later I decided to mention the incident in a speech I was giving, meaning to emphasise my opposition to bribery in business.

Unfortunately, I obviously failed to communicate the gist of the matter as clearly as I should have, because next thing, the newspaper headline 'Ackerman and Bribery' appeared. It was an awful line because it gave the impression that I was involved in some sort of bribery scam, yet there I had been, telling the audience in my speech how two men had come into my office wanting money to bribe and how I had refused. It was all very vexing, especially as I'd given the instance as an example of integrity.

The issue over the Constantia store culminated domestically when a sharp rap on my office door preceded the grand entrance of Wendy, immaculately dressed in her best pin-striped business suit, carrying an official-looking envelope which she placed before me on my desk. It was her resignation. Her feelings over what should or should not be placed on the Constantia site ran so high that she was presenting me with an ultimatum, one concerned with rather more than the disputed site too. I could keep my Director of Social Responsibilities – and, it was made clear, my wife too – or I could go ahead with opening a hypermarket in Constantia and lose her on both counts.

This of course settled the issue once and for all. Today, there is a lovely development – Constantia Village – in the disputed area, with not a trace of a hyper anywhere on the horizon.

CHAPTER 17

Political Twists and Turns

It was perhaps ironic that just when I was grappling hardest with organisational problems within Pick 'n Pay, I was almost *required* to become more politically active. As the 1970s progressed I found I was fighting on a broader front because my stands on behalf of our people within the company, or on consumer issues, had turned me into a spokesman, a figurehead. My speeches and actions attracted a lot of publicity and I found that people really listened when I spoke at the functions and events packing every page of my diary.

My family thought I was nosing around on the fringes of politics and urged me to participate more decisively. I remember having a family meeting about it.

The Urban Foundation, started in 1977 on the initiative of Harry Oppenheimer and Anton Rupert among others, presented me with a perfect opportunity to become more actively involved, as my family thought I should. The Urban Foundation, under the direction of ex-Judge Steyn, came into being because more and more business people were saying, 'We've got to do something, we can't just sit on the sidelines watching things go from bad to worse,' exactly as I was saying within my own company.

Initially, about two hundred businessmen met at the Carlton Hotel in Johannesburg to discuss this wonderful idea. I got up at the meeting to suggest a form of fund-raising based on tithing, exactly as churches tithe members. I thought a business tithe could be worked out as a percentage of profits, to be used for the purpose of improving living conditions in black urban residential areas. The idea of tithing, incidentally, has very recently been revived by the National Business Institute, which believes it can raise vital funds for promoting tourism through this sensible route.

Both Wendy and I became very involved with the work of the Urban Foundation, sitting on both national and Western Cape committees. The privately funded organisation embarked on projects to the value of nearly R5 million within 18 months of formation, and did excellent work right up until it was disbanded in the early 1990s.

Inasmuch as I still hesitated to commit myself to any formal political role, it became crystal clear during the 1970s that all social issues in South Africa had a political connotation. When a lost limb or a broken back among your own people happened because they were conscripted into military duty, that was political. When issues of food prices for poor people or matters of housing, welfare or medicine impacted adversely on both your customers and your staff and their families, that was political too. It was simply impossible to separate politics, put them on a shelf of their own, out of sight and out of mind, when nearly everything that happened was a result of the political dispensation in South Africa.

When racial tension was strung taut as razor wire a month after the Soweto riots, for instance, the government chose this time to reject outright the recommendations of their own commission that coloured people should immediately be given a greater say in political decision-making. That statement – a political one – had a direct bearing on the lives of the majority of our employees in the Cape, so how was it possible to keep politics out of the workplace?

Among the influential people I spoke to at this time, there was, however, consensus on one point. They all agreed that virtually every word written about South Africa and read abroad reflected the bad and destructive elements in our country. To those of us who did not want to be apologists for the government but who believed that if we were given a chance we could change the country from within, this situation was unfair and unnecessarily destructive. There were many businesses, organisations and individuals working hard at what I call the nuts and bolts, working from within to make meaningful changes. And we weren't doing too badly either.

The main trouble about standing up to be counted, tackling issues impacting on day-to-day life, was that you were always fighting at least two adversaries. You might enter into deep public discussions with influential people overseas to point out that sanctions and isolation impeded progress and only hurt those they meant to help, yet still get slammed back home in South Africa for meddling in politics instead of sticking to commerce.

I once suggested that if one hundred large local companies adopted policies of equal opportunity and salary on merit, tension could be reduced without government having to change legislation. The business community was enthusiastic about the idea, but official reaction was churlish and aggrieved – uncalled-for intervention and meddling, they said.

Tony Heard, editor of the *Cape Times*, wrote a strong editorial asking whether business was prepared to declare that enough was enough and to *do* something at last about the deteriorating situation in South Africa. I phoned Tony and told him I was ready to take the gloves off. From that time I became much more openly outspoken, which was about the same time I first met Secretary of Information Dr Eschel Rhoodie.

At 38 years of age, Dr Rhoodie was the youngest man ever appointed to high office by the National Party. When his past was later being dissected, it was revealed that he had never belonged to the powerful Afrikaner secret society, the Broederbond, which was almost obligatory for admittance to the higher levels of Afrikaner power. Instead, he had established himself as a maverick operator during service with the South African Information Services in Australia, the USA and Holland. Dr Rhoodie had no time for the constraints of conventional attitudes towards making friends and influencing people. He had formulated his own unconventional plan, targeted at those who formed opinions and made decisions overseas, to change their uniformly poor perceptions of South Africa.

Later reports revealed that when Dr Rhoodie presented his R64-million plan for influencing international opinion in South Africa's favour, Prime

Minister John Vorster warmed to it immediately. Finance Minister Dr Nico Diederichs agreed there would be no audit of the funds allocated for Dr Rhoodie's plan for five years. It was all strikingly unconventional, but when scandal erupted in 1978 – scandal in which I was embroiled in a fairly minor way – over what the funds had been spent on, there was an unseemly scramble on the part of government to deny having given Dr Rhoodie a free hand.

At my first meeting with Dr Rhoodie he said he was speaking to me because I was a prominent businessman with well-established contacts abroad, and also because I had spoken out against sanctions and embargoes, advocating change through economic development instead. Eventually, through Dr Rhoodie, I became one of five original trustees who formed the South African Freedom Foundation (SAFF). The SAFF was partly funded out of the trustees' pockets, but it was known from the outset that some funding came from the government.

In my own case, I became a sort of unofficial ambassador for South Africa, setting out to inform influential people of efforts to improve the lives of ordinary black people at grassroots level. I travelled extensively, as I had always done, and spoke as I always had, using real examples of the non-racial structures within Pick 'n Pay and the company's social commitment programmes to show that there was good in South Africa. I had to travel abroad so often that I was granted an exchange control exemption to allow me to buy a flat in London – with my own money – to use as a base.

Probably one of the most controversial stands I took in the 1970s, and one that is very unfashionable to own up to today, concerned the South African government's homelands policy. It is virtually impossible to find anyone now who is willing to admit that they thought there might be positive aspects to the homelands policy, but then it is also quite difficult to find anyone who admits to having voted for the National Party at all.

I first toured homeland areas near Pretoria in 1975 and spoke with the Bophuthatswana government. I saw an enormous amount on the positive side. Yes, there was a lot of squalor, a lot of squatters, but I also saw African businessmen building up chains of stores, owning land, owning houses. I saw 32 schools, a hotel school, plans to build an 18-hole golf course. All this was, I thought, at least something which allowed black people to hold their heads up higher, something better than the absolute yoke of repression under which they lived in urban white South Africa.

Since the early 1970s I had been speaking out against the ban on white capital investment in black homelands and the hopelessly restrictive clauses in the Group Areas Act, which demarcated trading areas by race. These nonsensical restraints worked disastrously against the interests of black consumers. As a direct result of big food chains being barred from trading in the black areas, it cost less to purchase a loaf of bread in the plush white residential areas of Johannesburg's northern suburbs than in Soweto. The bargaining power of big chains like Pick 'n Pay and the OK was not allowed to put cheaper food on township shelves, where it was so desperately needed.

In an effort to overcome restrictions on opening stores in black areas, I started discussions with Sam Motsuenyane of the African Chamber of Commerce (NAFCOC). I suggested that we could think about opening supermarkets jointly. The suggestion was to put in place an 80–20 percent deal, with Pick 'n Pay giving NAFCOC an 80 percent equity, while we retained 20 percent. Sam and I had many deep meetings about this proposal. We went together to see Interior Minister Connie Mulder and Prime Minister Vorster, and eventually got the government go-ahead for the scheme.

All of a sudden, I received a letter from Sam saying that the NAFCOC board had turned down this most imaginative scheme, which, after all, offered black entrepreneurs 80 percent for nothing, allowing them to open supermarkets in black areas backed by our buying power, expertise and experience. The NAFCOC board's decision to spurn capital and expertise in the 1970s because it was white was a tragic mistake, which they have accepted today. It would have been an absolutely marvellous pioneering thing and, had it happened, those founding people would have had a thriving chain today with what would probably be the biggest black holding on the Stock Exchange.

In my SAFF role as unofficial ambassador, I took information such as the NAFCOC initiative abroad to show that some pragmatic, practical

BUSINESS

SOUTH AFRICA

INCORPORATING BUSINESS EFFICIENCY

VOL. 5 NO. 6   JUNE 1970   50 CENTS

Pick and Pay's Raymond Ackerman: Doing our own thing.

Gus Ackerman

Gus's brother Mick

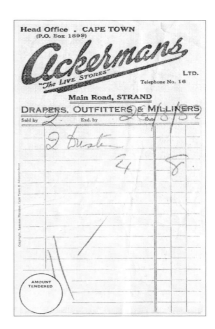

Below: Staff of an Ackermans store

17 MONDAY (48—317)

The Rising bell went at 5·45 and we all got dressed into our cadet clothes! After breakfast Oke, Bugs & I kept together and set off for the station. Mr O'Douglas gave us a lift down. We caught a packed train 6·40 and were in our positions in town by 7·00 (3½ hours to wait). Thousands upon thousands were there to honour the king and we were lining Adderley street right in the front. For two hours we waited doing nothing - people fainted all over the place. At 9·30 the Governor General Van Zyl & Field Marshall Smuts came down the street to meet the King on the Vanguard. At 10·20 we saw a guard of honour of 20 horsemen coming up from the docks, and behind them the King, Queen and the Princesses, it was thrilling seeing them at about 4 yds distant! After the procession had gone past we ran & caught the first train. At Rondebosch we had a drink and at school Riley gave us a swim. After lunch we were allowed out till 10·pm. Ken drove me to the beach & we came back at 5·00 pm. We played Billiards and Ping Pong & then had a treat supper. After that we listened to the celebrations in town over the wireless & played Ping·Pong. Dad brought me back to school. It was a

very hot day but one that I shall never forget.

A diary entry recording the Royal Visit of 1947

Above: Moyra, Ken and Raymond with their mother Rachel

Left: The Bishops First Team full-back

Raymond Ackerman, June 1951 (Photo: Arthur English)

Papal blessing on the NUSAS tour of Europe, 1952 (Raymond Ackerman is to the left of the student in the UCT blazer)

A Night School in Cape Town   (Photo: *Cape Times*)

Opening a new Checkers store, with Wendy Ackerman standing behind Raymond

The Modern Merchandising Methods seminar in Ohio, 1957, with Raymond Ackerman seated second from the right in front and Wendy Ackerman on the left

Wendy and Raymond Ackerman at the MMM seminar

The first Pick 'n Pay supermarket, in Belvedere Road, Claremont, Cape Town

The Ottery hypermarket

Turning the first sod on a new development

The aftermath of the fire at the Blackheath store, with John Lawley's marquee open for business in the background

Pick 'n Pay employees showing the keys to their own houses

Taking on the oil barons and the government

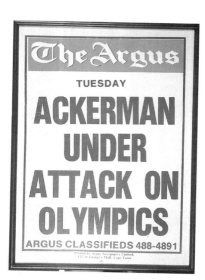

The Argus

TUESDAY

ACKERMAN UNDER ATTACK ON OLYMPICS

ARGUS CLASSIFIEDS 488-4891

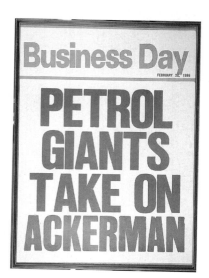

Business Day

FEBRUARY 22, 1996

PETROL GIANTS TAKE ON ACKERMAN

THE SUNDAY INDEPENDENT

ACKERMAN RESCUES STORMERS

May 231999

CAPE TIMES

BUSINESS REPORT

FRIDAY, MAY 9, 1997

PICK 'N PAY RUFFLES BANKING FEATHERS

Wendy Ackerman and Nelson Mandela at an event in aid of the Nelson Mandela Children's Fund

Raymond Ackerman, Adelaide Tambo, Steve Tshwete and Ngconde Balfour at the time of the Cape Town Olympic bid

(Photo: Graeme Robinson)

solutions were being tried by people in South Africa who were as genuine in their desire to see change in our country as those touting sanctions and isolation as the only means, particularly as sanctions so desperately hurt the most vulnerable sections of South African society.

I remember pleading with Desmond Tutu, then a Bishop, when he was secretary general of the South African Council of Churches, on behalf of farm workers living in Paarl, Worcester and Wellington. Bishop Tutu's campaign for the Council of Churches had persuaded British importers to stop buying South African wine and fruit. This inevitably caused a major slump in those labour-intensive industries. As jobs were lost, already desperately poor farm workers came face-to-face with the spectre of starvation. To help alleviate their plight, we set up soup kitchens outside our country stores and fed queues of hungry men, women and children, just as they did in America during the Great Depression.

I appealed desperately to Bishop Tutu to consider the results of his Council's campaign, but he refused to be moved. The end justified the means, he said. His attitude was in direct opposition to the stand taken by the Zulu leader Chief Mangosuthu Buthelezi. He cooperated in an anti-sanctions campaign with myself and other business leaders which at least gave people overseas another perspective. Although it has subsequently been accepted that sanctions did play a vital role in speeding up the demise of apartheid, I respected the stand Chief Buthelezi took in the 1970s against sanctions and disinvestment, at a time when it was not popular for a black leader to do so.

An annual family skiing holiday in the Swiss Alps had become a tradition in our family. On such holidays in the 1970s I was able to further my work for the SAFF through friendships Wendy and I formed with a group of British politicians, some of whom took Cabinet posts after Margaret Thatcher's 1979 British election victory. One of these was Cecil Parkinson, Minister of State for Trade. I wrote personally to congratulate him on his appointment. In his reply he stressed the importance of forging and strengthening trade links between the United Kingdom and South Africa. Wearing my SAFF hat, I offered to assist in arranging any particular meetings he might want to have in South Africa. Through Cecil Parkinson's office and those of several other British politicians, crucial meetings were held in South Africa and in Britain aimed at lessening South Africa's isolation so as to foster the cause of change through economic development – the cause at the heart of my SAFF work.

Although some of the stands I was taking in the 1970s were no more popular then than they are now, I am proud of what I achieved with the SAFF. It is, for instance, a fact that through contacts which Wendy and I maintained with John Moore, the British Cabinet minister who so nearly became Prime Minister, British Airways stayed in South Africa. The influential people who were brought out to South Africa under the auspices of the SAFF saw that some good things were happening here, and that positive developments were supported by like-minded people across the racial divide.

Not all SAFF initiatives concerned overseas issues: we trustees of the Foundation often met with local government ministers too. In 1976, after a series of meetings with Interior Minister Schoeman, he accepted that the Nationalists had made mistakes and promised dramatic changes for the better in the administration of laws such as the Immorality Act, that most hated and derogatory piece of race legislation. We were also told of progress towards solving the impasse over South West Africa, about US Secretary of State Dr Kissinger's Angola initiatives and the situation in Rhodesia, about which Mr Vorster was meeting with Dr Kissinger in Zurich at the time.

The last of this series of meetings became a real red-letter day for me because I had heard prominent Nationalist government ministers admit to being sensitive about the lack of dignity afforded to black people. The way they had opened up and taken us into their confidence about what was going on politically at home and abroad was heartening. However, shortly after this series of positive meetings, Mr Vorster, speaking on the tenth anniversary of becoming Prime Minister, said that while he agreed the country was going through 'seriously dangerous' times, the only way of governing the country was by National Party policy and principles. If the policy failed in the future, he said, it would not be because of the *policy* but because of the weakness of those carrying it out.

One step forward – two steps back.

During the 1970s there was also a definite hardening of attitudes among all shades of political opinion and sharp divisions dictated by circumstances and experience. One evening, for instance, I sat at a dinner party listening to the guests discussing the riots raging around the country as dispassionately as though this was happening on the moon instead of on their own doorsteps.

I thought about a meeting I had held with our management people in Johannesburg earlier that same week, when we too discussed the rioting and unrest. I told them I thought it was wrong to expose any of our young people to potentially dangerous situations and that for the time being we as a company should stay out of the worst areas. I wouldn't want to send my son to manage one of those stores, so how could I expect anyone else to send theirs? The people at that meeting were involved on a day-to-day basis with the realities of riot and civil unrest. They lived with the dangers and the tensions, unlike those equally concerned but removed people bandying opinions back and forth around safe dinner tables.

Even though people in positions such as my own were aware through experience of what was going on at both grassroots and government levels, some encounters still shocked. Under the auspices of the Urban Foundation I attended a meeting at this time with black business leaders trading in Cape Town townships and black youth leaders. It was one of the most outspoken meetings I had ever attended and I was really shocked at what I heard on the labour opportunity situation. I was, of course, all too familiar with labour legislation – job reservation – which reserved certain categories and levels of work for various racial groups. In supermarkets, for instance, a black person could not be a cashier or manager, unless the authorities could be persuaded to look the other way, without special permission.

The ludicrous laws governing which race might do which job were one of the everyday irritations of being in business in South Africa in the 1970s. They were also one of the greatest causes of bitterness and strife, as I heard from the angry businessmen and youth at the Urban Foundation meeting.

As well as legislation reserving categories of work by race there were also preferential labour areas, designated according to racial criteria. The

Western Cape province, where Cape Town is situated, was reserved as a labour area for coloured people. Until the Urban Foundation meeting I hadn't realised how protected the Cape was for coloured people, nor how completely the labour laws excluded Africans.

It was deeply shocking to hear black businessmen from Nyanga, Langa and Guguletu – townships on the outskirts of Cape Town – pouring out their anger at being politically excluded, socially degraded and economically exploited. One after another, youth leaders at the meeting shouted about wanting to destroy everything rather than do anything positive, whether this served the interests of their comfort, education and economic development or not. They did not want to concede anything, because any lessening of protest action would perpetuate apartheid. I got up and slammed them, asking if they really wanted communism Angolan-, Mozambican- or Cambodian-style in South Africa, because that was the way things would go if we did not link arms and do something together to promote urban land tenure, education and employment.

The anger I heard expressed that day was sobering, frightening, but I still thought it had been a healthy exchange and good contact. At the end of the meeting we resolved to draw up a report setting out the views of the Africans for submission to the Cabinet committee then sitting. Until then, the views of black business people had hardly been heard at all – they were like invisible people living in the economic shadows of their own country.

* * *

However intense and concerted attacks on the National Party had been for its policy of apartheid, the party had always prided itself on its probity. When, therefore, the greatest can of worms ever opened within their Calvinistic confines showed them, at the highest level of government, to be deeply enmeshed in a web of lies, deceit and duplicity, the public was both astonished and outraged.

It was 1978, and this was the beginning of the Information Scandal.

As I have previously mentioned, Dr Eschel Rhoodie, the Secretary of Information at the centre of the scandal, enlisted me in the SAFF because

I was committed to finding ways to bring about non-violent change in South Africa and because I had a wide network of international contacts in business and politics. It was made clear from the beginning that most funding for SAFF work would come from government, but I funded many of my own efforts from my own pocket.

Although I was an avowed opponent of the Nationalist government and had fought them frequently over their apartheid policies, I recognised that there was a better side of South Africa that went largely unsung. I am not at all ashamed to say that I spoke out about the better things when it was appropriate to do so. I had shown influential opinion-makers from abroad non-racial initiatives aimed at improving the lives of ordinary South Africans and had taken people around our stores to show the non-racial make-up of our organisation, even then. Our SAFF initiative did not concentrate solely on bringing foreign visitors to South Africa. We also facilitated multi-racial meetings between various South African groups who needed to talk to one another.

When the Information Scandal broke in 1978, details of the quixotic adventure Rhoodie had embarked upon had the South African public gasping in disbelief. We learned that money, soon revealed to be tax-payers' money, had been showered over four continents. Some went to the 1976 presidential election campaign in the USA of Governor Jimmy Carter, some to President James Mancham of the Seychelles to help obtain landing rights for South African Airways, and some to secure a friendly voice at the Organisation of African Unity. There were bold efforts to buy into the American press and Britain's Independent Television News and many, many more projects ranging from the ambitious to the bizarre.

Perhaps the most brazen of all Dr Rhoodie's projects was the setting up of *The Citizen* newspaper to voice the government point of view in English. Not only was the existing English press at that time usually hostile to the government, but the government believed that much of the adverse publicity South Africa received abroad emanated from the local newsrooms of the English-language press. Accordingly, with the role of government tightly concealed, *The Citizen* daily newspaper was launched to put matters right, using R14 million of taxpayers' money, first laundered through a Swiss bank account.

In 1978, an audit of the Information Department's books, tabled in Parliament, castigated then unnamed Information officials for unnecessary extravagance. From this mild beginning an astonishing series of events was set in motion, and the wool of Dr Rhoodie's extravagant tapestry began to unravel. Revelations of government duplicity flowed thick and fast. At the earliest opportunity, Dr Connie Mulder, the Minister of Information to whom Dr Rhoodie supposedly reported, distanced himself from the mushrooming scandal, claiming outrage, innocence and affront at the accusations levelled against government.

By 1979 Dr Rhoodie was on the run from the South African government, who sought to put him on trial for misuse of public funds, hoping to divert attention from their own implication in the Information débâcle. Rhoodie, however, declined to take the role of scapegoat and fled instead to Europe. While he was lying low there, he told a BBC television crew who caught up with him about a 1973 meeting between himself, Minister of Information Connie Mulder, Prime Minister John Vorster and Finance Minister Dr Nico Diederichs at which he had presented his plan and lobbied for funds.

Dr Rhoodie said he had asked outright if those present understood what he meant by a propaganda war. Did they understand that this would be an effort, a programme, uninhibited by rules or regulations? Rhoodie said he had specifically asked whether he would, for example, be allowed to send a journalist who was writing anti-South African articles, to Hawaii with his girlfriend for a month's holiday to change the journalist's perspective. Could he buy politicians and editors fur coats? In each case all answers had been affirmative. Rhoodie also claimed, truthfully, that from the outset it had been agreed at the highest levels of Cabinet that funds allocated to his 'Information' activities would be used at his own discretion and would not be subject to any audit for at least the first five years.

Whenever I was called on to explain my part in the SAFF, and my use of funds, I stuck to my policy of telling the truth to whoever put questions because, of course, the Foundation fell under the searchlights of the

Information exposé. I never tried to deny the knowledge I had, nor disguise how money had been spent, and neither did the other four original trustees of the SAFF.

My take on Eschel Rhoodie's secret activities was that while his use of public funds to enrich certain individuals and finance dubious schemes was thoroughly wrong, by the end of the exercise his campaign had achieved at least some of its aims. For all the ridicule, and there was plenty, heaped on Dr Rhoodie's more unusual attempts to win friends and influence people, at the end of the 1970s South Africa still managed to buy oil and arms. Despite talk of disinvestment overseas investors remained attuned to the economic opportunities South Africa offered, and the major powers continued to ignore calls for sanctions. In spite of the Soweto riots, the deadlock over South West Africa/Namibia, and the international outcry over the death in detention of Black Consciousness leader Steve Biko, South Africa still had international friends.

In the early aftermath of the Information Scandal, Foreign Minister Pik Botha called a press conference. I was asked to consult with him as spokesperson for the SAFF prior to the press conference, at which he intended calling for the immediate disbanding of the SAFF, among other initiatives thought to have been embarrassingly funded. In the case of the SAFF, during the Information exposé it had been revealed that Mr Redvers 'Red' Metrowich, chief trustee of the SAFF and former South African Broadcasting Corporation political commentator, had been receiving a salary, the extent of which he always declined to reveal, from a government department.

Until a harried Red Metrowich approached me in the thick of the unfolding scandal, asking that I keep as much as possible about his activities covered up, I had absolutely no idea that he was on the government payroll or, as it later transpired, that he had squandered SAFF funds on various dubious publishing enterprises, entirely on his own initiative. So it was that I could refuse to disguise any facts with a clear conscience, because from my point of view there *was* nothing to hide.

For the same reason, when Pik Botha demanded my agreement on disbanding the SAFF prior to telling the press this would be done, I refused point-blank. The independent enterprises of Red Metrowich were the only misdeeds that could be associated with the SAFF, and about these the original trustees had been ignorant. Otherwise, I pointed out as spokesman, we at the SAFF had carried on with our work exactly as mandated by our own independent ideas. We had never covered up the fact that some government funding went to the foundation, and what funding was received had been put to good use – not as apologists for government policy, which we were overwhelmingly against, but to encourage investment in South Africa for the good of the country as a whole. Red Metrowich had been removed from his SAFF position and, instead of disbanding an otherwise valuable initiative, it made much better sense to allow us to build on the foundations already laid. We had decided to rename the SAFF the South African Forum, to which I was elected Chairman by my colleagues. We absolutely refuted government's right to tell us what to do with our own organisation.

I took the same stance at the press conference following the private exchange with Pik Botha. Disagreement between us became quite heated again, but I stuck to our resolve – the Forum was our organisation, which we would fund ourselves, if need be. No one would tell us what to do with it. Next day my disagreement with Botha featured largely in the press.

Pragmatism and practicality: these were qualities abundantly applied by so many organisations and individuals in the very thick of apartheid South Africa. When I read notes in my early 1980s diaries about the brilliant entrepreneur Sol Kerzner, then planning to build Sun City in the arid bush land of Bophuthatswana – a homeland which had started out as six separate, unhopeful tracts of land – I do not forget the bribery, scandals, corruption and misuse of funds which typified homeland administrations. But I do remember how Sun City brought jobs and prosperity to an otherwise hopeless region, becoming a glittering hotel, casino and entertainment fantasy palace equal to anything similar in the USA.

CHAPTER 18

Policy and Pragmatism

Prime Minister John Vorster glared down at the phone in his hand as though the receiver harboured a live enemy. 'Connie,' he said, addressing the misgivings his Interior Minister, Dr Connie Mulder, was obviously voicing on the end of the line, 'I have told Mr Ackerman that he *can* have the 99-year lease rights for blacks. I have told him he can announce this from a *helicopter* if he wishes, because I have made up my mind. So you, Connie, can just b– off!'

Slam!

That was how, on a cold, wet March afternoon in 1978, a concession was won. I had been seeing Connie Mulder, Chris Heunis and Prime Minister Vorster under the auspices of the SAFF and also on behalf of my own Pick 'n Pay people for discussions on the vexed question of land tenure for blacks. In early discussions, Chris Heunis was very difficult, but Connie Mulder was personable, flexible and intelligent. Once Chris Heunis's grave grumblings were removed from the equation, Mr Vorster, Connie Mulder and I talked our problems over very frankly.

By this time, all but the most fervent right-wingers in the government accepted that urban black people were not the temporary sojourners apartheid had hoped they would be. Migratory labour practices, influx control laws, policies declaring black people non-citizens in white South Africa, had all contributed to the destabilisation of urban black communities but had not stopped them from growing. Undeterred by harsh laws and evictions, black people declared their intention to stay permanently close to the cities, the economic hubs of the land, by doing just that.

Once officialdom grudgingly accepted a permanent black urban presence, the question of land tenure had to be resolved. Prime Minister Vorster had already come round to wanting theoretically to grant the same rights of land tenure to blacks as to whites, but with freehold land rights went voting rights, and granting voting rights to urban blacks was still quite unthinkable in 1970s South Africa.

The suggestion I put before Mr Vorster in March 1978 was that land tenure rights for blacks should go through under a 'bond-holder' title instead of a 'freehold' title. This type of tenure, in effect a 99-year lease-hold system, did not encompass voting rights but did allow the 99-year lease-holder to qualify for a mortgage bond and bequeath property to heirs. Giving millions of urban blacks the right to build homes would spark a boom in the building industry, creating thousands of new jobs. Black home-owners would vastly improve their economic standing, and the increased urban stability that was bound to result from black home-ownership would overlap into every sphere of society. Calls for the adoption of a 99-year lease-hold system had been put forward in South Africa for years by many businessmen, organisations and individuals.

The day I presented my version of a 99-year lease-hold plan to Mr Vorster – one which had been worked out in close cooperation with Wendy's social responsibility staff – he was at first very stiff because, intuition told me, he resented having to listen to a private person solving an official dilemma. So I made it abundantly clear that neither in my capacity as spokesman for the SAFF nor as Chairman of Pick 'n Pay was I trying to tell him how to run the country, as so many did.

He responded very well to this approach and soon loosened up, conceding that the simple device of changing freehold title into 99-year lease-hold bonds was a good solution. Henceforth, he said, 99-year lease-holdings for urban blacks would have his blessing.

Within a month of the meeting with Mr Vorster, the press was reporting a Cabinet decision granting all blacks full property rights in practice, in all black urban as well as rural townships. Under such headlines as 'Permanent Homes for Urban Blacks', newspapers reported that the new rights boiled down to granting blacks a permanent status outside the homelands, allowing them to buy property, sell it and bequeath it to their children in perpetuity. This was described as 'leasehold in name, but freehold in practice', which indeed it was.

Just a few months later I was able to record having had 'two very warm teas' with the first black Pick 'n Pay people to own their own houses, purchased through the first of very many assisted company housing schemes initiated over the years. The new home-owners were absolutely delighted – we were equally so. I wrote that it just showed what could be done in South Africa if only our policies could be more flexible and people could get homes in areas where they worked and were respected.

In 1978 I also had the opportunity to wring a major concession from Prime Minister Vorster with regard to the Clovelly Golf Club – founded by my father in the 1920s. You might recall that the policy was that the club was open, which in those days meant open to all religions. Now I wanted to make Clovelly even more open – this time open to all races. I went to see Mr Vorster, himself a golfer, about the matter and was greeted by a somewhat wary, 'And what do you want now, Mr Ackerman?' There must have been some special security scare going on at the time, because I remember that I had to sit at the opposite end of the room to Mr Vorster, making it necessary for us almost to shout to hear one another. It was really quite ridiculous.

Anyway, I told Mr Vorster the whole background of Clovelly, that the club needed new membership and that I wanted to open it to all races. He listened, looking reflective, then told me the obvious – that I couldn't do so because this would go against the Group Areas Act. I replied that he had already capitulated by letting us employ black managers at Pick 'n Pay, which was also against the Group Areas Act, so why not make another exception in the case of Clovelly?

Finally, Mr Vorster told me that if I could go away and get 86 percent of the Clovelly membership to vote in favour of becoming a multi-racial club, he would give us the go-ahead. I was understandably puzzled by the figure of 86 percent – why not a round percentage, why 86 percent? I asked. 'I don't know,' Mr Vorster replied, 'it's just the figure that came into my head.'

I immediately went away and convened a meeting at Clovelly at which over 90 percent of members voted to open the club to all races. So it was with Mr Vorster's obscure directive fulfilled that we were able to make Clovelly South Africa's first multi-racial golf club. Very soon, one of the most prestigious golf clubs in Cape Town, the august Royal Cape, hit the headlines by refusing to allow black players to participate in the South African Open Tournament which their club was hosting. Of course, they hid behind the Group Areas Act on this one. My son Gareth took extreme exception to Royal Cape's ban on black players and virtually insisted that Clovelly should offer to host the tournament instead.

We did so, winning high praise from the press for our stand, while the Royal Cape was roundly criticised. 'Royal Cape Bans Blacks' said the papers, after which I was never a very popular person at that venue, although I have since greatly admired the work the Royal Cape has done in the field of golf development.

* * *

In September 1978, after government had been forced into confession after confession about their knowledge of Dr Rhoodie's programme and funding of it, Prime Minister John Vorster cracked under accumulated strains and announced his resignation, making himself available for the ceremonial office of State President instead.

Prior to the Information Scandal, Dr Connie Mulder had always been regarded as Mr Vorster's natural successor. But not only had he occupied the hottest government seat as the minister responsible for Dr Rhoodie's policies, he had also told the South African public a barefaced lie when he stood up in Parliament to deny government funding or involvement in *The Citizen* newspaper. He was outvoted by the National Party caucus in the premiership ballot, losing to Mr P. W. Botha, who took over as Prime Minister in September 1978.

While the long drama of the Information Scandal had been playing out, the work of the Urban Foundation, with which I was still involved, continued effectively. A huge sum of money had already been raised in America for black housing. I thought this money should be lent to individual black urban-dwellers to buy their own homes – permitted under the 99-year lease provisions. The backbone of home-ownership schemes which Pick 'n Pay had in place over the years financed the building of houses with a combined company contribution and building society loan. Qualifying staff repaid loans in some subsidised way. I thought some of the monies raised in America through the Urban Foundation's enterprise could be lent to companies wishing to initiate housing schemes of their own, perhaps based on our group's tried and tested model.

At the beginning of the 1980s, with most of the world racked by recession, inflation and uncertainty, Pick 'n Pay was going forward with remarkable confidence. We announced plans for a new chain of super stores to challenge rival chain Checkers in the country towns, whereupon Checkers issued a challenge of their own. They intended engineering the greatest turnaround in South Africa's retail history, which demanded denting Pick 'n Pay's profits to bolster their own flagging figures. Such an ambition was a well-starred one to have at that time, because conditions were conducive to all forms of expansion. The South African economy was booming and consumers were spending lavishly.

Windfall profits of some R200 million had dropped South Africa's way as a result of astronomically high gold prices – US$835 by January 1980. The value of trading on the Johannesburg Stock Exchange zoomed up to over R3 million a day, equivalent to an entire week's figures less than a year previously. The first Budget of 1980 saw Finance Minister Owen Horwood announcing dream provisions such as cuts in income tax, increased pensions, subsidies and special funds for improving the lives of black South Africans.

It was paradoxical. In the midst of ever-simmering internal political tension, troubles on our border, international isolation and polecat status, South Africa was enjoying unprecedented prosperity.

Bolstered by the security of the windfall millions, Prime Minister P. W. Botha, who had already told whites in an early speech that they had to learn to *adapt or die*, nevertheless knew that attempts to move outside the ideological framework of apartheid would not be tolerated by the powerful white right-wing or conservatives in his ruling party. So he tried, instead, to moderate and modernise the image of apartheid, hoping, vainly of course, to make it more acceptable to black people.

While P. W. Botha grappled with his forward course, I was grappling with mine – namely the problem of how to cope with a company galloping ahead at such a massive rate. Apart from the ambitious new super-store programme devised, I knew that diversification was clearly called for within the company's endeavours. I had to analyse and assess how to do this, but my mind was absolutely boggled by the pace of the company's development. I was excited, but also cautious about doing too much, making the wrong move.

While I was casting around, thinking about possibilities, having long, intense debates with advisers, I was one day summoned to another meeting with Foreign Minister Pik Botha, who wanted further discussions on the SA Forum.

However, when we met, Pik Botha instead began to give me an impromptu summing-up of where he stood on the burning issues of Rhodesia, Angola and South West Africa. Hearing from him how serious matters were on our borders was hardly comforting when there was no dearth of bad news inside South Africa either. Serious riots over inferior education were blighting life in the Cape Peninsula, while the clash between Prime Minister P. W. Botha's reformists and the white far-right looked increasingly ominous. With South Africa engaged in conflict outside and within, danger was prosperity's companion at that turbulent time.

By the time Pik Botha eventually came to the topic actually on the agenda, nearly an hour and a half had flown by in a meeting for which minutes had been allocated. It was apparent that the bruising suffered as a result of Information Scandal revelations had healed, because Pik Botha was telling me that government wanted the South African Forum not only to continue, but to escalate our work on a contract basis. This seemed an opportune time to mention that I had been toying with the idea of relinquishing the role I held as the Forum's Chairman because of extreme work pressures.

Mr Botha would not hear of this at all, saying that government would only continue to participate if I agreed to remain in the chair. It was a gratifying response in view of the acrimonious exchanges between us the last time the Forum was discussed. I decided to drive home the advantage his vote of confidence gave to reaffirm the Forum's independence and our policy of not acting as fronts for government policies, which we mostly rejected, but as representatives of moderate South African opinion.

It was a good meeting, with good rapport, although as always I could not help feeling that Pik Botha veered too much to the emotional and was not cool enough. I also remember hearing for the first time at that meeting with Pik Botha how much faith the government had lost in the black leaders of their independent homeland creations like Transkei, where management was pathetic and corruption rife.

Ironically, following that piece of intelligence, within half an hour of leaving Mr Botha I was in another meeting talking with Chief Sebe of the self-governing Ciskei – Transkei's Eastern Cape neighbour – and four of his ministers. This delegation wanted me to take Pick 'n Pay into an agricultural project to help Ciskei people earn money and feed themselves. I was more than a little taken aback when Chief Sebe said that while his people felt that separate development, the euphemism for apartheid, was unequal and unfair, underneath many would not mind having it in their own country if it brought economic development and more money – the pragmatic politics of the hungry, needy and economically disempowered.

That night as I lay in bed, exhausted by a day of unremitting pressure, the meetings with Mr Botha and Chief Sebe buzzed round and round in my brain. Thanks to Pik Botha's disclosures, I now knew that South Africa was in deep trouble, and I knew I had to think equally deeply about the role Pick 'n Pay should take. Should we put our efforts into developing the independent states and homelands, or should we opt for an overseas diversification? Was it too idealistic to concentrate locally when this would create no insurance policy against mayhem in South Africa? Critical times. Critical decisions.

Just as I was nodding off to sleep, I woke with a start. With all my deliberations about Pik Botha's and Chief Sebe's politics, I had entirely forgotten to note down the results of two other meetings held that day. I heaved myself wearily out of bed, stumbled to my desk and noted that a good price for frozen chickens had been agreed and that I had found a reliable supplier of canned bamboo shoots.

Politics apart – for me, it was always business as usual.

PART THREE

NUTS AND BOLTS, NODS AND WINKS

'Doing good is good business'
– Bernardo Trujillo

CHAPTER 19

Building a Pyramid

'I have to tell you, Raymond, I have to tell you honestly, if it comes to a situation where it is in my family's interests to sell our shares in Pick 'n Pay because of what they are worth, because of what we could make, then that is what I would have to do.'

These honest words from my loyal friend and brother-in-law, Issy Fine, caused a coldness to creep into my business bones. What he was expressing brought me face-to-face with my worst fear: the fear of losing control of Pick 'n Pay as my father had lost control of Ackermans to Greatermans. Even my dismissal from Checkers in 1966 had happened because, exactly as in the case of my father, others were able to exert greater control over me than I had resources to counter.

If Issy felt that he might have to sell his shares – for which no one could blame him – who wouldn't succumb to the lure of a cash bonanza if the right offer was made? I had already sat down with my friend and adviser Harold Gorvy and worked out that at the current share price, other family members might well decide that they had to forgo family loyalty in the face of financial prudence. My brother Ken, resident in England, had indeed already sold shares and my father-in-law had intimated that he too might sell. For many local shareholders the prospect of selling shares in a South African business was anyway alluring at this time, when people worried about the future of their investments. Much capital was fleeing the country for reasons of expediency.

From the very beginning, I had always insisted on having full control of Pick 'n Pay to assuage my paranoia – as I have described it before – about being taken over, losing out. The first shareholdings issued in 1967 had been structured to keep the majority issue in my hands. Since then, events had rollicked along at such a pace, calling for vast cash resources to fund burgeoning supermarket and hypermarket developments.

By 1981 it had taken just 14 years to build Pick 'n Pay into a billion-rand business. On a visit to South Africa, Grant Gentry, ex-CEO of the great A&P food company of the USA, had expressed amazement at the rapid rise of our company, saying that it would have taken a lifetime to achieve a similar feat in America.

However, rapid growth was a hungry business beast to feed. Since Pick 'n Pay had gone public in 1968, Harold Gorvy had kept a watchful eye on developments and the need for funding. Therefore, over the years there had been a number of rights issues – more, with hindsight, than we probably needed to have released. At any rate, as a result I had been watching my family's shareholding in the company with concern, because we had slipped below the 51 percent holding that made me comfortable. Now, in 1981, I was hearing disquieting rumours that prominent South African businessmen, including Rembrandt's Anton Rupert and the late Jan Pickard, an original shareholder of ours, had been scanning share registers, intent on finding out the extent of my family's shareholding in Pick 'n Pay.

It was a dangerous situation, severely unsettling to one as paranoid as I am about keeping control. I could not abide the thought of being in a minority shareholding position, effectively just waiting for more powerful interests to swoop down and take over the majority holding in my company. This was a fear which Wendy shared. It was clear I was going to have to move fast to foil any take-over of the company.

The means I chose to achieve a new injection of capital while protecting my family's interests in Pick 'n Pay were designed around the creation of a pyramid scheme, which we called Pikwik.

In 1981 quite a few South African companies already had pyramid schemes in place. Anglo American had one, as had Anton Rupert's Rembrandt Group. But the Johannesburg Stock Exchange was wary about sanctioning pyramids, a reluctance they shared with most controllers of Western stock markets. The point about a pyramid is that it can be structured so as to allow a 25 percent holding in an underlying company to translate into a 50 percent holding in the pyramid company. The serious problem with pyramid schemes, however, is that theoretically the pyramid can go up and up.

Thus, the first pyramid could give a 50 percent holding in the pyramid company on an underlying holding of 25 percent; the next 50 percent on 12 percent; and the next 50 percent on 6,25 percent. Where a structure of multi-pyramids like these is formed, a 6,25 percent holding could practically translate into a controlling interest, which is patently wrong.

Because of such potentially unhealthy flaws, the Johannesburg Stock Exchange looked long and hard at our proposals for Pikwik. Negotiations were lengthy and difficult and we had to include some tough protective clauses prior to getting final permission to set up the scheme. I had to guarantee personally that Pikwik would only be used to hold Pick 'n Pay, that it would not be used for my family to go out and buy, for example, a hotel or a beach cottage. I also had to pledge that my family would never sell our shares in the pyramid unless the minority shareholders got the same deal, a unique undertaking in South Africa. Permission was eventually forthcoming, and Wendy and I effectively swapped our Pick 'n Pay shares for Pikwik shares, which remains the situation today.

Soon after issue, Pikwik shares rocketed, which was exciting and unexpected. I issued a statement about the formation of the Pikwik pyramid, telling financial reporters that my family had taken this route in order to keep control and avoid a take-over. Now that we had achieved our objective, we wanted to keep our eye on the ball and get on with normal business without having to watch our backs all the time.

Twenty-one years after the formation of the Pikwik pyramid, I am still fighting to make sure that Pick 'n Pay stays in family hands in the face of a decline in large family businesses throughout the world. Today, I can count large family businesses operating in South Africa on one hand, whereas twenty years ago in the retail sector alone the great chains of Woolworths, Greatermans and the OK were all family-controlled. Now, they have all gone to big conglomerates, to become cogs in the wheels of corporate juggernauts such as Sanlam, South African Breweries and the like. In so doing, I believe, those companies lost their personalities. I continue to fight very hard to stop our family identity in Pick 'n Pay from being swallowed up.

The issue of family succession in business is an interesting one. Throughout the world there have been many surveys on the impact of second and third generations in family businesses. Sam Cohen, founder of OK Bazaars, once remarked, 'I have a view ... that the first generation stick to their business and they die with their boots on. The second generation think, when they go into business, about how soon they can get out and cash in. The third generation don't even come in.'

I do not agree with Sam Cohen's assessment, obviously formed from his own disappointment. In the case of his company, as he pointed out, the young second generation simply didn't want to carry on. Two years after the death of Michael Miller, co-founder of the OK Bazaars with Sam Cohen, South African Breweries were banging on the OK's door bearing a take-over bid.

World-wide surveys have in fact shown that the third generation is often even stronger than the first. My father was the first generation. I am the second, and I haven't been too bad. The main inference drawn from comparisons between generations in business is that children of founders are less inclined to struggle and work because they grow up enjoying the fruits of their fathers' labours. My children are the third generation, but they have not always been in a comfort zone, any more than I was. My children have seen what it was like for our family to have very little. Gareth, after all, was nine years old when I bought Pick 'n Pay. He saw me having to start all over again, as did my daughters Kathy and Suzanne and Jonathan at a later date, being the youngest.

However, back at the time of the Pikwik flotation, as far as my family was concerned, the issues revolved around shareholdings and not succession, as they were later to do in the dramatic events of 1999.

Gareth was by this time working with me at Pick 'n Pay. He had long years of experience under his belt. Starting when he was still at school, he had worked with me during holidays and at weekends. One time I put him in charge of servicing and supervising our Cookiematic operation – imported biscuit-making machines we had in our bakeries. I remember that in this era he was forever dashing off with a bag full of tools to unclog some recalcitrant biscuit-making machine somewhere. Another time, he ran our Blue Ribbon butcher shops. I cherish the memory of a dinner Wendy and I had at that time with a branch of the Herber family, on holiday in South Africa from their transplant home in Canada. Robert Herber, once a colleague of mine and a cousin of the Herber who had thrown me out of Checkers, held forth for ages, reciting a well-rehearsed list of his children's remarkable accomplishments. Pausing briefly out of belated manners to ask what our eldest son was doing, Wendy told him, deadpan, that he was a butcher. We watched in high amusement as strained smiles and polite remarks of 'Oh, really?' were bandied round the table.

As each of our children did, Gareth spent a year in Europe after school before studying Social Science at the University of Cape Town. He chose this degree in preference to following me in studying Economics, because workplaces were in transition, with matters relating to labour and unions featuring ever more prominently in South African business. Gareth wisely wanted training that would allow him to work efficiently within this new-style commercial landscape.

After university, I didn't think it would be right for my eldest son to come straight into Pick 'n Pay. I thought he needed some independent experience away from my influence, so I spoke to several international retailing colleagues, including the dynamic Grant Gentry, then head of the giant American A & P group. Grant was prepared to take Gareth into an enterprise called Pantry Pride, a chain in the southern states of the USA which had been rescued after bankruptcy and was in the process of being revived. Because of these special circumstances, this was a very tough challenge, but it was a wonderful opportunity to gain world-wide experience in the intricacies of retail operations. At Pantry Pride, Gareth learned the nuts and bolts of retailing, but on a more scientific level than the pricing of ladies' underwear which my father had given *me* to do as training.

So, when Gareth finally joined me at Pick 'n Pay, he came with excellent experience and practical knowledge but was still required to work his way up through the ranks.

* * *

There was no doubt: Pick 'n Pay had never been in a stronger financial position than following the Pikwik flotation, which had pushed shares up to a phenomenal R98. International recognition came too when the CIES – the Paris-based International Association of Food Chains – invited me to give a presentation on the whole Pick 'n Pay story at an upcoming San Francisco conference.

I had once been reluctantly torn away from the book I was reading in a dark corner of a Swiss hotel lounge – prised like a reluctant crab from the protective shell I always adopted in order to read peacefully when we were on family skiing holidays in Davos – by Wendy's insistence that I should meet Rudi Suter, head of the European retail chain Migros. That introduction turned out to be one of the most auspicious of my business career because through Rudi Suter I was invited to join the CIES. As a member and later Chairman of the CIES for one term of office, I was able to help keep South African business on the international map during the long period of isolation that the country went through. Membership of the CIES also gave me opportunities to discuss South African problems, such as sanctions and disinvestment, with people of the stature of John Major and Margaret Thatcher of the United Kingdom, Brian Mulroney of Canada, Chancellor Kohl of Germany and Jesse Jackson, Andrew Young and Colin Powell of the USA. I was able to rub shoulders with high-profile people such as these when I was introduced to them at CIES conferences around the world.

The myriad matters that went into the day-to-day running of Pick 'n Pay had formed a complex and demanding pattern at the time of the Pikwik flotation, mainly because of the management style I chose to follow. The company was really on the move. During one week alone I worked out that I had been in touch with over 2 500 people within the company. Over a couple of weeks, I visited all eight hypers and 54 stores in the supermarket division, shaking everyone by the hand. I wrote in my diary that I knew exactly how Henry Kissinger, whose shuttle diplomacy was much in the news then, must have felt, as I too flew from meeting to meeting, place to place.

Then increasing disquiet among South Africa's business community over the course of affairs at home and abroad prompted Prime Minister P. W. Botha to call a conference. Six hundred top business people, myself among them, were summoned to a Johannesburg hotel to hear a policy update. Addressing the conference, Mr Botha said he was well aware of our grave concerns but asked us to accept that government was serious in its endeavours to secure effective participation for all South Africans – conditional only on the maintenance of stability. This was, of course, a very ambiguous statement open to varied interpretation, so reaction to Mr Botha's remarks was predictably mixed. Some found his address 'interesting', some 'uninspiring', others 'optimistic'. Harry Oppenheimer, who had publicly told P. W. Botha that if substantial progress was not made quickly towards genuine political power-sharing and social justice, the country was headed towards armed revolution, said, 'The Prime Minister is still on his reformist course; I am not sure how fast, but it is something anyway.'

Soon afterwards, the Black Sash, a respected human rights organisation, protested that the business community present at Mr Botha's meeting had tended towards accepting platitudes while ignoring the growing debasement of civilised standards in South Africa. The Black Sash protest followed a fresh wave of trade unionist detentions then in progress and the ongoing general practice of detaining suspects without trial.

Only three businessmen, of whom I was one, responded to the Black Sash protest. I told the organisation that it was definitely not my own policy nor that of my company to support detention without trial – we were totally against it. I intended raising the matter at the first opportunity, but there was so *much* going on, so *much* that needed careful analysis and thought, quite apart from the 'ordinary' business of running a large company going through a period of rapid expansion. Sometimes it was hard to know where to begin, especially when mounting international pressure was pushing South Africa further and further into isolation.

There was a marked increase in union militancy at this time, which in a way was unexpected and even contradictory, since the only sector of black life to benefit thus far from Prime Minister Botha's promised reforms had been the black trade union movement. But black union leaders had turned overtly political because trade unionism was the only political forum open to them. We had experienced increased union aggression at first hand through a difficult strike at our Norwood hyper in Johannesburg. By the time the strike was over, I had to conclude that even after the increases awarded, wages across the board were still too low. Clearly a long season of strife lay ahead. I thought about the pros and cons of adopting a strong policy change, because the Norwood strike had proved that a hypermarket could run on a skeleton staff, still look good and still achieve terrific productivity.

Perhaps the time had come to consider cutting *numbers* dramatically, paying those remaining much higher salaries. How this could be achieved without losing our commitment to the consumer was an issue flowing strongly from this contemplated new strategy, which I mention to illustrate the fluidity within the South African business community at this time – a fluidity dictated by the changing demands of the union movement among other potent forces.

A few years down the line, the fall-out from union activism would put the backs of the South African business community firmly against the wall. Some of the worst results of political repression were still to come home to roost.

As our wider world steadily contracted, efforts towards reform limped slowly along at home. The newly constituted President's Council was a case in point. The multi-racial Council, comprising government-appointed white, coloured and Asian members, was charged with advising on constitutional reforms. Blacks were entirely excluded from Council membership. One of the President's Council's first recommendations was that areas from which blacks had been forcibly removed should be rezoned and returned to the evicted communities as a symbol of reconciliation.

Mr Botha rejected this small but immensely emotive concession outright. It was very ominous to those of us watching desperately for meaningful change, seeming to point to a basic unwillingness on Mr Botha's part to really dismantle apartheid.

As for our company, we chose this time of turmoil over residence to deposit R1 million with a Natal building society to subsidise home loans for our black staff living in Natal. As always in South Africa, business had to carry on and do whatever it could.

The contradiction between P. W. Botha's reported desire for reform and his unwillingness to embrace the consequences ended up alienating him from all shades of political opinion. Liberal whites joined the majority of black opinion in rejecting reform initiatives because they excluded Africans. Conservative whites, who believed Mr Botha planned to remove the very cornerstones of apartheid legislation in which they saw their only hope of survival, mounted their own rebellion. Mr Botha eventually expelled 16 arch-conservatives from his ruling National Party for failing to support reformist racial policies. This led the spokesman for the rebels, Dr Treurnicht, to form his own right-wing grouping – the Conservative Party.

Dr Treurnicht's exit moved a man of destiny closer to centre stage. This was Mr F. W. de Klerk, whom I soon came to know and respect, first when he accepted an invitation to open one of our new stores located in his Vaal Triangle constituency. Early in the 1980s Johann Rupert – Anton Rupert's son – orchestrated one of many business initiatives aimed, over the years, at increasing the pace of change. Mr De Klerk joined those of us involved with the initiative for lunch at the Mount Nelson Hotel, where Wendy took the opportunity to tackle him about the rise of the South African right-wing. That far back Mr De Klerk's frankness and openness, although there was no doubt he was basically quite a conservative man, were a breath of fresh air.

Meanwhile, again wearing my commercial hat, I gave an address to the annual CIES Executive Congress in 1982, which I called 'Revolutionary Changes in South African Retailing'. I noted that as the face of super-market trading was changing in South Africa, so America too was passing through a trading revolution. There, chains were closing down shops in regions which were over-stored and unprofitable. This phenomenon was of great interest to me because I had started to isolate what I believed ailed our rivals, Checkers, in their attempts to hold steady and expand in the face of Pick 'n Pay's rock-solid performance countrywide.

Retailers, then, loved to say what *market share* they had. They worked tirelessly towards growing market share, which I had come to view as a dangerous philosophy. Checkers set out to increase their market share in the 1980s by opening outlets far and wide. Their policy was to get at Pick 'n Pay by putting stores down to improve their market share. But the number of stores they put down didn't matter, because they were not making a profit, which is precisely the risk inherent in placing market share above profitability. By contrast, I resolved not to care how *many* stores we had, so long as each and every one of them made a profit. As a result, speaking with the advantage of hindsight, we went roaring ahead in profitability while Checkers went steadily downhill on their endless chase after market share.

Mind you, in one of those paradoxes of business, the single most important factor in bringing my company's Australian dream crashing down was being blocked against establishing more than one store when we badly needed to open more outlets.

Strange the twists fate takes.

CHAPTER 20

Going Down Under

As we concentrated on putting the final touches to the Pikwik pyramid in place, another page turned, revealing a character who carried the key to a door I had been wanting to open for years. This was Mr Jack Liberman from Melbourne, Australia, and the key he held was to open the door to the overseas outlet I had come to believe that Pick 'n Pay needed.

Jack Liberman was introduced by one of our South African suppliers. As soon as I began talking to him – and I cannot explain this on any grounds other than instinct – pieces of a puzzle fell into place. The quest to find the right vehicle for taking Pick 'n Pay forward in strength and security had continued. Ideas for local investment in South Africa's independent and homeland territories had not been abandoned, but it had become clear that the business needed an overseas outlet as well. I personally very much wanted an asset outside South Africa – yes, as a hedge against everything here going up in flames. I had looked at possibilities in Europe, in America and in Britain, but nothing thus far had felt right.

The Liberman family ran a chain of convenience stores in Australia as well as many other factories. They were real Australian entrepreneurs. After I had taken Jack Liberman around our hypers and gone through some of the intricacies of running those huge stores, he was very impressed, very excited, very enthusiastic. Australia, he told me, was wide open for the introduction of our hypermarkets.

I started to experience the familiar adrenalin surge, precursor of something new, exciting and challenging. I lost no time in starting deep discussions with Hugh Herman, after which we assembled our decision-makers and structured a deal to put to Jack Liberman. With hindsight, the deal was probably put together too rapidly, although we did try to temper our enthusiasm with objectivity. I should also record that while I went ahead with the Australian venture with enthusiasm and belief in its rightness, there was always a small place in my ultra-sensitive business gut that stood aside and wondered if the Australian adventure *was* as right as it seemed.

At any rate, the final agreement reached with the Liberman family was that they would put up most of the money if we would provide the expertise to open up in Australia. We were to provide one-third of the capital in exchange for a 33 percent stake. At that time the Australian dollar and South African rand were almost one to one in value – rather different to the overall weakness of the rand against foreign currencies today. I anticipated plenty of trouble in getting permission from the South African Reserve Bank to move money out of South Africa into Australia because all foreign exchange transactions were scrutinised in the light of the rand being under siege. Nevertheless, we finally got the necessary approvals, and the way was open for Pick 'n Pay's Australian début.

Hugh and I left for Australia soon after our initial talks with the Libermans, to see for ourselves whether Australia was as ready for hypermarkets as Jack had suggested. Coming from the isolated outpost of southern Africa, we were surprised to find supermarket development in Australia well behind ours. Jack, we soon concluded, was absolutely right – Australia was ready for the introduction of hypermarket shopping.

After applying the same formulas I used to decide how many hypers South Africa could sustain, Hugh and I between us concluded that Australia could ultimately support ten hyper stores. This being the case, I saw our first foray into Australia as very much a beginning, the start of a continent-wide presence for Pick 'n Pay across Australia. But to build a chain we needed the first link, and I accordingly left Hugh searching for an Australian hyper site while I returned to South Africa and arranged to sign the final deal with the Libermans.

On my return to South Africa I found that the press had already got onto the story of Pick 'n Pay going to Australia, which I played down without denying the fact. I was feeling terribly pressurised at this time, plagued by headaches and often exhausted – the Australian venture was only one card in Pick 'n Pay's pack. This being the case, it was just as well I didn't realise that I was only at the very beginning of a time of unprecedented tension that would demand extremes of emotional and physical endurance.

We were in the midst of dealing with a kidnapping crisis when I heard that Hugh Herman had secured a wonderful site in Brisbane for our first Australian hyper. I had spent an entire night next to the phone keeping in touch with developments after a two-year-old boy had been snatched from our Brackenfell hyper store. I had immediately doubled the reward his father offered for the boy's return, which meant that I had to stay alert and near a phone all night in case the kidnapper made contact. When Hugh phoned next morning with his good news, I seemed to be hearing it through a cottonwool cloud of fatigue. There were still 17 tense hours to go before the kidnapped child was found abandoned in a suburban telephone booth.

The site Hugh had found was in the Aspley suburb on the outskirts of Brisbane, a lovely city with a relaxed, cosmopolitan atmosphere very like the feel of South African coastal cities. The Brisbane site had a creek running through it, which would require draining, but was otherwise perfect.

With the first hyper site chosen, it was time to start selecting a team to put our Australian plan into play, because our deal with the Libermans called on us to provide a South African management team experienced in hypers to get the Australian store up and running. Other hyper staff would be locally employed Australians. I chose one of my most experienced and best-performing managers, David Goldberg, to head up our South African contingent and asked him if he would agree to take my son Gareth onto his team. I felt that Gareth would be a valuable member of the pioneer team with his operations and planning experience, even though I was aware he would encounter difficulties in finding his own level as an individual who also happened to be the boss's son.

The South African contingent went to Australia on assignment, but because things were so difficult at home at that time, many were keen to go, seeing it as an ideal 'look-see' opportunity.

As we readied ourselves to move into Australia we did, of course, anticipate opposition – as a South African company how could we not? But we believed that numbers were in our favour; the team of South African managers was so small that they were an insignificant number when measured against the overwhelmingly greater participation of our Australian partners. The Libermans were the majority shareholders, and from the beginning Australian architects and builders, suppliers and store staff were part of the plan.

Still, the international outcry against South Africa was building to a shrill climax and protest was better organised, better focused and more effective on all fronts than it had been before. Even in anti-South African sports demonstrations, protesters were better organised. When the rugby Springboks toured New Zealand in 1981, they were harassed by protesters sufficiently organised to form a human wall which closed local rail services and two motorways for hours. Protesters threw smoke bombs onto pitches and exchanged blows with pro-tour rugby fans in angry scenes.

As news of our proposed arrival on Australian shores built into a big story, we attracted the ire of Australian traders who plotted and planned to avoid having to share a slice of their cake with the South African interloper, Pick 'n Pay.

* * *

As soon as I had shaken hands with Australia's Labour Prime Minister Bob Hawke, I realised that my trepidation about meeting him was misplaced.

I met Mr Hawke at a social function some time after Hugh Herman and others involved in Pick 'n Pay's move into Australia had sought his help in overcoming the huge opposition we faced over opening our hyper store in Brisbane. Being a staunch opponent of apartheid he had not felt able to assist. I was therefore expecting to meet a stiff, resentful premier. However, to my surprise Mr Hawke turned out to be pragmatic and down-to-earth.

He was soon telling me that although his politics were left-wing and he was indeed fiercely anti-apartheid, he had cause to be grateful to two South Africans. When he had been a Rhodes Scholar at Oxford University, he one day participated in a particularly hair-raising Rag stunt – a horse and cart race. When his cart reached a fair speed, a sudden lurch pitched him out, flinging him into the path of oncoming horses. At the moment he hit the ground, two white flannelled figures rushed through the barrier and pulled him out almost from under the very hooves of the horses, thereby saving his life. The heroes turned out to be two South African cricketers, Roy McLean and Jackie McGlew, who were members of a touring Springbok team then visiting Oxford.

Since that time, Mr Hawke told me, he had always thanked the South Africans for his life. They still exchanged gifts each year and kept in touch. He then went on to tell me that although his party was sympathetic to the ANC and he wanted to protect the interests of Australians against outside business intervention, he also saw *any* initiative which brought money and jobs into Australia as advantageous. Prime Minister Hawke was caught in a bit of a squeeze, really. In the end he told me, as he had told Hugh Herman before, that while he would not help us with setting up in Australia, he would not hinder us either, which was the fairest stand he could take.

The torrent of opposition that had poured over us since we announced our intention of opening an Australian Pick 'n Pay had surprised even us beleaguered South Africans, used as we were to polecat status. On the surface, opposition seemed to be directed against us on the grounds that we were a South African company. The reality, however, was rather different. Behind the front of opposing us because we hailed from apartheid South Africa, Australian traders were engaged in a calculated strategy which united union and political opposition in repelling an invasion of their trading turf.

I am not saying that there wasn't real abhorrence for apartheid or some genuine desire on the part of unions to show solidarity with their South African counterparts, but I am saying that as far as the Australian traders were concerned, all the anti-apartheid angst provided a convenient cover for their true commercial motives. The need to protect their trading turf was also the real reason behind later assertions that the arrival of Pick 'n Pay in Australia would cause the country to become over-traded – a ludicrous idea when you think of the size of Australia.

Events in South Africa in the early 1980s hardly helped to promote our cause either. All news coverage coming out of our country was depressing, showing crowds of militant black people – sometimes schoolchildren and youths – being controlled by snarling dogs, guns and armoured vehicles. Bullets flew and black people died in dusty township ghettos. It was widely believed that the state of affairs in South Africa was deteriorating and that the rest of the civilised world had a duty to apply pressure in the form of sanctions and exclusion to bring apartheid down.

Looking back on the lead-up to the opening of our first Australian hyper, I can still close my eyes and relive how it felt to promote the positive side of South African life in the face of such a crushing wall of antagonism. I gave numerous interviews to radio and television reporters, explaining that Pick 'n Pay's policy of social responsibility within and without the company, the proven non-racialism we practised, in fact aligned us with opponents of apartheid. The only difference was that as a company we chose to take the path of economic empowerment above violent conflict.

I also discussed the unique approach to business developed in Pick 'n Pay and my own attitude to the commonly held maxim that the aim of business should be to maximise profits. Many business schools at that time taught, as indeed some still do, that the reason for being in business is to maximise profits. But through the guidance of my mentors Professor Hutt and Bernardo Trujillo, I had developed a different philosophy.

I explained the Pick 'n Pay structure to Australian journalists, how the 'four legs of the table' principle balanced the company equally on the four legs of administration, merchandise, social responsibility and people, with consumer sovereignty supreme on top. There was no doubt that we would have been far less successful if our aim had been to maximise profits. Yet, by not pursuing market share, not actively operating for maximisation of profit, we had become the largest food retailer in South Africa and had shown a consistent rise in profits. In plain English, the more we gave and the more actively we pursued our core policies under the 'people' and 'social responsibility' legs of the Pick 'n Pay table, the more we gained. The more we cared for customers, the more they supported us. It was obvious that many listeners in Australia were fascinated by this unconventional approach to business and, left to themselves, would have liked to heave out the political baggage to hear more.

I also had many long discussions with union leaders and the Australian building industry organisation, BOMA, even showing a film specially produced to show how progressive and liberal our company's labour policies were. At a later stage, I was able to tell Australian union representatives that more than eight hundred people had approached our Brisbane hyper in the hopes of obtaining one of the four hundred full-time jobs on offer. Surely this proved conclusively that ordinary Australians were more interested in work than in the origins of the employer?

At one time, on the run-up to gaining Federal Government approval for the Brisbane hyper, opposition to Pick 'n Pay's Australian début took an especially ugly turn. An article expressing the views of various opponents contained one of the worst anti-Semitic statements I have ever read. The horrible opinion stated baldly that Australian traders didn't want a South African business in their country and, most particularly, not a Jewish one. The distasteful tone was redolent of German attacks on Jewish business in the 1930s, and I lost no time in going public with a counter-statement because I refused to take the anti-Semitic slur lying down. I did not believe that Australian businessmen in general supported racist propaganda of the kind that once came out of Hitler's Germany and, of course, in the majority they did not.

The most important sector of the Australian public from our point of view – consumers – first reserved judgment and then mostly came round to welcoming the advent of hypermarket shopping down under. Australian consumers liked the sound of our 'caring for the customer is everything' policy. Nearly four hundred thousand people lived within thirty minutes of the proposed Brisbane hyper, so interest in the saga of whether we would get permission to open was intense.

While all the lobbying for and against the Brisbane hyper was in progress, I flew endlessly back and forth between Africa and Australia and learned to live with jet lag. On one of the last visits I made to Brisbane before building was finally allowed to proceed, I met Beryce Nelson, Member of Parliament for Aspley. She was most impressed that I had come especially to see her, although she was somewhat sheepish, because she had been most vociferous in opposing our entry into Australia. We settled down to tackle the points she had raised against us, and by the end of the interview an enemy had been turned into a friend. From then on Beryce Nelson spoke warmly on our behalf.

While I was on the telephone in my Cape Town office, dealing with an irate customer who had been locked in the lavatory at our Brackenfell hyper, the word came through that we were at long last cleared to start trading in Brisbane. She went on and on while my secretary, June Hanks, jumped up and down in front of me, grinning and silently applauding the Australian news. The Queensland Retail Traders' Association, which darkly prophesied major survival problems for all retailers in northern Brisbane once Pick 'n Pay arrived, had finally been over-ruled.

Now building work in Brisbane proceeded apace. We set an opening date for November 1984 and the team sent to open the hyper swung into serious action. There were some problems among the management team, but mostly they were related to the normal issues that arise around organising such a mammoth exercise as building, stocking, staffing, training and finally opening a new hyper. The Brisbane hyper was an A$23 million investment – a huge enterprise. While we had all the experience of our South African chain behind us, there were problems peculiar to Australia that had to be ironed out.

In exactly the same way as the suppliers' boycott of our first South African hyper had worked in our favour, putting us on the map and the public on our side, so our teething troubles with the labour unions and our struggle to get official sanction for the Brisbane hyper gave us a terrific boost. Everyone knew about us, everyone wanted to experience shopping in a hyper. In addition, numerous interviews I had given on the role of business in bringing about change in South Africa erased much of the criticism against us. Prominent spokesmen from the Australian building industry organisation said that their entire attitude about South Africa had changed since hearing my side of the story. This was not, alas, to be a permanent conversion.

On the morning of the Brisbane opening on 7 November 1984, I had to have a radio debate with a leading Aborigine who had issued a statement saying that the new hyper should be subject to total boycott because of apartheid. Again, I had to be very clear – and how tiring it had become – that Pick 'n Pay was a non-discriminatory employer and that he, like all anti-South African protesters, should take the time to find out how much hypocrisy there was, how many supposed opponents piously supported sanctions against South Africa while continuing with business as usual. Of course, discrimination against Aborigines in Australia was every bit as bad as discrimination against blacks in South Africa. It just happened that in Australia it was the majority oppressing a minority instead of the reverse situation in South Africa.

In the event, voices raised against us on opening day in Brisbane were entirely lost in the terrific reception we experienced. It was a spectacular day! Consumers poured through our doors in such numbers that we had to resort to admitting people in batches. The first day's trading figure was a thrilling A$600 000, but it wasn't that which really counted. It was the warmth of the welcome, a warmth which placed that day among the major highlights of my life.

The Premier of Queensland, guest speaker at the opening, praised us warmly for having come to Australia and thanked us for creating over three thousand new jobs in the building and operation of our new enterprise. I was particularly happy to see Jack Goldin, the super-successful retailer who had founded the Clicks empire and from whom I had originally bought Pick 'n Pay in 1967, at the Brisbane opening. He too was very warm and excited, because he had been in at the beginning, so to speak, of the great adventure that was Pick 'n Pay. At that time he was about to take Clicks into Australia too.

In the midst of all the excitement on opening day, my dynamic manager, David Goldberg, dropped a bombshell. He told me he now felt that his loyalties lay with our Australian partners, the Libermans, and not with us. I was as flabbergasted as I had time to be that day. David's swing in loyalties really hurt me very deeply. Later, I tried to reason with him to affirm that although we had a minority shareholding in Australia we were in charge of the actual running and the management of the Australian Pick 'n Pay. David countered this by saying that no matter how shares and responsibilities were allocated, the plain fact was that Jack Liberman was in Australia and I was in South Africa – and he preferred to be answerable locally, which I did understand.

David Goldberg's stance was the only disappointment on an otherwise perfect opening day in Australia. Pictures of the event appeared on every single Australian television station that evening, while a programme on the launch made by South African broadcaster Nigel Murphy for the SABC went out across the globe. I wrote that this had been a day that could very nicely change Australian retailing, just as we had changed South African retailing with the opening of hypers here. However, I remained very aware of the fact that any fool can fling open the doors of a new store and attract crowds. It's what happens afterwards that counts. The aftermath of the Brisbane opening was going to be just as important as the launch.

Although we had succeeded magnificently in shaking up the Australian retailing establishment, much hard work lay ahead if we were to reach our target of opening ten hypers across Australia.

* * *

A hypermarket does not thrive in isolation. This is a fundamental principle. In spite of the size of a hyper, it has to be at least as comprehensive as a supermarket – the product range carried by the hyper cannot be narrowed. This being the case, a vast range must be purchased, and the only way to do that and end up with low-price goods is to buy on a massive scale for a chain rather than one store. Administratively, running a chain of hypers streamlines processes, making everything more efficient, as is the case with supermarkets as well.

Mindful of this because of our South African hyper experience, Hugh Herman and I started searching for a second Australian hyper site just days after the Brisbane opening. At that time we naïvely believed that opposition had been overcome and we would be left alone to concentrate on the purely practical aspects of expansion. This proved to be a grave miscalculation.

When Hugh and I finally found the perfect site for a second hyper on the outskirts of Melbourne, and had earmarked another in Sydney – which, ironically, later became the site that housed the 2000 Olympic meeting – union action against Pick 'n Pay became ugly and determined. There was absolutely no way they were going to allow any member of any building or affiliated trade or profession in Australia to so much as lay a finger on the Melbourne site. The fight between Pick 'n Pay and the Australian unions over Melbourne went on for a protracted period of time, during which I was amazed to discover the scope of vested interests ranged against South Africa. At one meeting with union leaders I was most surprised to find representatives from the ANC and from SWAPO. The ANC man, a very nice, courteous person, explained that the ANC in Australia were not against me personally; they were just against any contact with South Africa, whether through sport or business.

In the end, and over a two-year period after the Brisbane opening, the forces ranged against Pick 'n Pay in Australia prevailed. Although more than a million shoppers had passed through the 89 checkout points at the Brisbane hyper within six months of opening, expenses were too high for one operation. Nevertheless, problems of a commercial nature, as of management style, prices and ranges, could have been solved. We had the experience, the expertise and the will to overcome any trading problem – save that of being prevented from opening more stores.

We could not survive on one store – to thrive, we had to expand into a chain, and on that front we were totally blocked. In the end, we came to an amicable agreement with the Liberman family, who were honest and decent. I don't think I have ever come across people who honoured their word quite so fully, right the way through the good times and the bad. In the final agreement, we gave the Libermans the right to take over our South African interest in Australia. Like us, they had not been prepared for the total onslaught against Pick 'n Pay in their country and felt it was better that we should withdraw.

When the Liberman acquisition deal was signed in Melbourne, I got into a taxi and asked to be driven out to the site on which we had wanted to put our second Australian hyper. It was then just a huge, open, dirt parking lot. I stood in the middle of the ground with dust eddying round my feet and thought about all the energy, enterprise, hard work and courage that had gone into putting Pick 'n Pay in Australia. Standing on that dismal site, dismal because it was empty, a mere speck in a vast area of barred opportunity, I tasted a defeat that was especially bitter because there was absolutely nothing more I could have done to avoid it.

It was one of the saddest days of my life.

CHAPTER 21

What, No Rubicon?

In the heyday of their secret operations, Dr Eschel Rhoodie and his confidants had dubbed Mr P. W. Botha – then Minister of Defence – 'the Pangaman' for his ruthless removal of anyone who displeased him. Looking from uncomfortably close quarters into Prime Minister Botha's angry face, I now could see their point. Grabbing my lapel and shaking me furiously, Mr Botha shouted, 'How *dare* you come and bother me about *bread* when I have so many serious matters to worry about.'

With that, still firmly in the grip of a heavily breathing Mr Botha, I found myself propelled towards the door and unceremoniously thrown out into the corridor. Once I had reassembled my suit and collected my shaken wits, I had to admit that my timing had been bad. Mr Botha was under extreme pressure, having to grapple with serious economic problems and widespread civil unrest within South Africa as well as attend to issues on a broader front.

I had gone to see Mr Botha as part of a South African Forum delegation. After scheduled general discussions, each of us had been allowed to put questions of our own. It was my choice of topic – the bread price – which proved so provocative.

However, there was no getting away from the fact that for the very poor people of South Africa, there was no issue of greater importance than what they had to pay for bread – often the only food on their tables. The particular bread-price confrontation which got me thrown out of Mr Botha's office had started when government announced an increase in the cost of white and brown bread, coupled with a rise in General Sales Tax. I considered this dual hike to be a tragic mistake. The consequences of putting up the price of bread in the face of the serious political unrest sweeping the country seemed dire to me. I had been to see Finance Minister Owen Horwood, hoping to convince him to rescind the increases at that sensitive time, but he had been barely interested, having just returned from a dramatic meeting with the International Monetary Fund, which was under pressure to call in South Africa's foreign loans.

Clearly, government was too preoccupied on all fronts to think about bread, so I put together a plan calling on other food chains to join Pick 'n Pay in setting up a private bread subsidy. If we all agreed to put R1 million into the fund, we could easily hold bread prices down for the foreseeable future. Here again, my approaches fell on stony ground. Mr Gordon Utian, Managing Director of Checkers, summed up the consensus attitude when he said he did not want to support a scheme that was unlikely to get off the ground. Nevertheless, we decided to go ahead with our own R1 million subsidy, which attracted warm approval. I was interviewed for an American analysis, broadcast on a Washington, D.C. radio station, into the social implications of price fluctuations on basic food. Also, on my travels up and down the country I came to realise how much the bread subsidy meant to the employees of Pick 'n Pay, who were proud to be associated with a company demonstrating social responsibility.

When the business magazine *Finance Week* wondered whether I had the right to donate R1 million from the point of view of shareholders, I told them that I absolutely did and that I was happy to be challenged on the point because social peace was so critical to South Africa.

Once the financial press took an interest in the bread-price issue, government were soon persuaded to review their dismissive attitude because they were being shown in a very bad, uncaring light. Owen Horwood's secretary told me that both Horwood and the Cabinet were very annoyed that I had publicised the bread issue. I immediately pointed out, in the press, that it had been an announcement from the Minister of Agriculture, another minister who had refused point-blank to meet with me, which first alerted the media.

At this stage, because of the insensitivity and rudeness of the government and their refusal to discuss this issue of burning concern to ordinary people, I announced my intention to form a Consumers' Party to fight the government on price issues. Now the fat was really in the fire. Cognisant of having been returned to power with a reduced majority at the last general election and haunted by the prospect of more migrant Nat voters, the government quickly changed its tune. Invitations suddenly flew from this, that and the other minister to me saying they would see me *immediately* to sort out the vexed question of bread.

My rather rash remarks about forming a Consumers' Party generated a degree of approval and enthusiasm which not only surprised but alarmed me as well. I hardly had time to manage what was already on my plate, was plagued by tension headaches and exhaustion from overwork, and was certainly in no position to take on anything more. Accordingly, I just issued a few more statements quietly pointing out how carefully the government needed to think before imposing inflammatory price hikes on an already simmering national situation.

South Africa's black majority were losing patience with the temperate voices of moderates, a fact surely as clear to the government as it was to the rest of us. Oliver Tambo, exiled leader of the banned ANC, had already declared ominously, 'Never again are our people going to do all the bleeding.' Even before Mr Tambo's chilling declaration, a shift in the ANC's campaign against the government became evident when four blasts destroyed South Africa's first nuclear power station then being completed at Koeberg in the Cape – a major coup for ANC militants. Soon after, a huge car bomb exploded outside the Pretoria headquarters of the Air Force, killing nineteen and injuring two hundred, mostly civilian pedestrians.

Against this backdrop of severely unsettled conditions – socially, politically and economically – it was harder, on the one hand, to maintain confidence, but increasingly more important, on the other, to be seen to be doing something about the deteriorating situation around us.

As heartbreaking pictures went around the world showing mothers evicted from their shacks in squatter settlements in the depths of a bitter, wet Cape winter, putting their children into plastic refuse bags to shelter them from the elements, Wendy and her team devised a scheme to house some of our lower-paid employees in their own homes. Pick 'n Pay invested funds with a building society. On the interest earned, housing for weekly paid black employees was subsidised. At the time, mortgage interest rates had climbed so high that even the rich were gasping. It seemed impossible, although it was true, that ways could be found to allow quite low-paid workers to own their own homes. But, no matter how many home-loan schemes we initiated over the years, and there were very many, there were never enough houses to go round.

If the succeeding Nationalist administrations had turned away from their obsession with apartheid ideology earlier and given free rein to the forces of creative energy locked within the progressive sector of South African business, millions more black South Africans might have today owned their own homes. By clinging to the clearly untenable and immoral notion that urban black people were temporary residents, so much time was wasted and energy went fruitlessly into containing the uncontainable.

When Prime Minister P. W. Botha proposed introducing a tricameral system of Parliament to give some political voice to Indian and coloured people – not to Africans – a national whites-only referendum was called to give majority white approval.

Furious debate ensued between those whites who disapproved of the tricameral system because it excluded Africans and those who believed any step forward was worthwhile. To dissenters, exclusion of the African majority and a system of separate parliamentary chambers to which white, Indian and coloured members were elected by their own race groups were toothless, insulting and irrelevant: a time-wasting diversion from the real liberation struggle. Those in favour – and I was among them – believed that something was better than nothing, and that this was at least a start.

The tricameral system proved to be unwieldy and patronising in limiting the jurisdiction of the Indian and coloured parliamentarians to 'own affairs', that is, matters affecting their own race groups but not matters of national import, such as defence. But it *was* an attempt to reach beyond an oppressive heritage of prejudice and fear, and it did eventually see two men of colour included in the Cabinet for the first time in the history of South Africa.

The tricameral debate created sharp divisions in my family. I was threatened with being sent to Coventry if I insisted on voting in favour. My daughter Suzanne, who was then as deeply involved in political and social responsibility activities as I had been in my student days, was particularly critical. She was coming to the end of a successful year chairing her university's Rag Committee. She and her young contemporaries, who poured in and out of our house at all hours, engaged me in endless heated debate over what they saw as my misguided attitudes. They perceived me as a prime candidate for re-education. Another event which did not garner approval at home was my attendance at the signing of the Nkomati Accord. I went to the sweltering, malaria-ridden bush area near Komatipoort, principal gateway between Mozambique and South Africa, with some three hundred fellow guests at the invitation of the South African Department of Foreign Affairs to witness the signing of an historic non-aggression pact between the two countries.

The Nkomati Peace Accord had tremendously important implications for both countries. In the case of South Africa, if the peace held it could bring about peace in Angola, where, despite the signing of an agreement withdrawing South African troops, fighting continued. At that time military obligations – two years full-time conscription with regular part-time obligations – impacted on the lives of the majority of white South African men. 'Going to the border' (with Angola) on military call-up was an accepted condition of white South African life in the 1980s, a hindrance to careers, a worry for families and an ongoing logistical nightmare for employers.

* * *

The scope and intensity of media speculation sparked by a minor remark about an impending event of an overwhelmingly dull nature, made early in August 1985 by Foreign Minister Pik Botha, have remained forever inexplicable.

Pik Botha told a gathering of foreign diplomats that further policy reforms *might* be forthcoming in South Africa and that the State President – the title adopted in place of Prime Minister – Mr P. W. Botha, would make an announcement in this regard when he addressed the Natal congress of the National Party on 15 August.

The foreign press, in particular, instantly latched on to this mild and ambiguous remark, and began speculating wildly. Global publication *Newsweek* speculated about a 'giant step away' from apartheid, while *Time* magazine advised readers to expect 'the most important statement since Dutch settlers arrived at the Cape of Good Hope 300 years ago'. International broadcast networks scurried to set up live coverage – the first afforded a South African premier – for President Botha's address.

In the event, speaking in an aggressive tone of voice, Mr Botha informed South Africans and millions of overseas viewers that he rejected the concept of one-man one-vote, that he was not concerned with foreign demands and that he was not prepared to lead white South Africa down the road to abdication and 'suicide'. He was also not prepared to deviate from his stand that Nelson Mandela would not be released from jail until he renounced violence.

Towards the end of his speech Mr Botha informed his audience that he would continue with reforms. 'I believe', he said confusingly, 'that we are today crossing the Rubicon. There can be no turning back.' But while South Africa and the world had indeed waited for Mr Botha to cross the Rubicon, he had done nothing of the sort.

The President's Rubicon speech aroused massive hostility abroad and triggered a huge financial crisis. Chase Manhattan bank had already demanded the immediate repayment of their loans following the declaration in July 1985 of an indefinite state of emergency, imposed as an attempt to counter worsening civil unrest throughout South Africa. Within the first few days of the imposition of the state of emergency, a security police swoop had netted nearly eight hundred, mostly black, people who were detained under harsh new security regulations. The European Community condemned events in South Africa and France announced it would immediately suspend all new investment. The United

States stopped short of condemning the South African government publicly then, but indicated that 'quiet pressure' was being brought to bear to resolve the crisis.

No sooner had President Botha dropped his bombshell at the Natal convention than other foreign banks followed Chase Manhattan's example and demanded the immediate repayment of their loans. But South Africa could not afford to pay back enormous outstanding foreign debts at such short notice. When a worried Dr Gerhard de Kock, the President of the South African Reserve Bank, travelled abroad to see if he could secure new loans, he found that South Africa had overnight become a pariah in world financial circles.

To me, P. W. Botha's disastrous Rubicon speech came as a further setback in a year already marred by travail and tribulation. Following the departure of Senator Teddy Kennedy in January 1985, after an acrimonious visit to this country, anti-South African lobbyists shifted into top gear. Senator Kennedy's public pronouncements against foreign investment in South Africa highlighted world-wide hostility prevailing against companies who still chose to invest here.

To those of us who had been working hard for years to argue against and prevent disinvestment, it was becoming increasingly difficult to counter the bad news coming out of South Africa with positive facts. As internal unrest, violence and acts of sabotage edged us ever closer to anarchy, they also made the case against investing in South Africa increasingly persuasive. Since the outbreak of severe internal unrest in September 1984, American companies had been withdrawing steadily. In 1985 alone, forty American companies sold their South African interests. Within two years, American investments declined to less than $1 billion from the 1982 figure of $2,4 billion.

Among the migrant companies to withdraw up to 1988 were major firms such as Coca-Cola, Eastman Kodak, IBM, Ford and General Motors. In each case, company withdrawal had serious ripple effects. In the case of Eastman Kodak, 460 employees lost their jobs, all supplies of Atex computers used by major newspaper groups were halted, and Kodak photographic equipment, video cassettes, motion picture films, X-ray film and floppy disks were no longer available locally.

A few days after Senator Ted Kennedy left, I had a chastening meeting with Dick Scissors of the US Embassy and two visitors from the US Department of Commerce. These visitors wanted ammunition to fight the disinvestment lobby in the United States. It really was frightening to hear, at first hand, how strong and determined the anti-South African lobby group was in Washington, particularly as events at home played so well into their hands.

Soon after my meeting with Dick Scissors, I also met the Chairman and President of Kelloggs, Bill La Moth. During our discussion he told me that he too was in South Africa to gather ammunition against the USA disinvestment lobby. Coming from exactly the same position as myself and other like-minded South African business people, the Kelloggs Chairman believed that providing jobs and incomes for black people served the interests of the poor far better than pulling out to appease a principle. As I had once told Archbishop Desmond Tutu – you can't eat principles. Did those who had incomes and food and security really have the right to say that poor people in South Africa should suffer to further the cause of isolation?

I was feeling especially sensitive about this issue, having travelled under the auspices of Operation Hunger – a respected, energetic charity of which both Wendy and I were trustees – to visit and talk to hungry people all over the country. The founder of Operation Hunger, Ina Perlman, had revealed ghastly statistics showing that over two million children in South Africa were visibly malnourished, and one child died every 15 minutes from hunger-related causes. On my visits I saw the evidence at first hand and resolved that much more money from our social responsibility budget would in future go into school-feeding schemes to help alleviate hunger at grassroots level.

As I travelled around, I wondered how those pushing for disinvestment squared their consciences with the fact that every black migrant worker retrenched from work in a city or down a mine plunged an average of nine dependants into abject poverty and hunger. Was it possible to accept without flinching the end justifying the means?

As soon as I returned to Cape Town, I called an emergency board meeting. We resolved to slash profit margins on a broad range of foodstuffs, and immediately release a sum of R10 million to reduce the prices of a wide range of food and other lines. Negotiations with suppliers raised contributions of R2 million towards our efforts at putting a cap on price increases. A heartfelt appeal went out to all manufacturers of food to follow this lead.

* * *

Post-Rubicon, even the friendly voices of staunch anti-sanctions leaders such as Margaret Thatcher and Ronald Reagan were starting to waver. I knew, in common with countless others, that something really had to be done to reverse the disastrous effects of President Botha's costly error.

As a start towards making a contribution, I thought that if I could organise leading figures in commerce, industry and finance to speak out in unison, we could achieve great things. I knew many prominent people shared the opinion that constructive actions by business could bring about change without violence. I was sure that we had a part to play, that the time had come for leading figures in the commercial, industrial and financial spheres to show they were willing not only to talk but to do something constructive.

In the first phase of what came to be called the Business Initiative, when I was making contact with other leading business figures about joining me, Dr Allan Boesak, then President of the World Alliance of Reformed Churches, was organising an initiative of a different nature. He called for a boycott of white shops in the Cape, saying that white South Africa could not survive without black buying power. The boycott was soon in place and was generally heeded. Once again, small traders whose livelihoods depended on supplying the big retailers or who traded on the peripheries of big stores were most sorely affected.

The consumer boycott hit traders very hard and unleashed a fresh wave of violence. People marching to protest against the detention of Dr Boesak died in horrible clashes with the police. Checkers and Woolworths stores were attacked and had windows smashed. Although none of Pick 'n Pay's stores suffered similarly, when the boycott was finally called off we had a long, hard battle to recoup all the business lost. We did eventually recover and never dropped profit during that testing time, which is more than can be said for many small traders who were sent to the wall, never to recover at all.

In the thick of the 1985 boycott, Dr Frederik van Zyl Slabbert and Colin Eglin of the Progressive Federal Party invited me to attend a meeting of their National Alliance Convention in Johannesburg – a group which had similar aims to my Business Initiative but which believed in more radical means to achieve its ends. I accepted for the contact it would afford with other leaders and the opportunity to further the aims of the Business Initiative.

I went to the big September 1985 National Alliance Convention meeting, having already persuaded a lot of useful people to join the Business Initiative I was spearheading. Tony Bloom of Premier Milling had been a co-founder of the Initiative from the start, but there were surprising refusals from companies, such as Anglo-Vaal, whose attitude astonished me.

During a lunch break at the National Alliance Convention, I shared a table with Allan Greenblo, editor of *Finance Week* magazine; the Inkatha Freedom Party leader, Chief Buthelezi; Tommy Bedford, ex-Springbok rugby captain; and Vincent van der Bijl of cricket fame. Discussion over lunch was lively and interesting, focusing largely on the special problems Chief Buthelezi was encountering because of his stand against sanctions. There were massive differences, too, between his Inkatha Freedom Party and the ANC. After lunch there were calls to form a steering committee. Morné du Plessis, Springbok rugby hero, put my name forward, saying he would like me to represent the young Afrikaners, who had no one to turn to.

Suddenly, at the end of the meeting, I was whipped into a makeshift studio, where Chief Buthelezi was appointed Chairman of the steering committee in a blaze of publicity. I lined up with two or three other members of the committee on one side of Chief Buthelezi, while Dr Van Zyl Slabbert stood on the other side. TV cameras whirred and press bulbs flashed. I spoke to the BBC on the role of businessmen in South Africa and gave interviews to reporters from black TV and radio stations. It was quite an occasion, one I felt could really be the beginning of a whole groundswell movement in South Africa, just as I hoped the Business Initiative would prove to be.

It was also, coincidentally, our twenty-ninth wedding anniversary, but all Wendy and I could do to celebrate that evening was talk on the telephone.

As it happened, I was soon to find the National Alliance far too political for my taste. I could not agree with their refusal to condemn all the burning and pillaging going on throughout the country, so I soon resigned.

When 84 leading figures had committed to participating in the Business Initiative, Hugh Herman and I attended a lunch at which the head of the American corporation Johnson & Johnson and one of his top local men gave us an incredibly valuable update on the disinvestment campaign in the United States. They told us they had been summoned to attend a meeting with President Reagan and Mr George Shultz, US Secretary of State, to discuss beleaguered American investments in South Africa.

In spite of all that was happening, some American companies wanted to keep their South African investments. To this end, a group of them decided to create a Corporate Committee comprising American and South African companies to help the Americans keep their investments here. The Johnson & Johnson men were most impressed by what Hugh and I had to say about our Business Initiative and felt we were ideally placed to manage their Corporate Committee initiative, especially as the United Democratic Front, South Africa's main anti-apartheid political coalition, had written to us to say they thought the Business Initiative was doing a great job.

But doing a great job was not at all easy. For someone with so much piled on my overloaded plate, the work was very time-consuming. Then, elements working within the Initiative who had the same objectives, and therefore ought to have been able to work in unison, often pulled in different directions, which was unnecessary and frustrating. I know that if all the forces ranged against the stupidity and wastefulness of apartheid could have spoken as one concerted voice, much more could have been achieved much earlier.

The American Corporate Committee initiative ended up dissipated and ultimately useless because of a senseless dispute over which five businessmen should represent South Africa. Ironically, Harry Oppenheimer and Gavin Relly, both forceful, thoughtful and consistent opponents of disinvestment, effectively put paid to the Corporate Committee initiative, although with the best of intentions. It was, nevertheless, their insistence on choosing the five to represent South Africa that ultimately caused the Corporate Committee initiative to come to a fruitless end.

Also at this time, some of South Africa's financial giants – Anglo American, Sanlam, Barclays National and the Rembrandt Group among them – were talking to the banned ANC in an initiative of their own. However, President Botha soon brought the talks with the ANC to a complete halt, even as Gavin Relly protested that they were merely having discussions in pursuit of peaceful solutions. Once again, President Botha had committed a tragic error.

Shortly before the publication of our Business Initiative's trademark full-page press adverts setting out in point form our formula for accelerating the reform process without resorting to violence, I came under a lot of pressure to let the initiative die a quiet death. Dr Denis Worrall, South African Ambassador in London and a sympathiser of our cause, phoned me following front-page reports about the initiative in *The Times* of London. He advised me in a friendly but firm fashion to lay off because, he felt, this was not the right way to handle government at this time. Suddenly, other leading personalities changed their minds about adding their names to our planned press campaign, among them Chris Saunders of Tongaat, Tertius Myburgh of the *Sunday Times*, Gavin Relly of Anglo American and Jan Pickard. They each apparently agreed that the time was not right to challenge the government.

But when *would* the time be right? I didn't want to wake up in a few months' time to find that the crisis had irrevocably reached the point of no return. Accordingly, 89 co-participants in the Business Initiative went to print.

The campaign netted some very positive results in terms of invitations to address the international media on our 'alternative' approach to bringing about change in South Africa. I gave a major interview to the BBC and one to CBS – the Canadian Broadcasting Service – filmed in the Parliament buildings. This interview pitted me against two staunch supporters of sanctions and disinvestment. Feedback from America regarding this interesting piece of television was very positive for our cause: people apparently felt that our view was practical, honest and pragmatic.

However, by the end of 1985 it had become so much harder, not only to persist in speaking out against disinvestment and sanctions, but to keep faith with the belief that the government would eventually dismantle apartheid, would take the steps necessary to re-establish South Africa as an honourable country in the world. It was difficult if not impossible to see any kind of future, let alone a peaceful one, as rioting in the Cape continued unabated. Around Durban, rioting was so severe that newspapers showed pictures of hospital reception areas looking like First World War casualty stations. For the first time, a Markinor poll ominously revealed that a clear majority of black South Africans saw civil war as inevitable.

How much worse could it all get?

* * *

One early evening in 1986, sitting in my office and nursing one of the tension headaches that plagued my life, I wrote: 'When I write my memoirs one day, this period must go down as the most difficult and pressurised time from every angle we have ever had. I know we have had pressurised times before, but not from an emotional, political and morale point of view.' With hindsight, that time could be placed on the nursery slopes compared to what still needed scaling, but of that fact I was fortunately ignorant.

The path of politics – South African-style – in early 1986 was marked by the usual contradictions. President Botha announced in a conciliatory speech that South Africa had outgrown the outdated concept of apartheid. He hinted that ANC leader Nelson Mandela might be released from prison on humanitarian grounds. Then, barely one month later, he unleashed a humiliating repudiation of Foreign Minister Pik Botha in

Parliament, chastising him in typical finger-wagging style for having dared to surmise that there might one day be a black South African President.

Next, Dr Van Zyl Slabbert dropped a bombshell of his own by announcing his resignation from politics. I thought this was a very sad move, but could identify with his suspicion that government were just issuing words without really meaning what they said.

Then, President Botha announced the repeal of the Urban Areas Act, which involved the removal of the hated pass laws and the release of those imprisoned for violating them. But, as the country basked in a little favourable global media coverage as a result of the repeal, the South African Defence Force suddenly launched a combined air and land attack on the capitals of three neighbouring Commonwealth countries – Botswana, Zambia and Zimbabwe. The attacks were supposedly aimed against ANC strongholds but political commentators believed that the raids marked a major turning-point in the course of P. W. Botha's government: he seemed to have abandoned his attempts to reform the apartheid system, choosing instead to crack down ruthlessly on opponents.

As though in confirmation of this, a nation-wide state of emergency was re-imposed after having been lifted three months earlier. The security forces were given virtually unlimited powers, severe restrictions were imposed on the media, and thousands of anti-apartheid activists were detained. Soon the government released the names of no less than 8 500 people, some of them children as young as 12 years old, detained under the emergency regulations. Mr Botha said the measures were necessary because the security of the country was at risk from the planned violence sweeping it.

He also predicted, accurately, that the stricter security measures would bring criticism and punitive measures from the outside world, but added that the world should take note and never forget that South Africa was not a nation of weaklings. Considering the fact that limpet mines were exploding in South Africa every week and that, on average, there was one unrest incident every half-hour, 24 hours a day, it was just as well we *weren't* weak.

At this precise time, I took my son Jonathan to the navy to serve his period of national service. Going into the navy was his own decision. He felt that if he went instead to college in America he would probably never come back, and he wanted to keep his options open because he loved South Africa and wanted to stay. It was not a pleasant situation for any of the parents, wives and girlfriends saying goodbye to their young men in Simon's Town. But such scenes were being repeated throughout the country, and had been happening for a long time.

President Botha's prediction of increased punitive action against South Africa soon came miserably true. Britain considered imposing a range of sanctions against South Africa, although Geoffrey Howe, Margaret Thatcher's Foreign Secretary, still called for deeper Western involvement to bring about reform and an end to apartheid.

The Commonwealth mounted their own tough sanctions campaign banning air links, new bank loans, consular facilities, as well as the import of uranium, coal, iron and steel. Tourism promotion, new investments and reinvestments of profits earned in South Africa were banned and taxation agreements ended.

Before much longer, President Ronald Reagan's veto was to fail, and the USA enforced sanctions too. As a result, Secretary of State George Shultz warned that allowing South Africa to slip into a state of political and economic siege could so erode the base for future governments that they would find it impossible to meet the country's pressing social and economic needs.

Sage words indeed, as the overall situation became increasingly desperate. Two of my most important and valued people in Pick 'n Pay – René de Wet and Sean Summers – had come into my office to see me, both distressed and depressed, to say they felt they had to leave South Africa for the sake of their children or for their own sanity. I spoke to both of them for hours. I knew exactly what pressures had brought them to my office and I knew they were expressing doubts and fears increasingly common in the hard-pressed South African business community. Both René and Sean did eventually decide that it was better to stay and work towards change rather than joining the exodus of the disillusioned, but it was a tough decision for anyone to have to make.

Feeling under siege from every side, I joined with seven other top businessmen at this time in making a desperate appeal for the immediate and unconditional release of Nelson Mandela and the unbanning of the ANC. We pointed out, as leaders of companies with combined assets of R35 billion, that South Africa was doomed unless the ANC became a participant in negotiations on the country's future. From the government there was no immediate response.

Meanwhile, I travelled to England with Wendy, hoping in vain for a holiday respite from strife-torn South Africa. Shortly after arriving, I was asked to appear on a television discussion panel to question South Africa's Ambassador to Britain, Denis Worrall, a member of the Pan-Africanist Congress and a black South African leader.

In preparation I spoke to an ex-Minister of Justice from Uganda who had taken up a professorship in Wales, and an exiled ANC journalist, and was amazed by the opinion they shared that South Africa was fast running out of time. Just before going into the London television studio for the live panel debate, I received the ghastly news that a Russian limpet mine had exploded in our Montclair store in Durban. Our employee Mrs Monica Strijdom, wife and mother of young children, later died of injuries sustained in the blast, which was a terrible tragedy.

With the sad news of the Montclair bomb uppermost in my mind, I found myself in a difficult position, placed on a panel with people who were not only violently anti-South Africa but also opposed to everything those of us in favour of non-violent change were trying to do. The bottom line was that my fellow panellists did not want to recognise anything being done by anyone who was not black. Although they would not admit this, according to their dogmatic views all representatives of the white race had to be lumped into one foul camp. I stuck to my position – the middle-of-the-road, businessman's view – and said how strongly people like myself backed non-violent change to bring South Africa to a non-racial, multi-party democracy.

* * *

When it was reported that Barclays National Bank MD Chris Ball and his family needed armed guards to protect their lives, fellow business leaders received an uncomfortable reminder that the results of being identified with opposition to the government, even just by association, could be swift and nasty. The Ball family's need for protection arose after advertisements appeared calling for change, which President Botha alleged were paid for out of funds advanced by Barclays. In a natural Nationalist progression, communist sympathies and links with the banned ANC were hinted at. Fanatical right-wing elements responded by spray-painting insulting slogans on bank properties and issuing dark, veiled threats.

Chris Ball, who would feature markedly in the later Cape Town Olympic bid, made the mistake of initially denying that Barclays had knowingly granted funds to pay for the advertisement. As for myself, I remember discussing with Issy Fine the importance of keeping a cool head as a business leader, not being panicked into making statements you would regret in South Africa's fraught political climate.

With other business leaders, I rallied to the support of Chris Ball, who subsequently joined the exodus of businessmen leaving South Africa. Tony Bloom, the committed campaigner who had always spoken up for peaceful change and with whom I had worked on the 'There Is a Better Way' initiative, also relinquished his position as Group Chairman and CEO of the Premier Group and departed from South Africa. There had been a personal tragedy in Tony's family which necessitated a move to the United Kingdom but, although he played this down, I believe scurrilous attacks against the stand he adopted in South Africa took their toll and influenced his decision to leave. Tony's name was added to the increasing list of talented leaders joining the brain drain. Soon after his departure, Who's Who of Southern Africa started including a chapter entitled 'Who's Where' – listing the whereabouts of super-charged South Africans from the fields of business, sport, the arts and academia. It made a most depressing read.

Apart from verbal attacks, actual physical attack became an immediate problem in my family when the Johannesburg home of Gareth and Mandy was twice attacked. At the time it was thought this could be traced to union resentment because Gareth and his family made good targets for getting at me. Since discovering that a 'contract' had been taken out on my life in the 1970s by rival traders, I had received quite a number of death threats and would receive others in future. When I spoke to the security police about the attacks on Gareth's Johannesburg home, they assured me they would come to the aid of my son's family if there was a problem, but I decided not to put this to the test and brought them to Cape Town for better security.

Security concerns are facts of modern life familiar to high-profile people the world over, but many of the issues that arose out of running a South African enterprise would never occur in the lives of business people operating elsewhere. True, South Africa was far from being the only place on the globe where speaking out against the government could bring down extreme retribution in one form or another, but I cannot think of another developed economy where it was essentially impossible to separate politics from business. The policies of apartheid sat next to us at board meetings, forming a silent quorum dictating decisions, if so permitted, because they impacted on every facet of business one way or another.

As an instance, take the bizarre situation which arose early in 1987 when President Botha, fond of haranguing business for meddling in politics, demanded that we should deduct money directly from employees who were withholding rents for government-owned township houses as part of an anti-apartheid civil disobedience campaign. We were supposed to hand deductions over to the government landlords – a preposterous idea.

Both Wendy and I continued to work towards the ideal of peaceful change, even if it was becoming increasingly difficult to keep sight of the goal posts. In May 1987, the whites-only general election divided the electorate into those unequivocally against reform and those who recognised, however reluctantly, that South Africa had to change, that changes had to be negotiated with black leaders, and that a detailed vision for the future could not be spelled out before such negotiation happened.

The result of the election reflected a decided swing to the right. My son Jon and I sat up all night listening to results coming in. By morning the Conservative Party dissidents evicted from P. W. Botha's government for refusing to embrace reform were established as South Africa's official opposition. But, in the scheme of South African politics, the Conservative Party was at least only moderately rightist compared to the extreme Verwoerdian-style apartheid candidates who had also contested the election but lost heavily.

I was not depressed by the result because I thought the message should now come loud and clear to the government: escalate the pace of change to appease the slim majority of white voters who had shown, by voting for the National Party rather than the extreme right, that they accepted the need for change. While the not-so-subtle nuances of South African politics made some contextual sense to insiders, it was much harder to explain the convoluted path of our political system outside the country, which Wendy and I always seemed to be trying to do.

When Wendy gave an unusually long interview to the London *Telegraph*, telling them that 41 percent of Pick 'n Pay's management were already black, and that she controlled the company's bursary scheme to help educate both adults and children among our staff of 25 000 people, she made the point that the world was losing sight of the fact that normal, everyday life was going on in South Africa, just as it was in Britain. Hysterical media coverage was completely ignoring the good things happening at home. When she made a live speech in similar vein later, Wendy's British audience reacted with thunderous applause. To us harried carriers of a generally unpopular message, reactions of approval meant a great deal on our overseas travels.

At home, an interesting slant was put on the virtue of pragmatism following an historic meeting between 54 white businessmen who travelled out of South Africa to meet with a delegation of the banned ANC led by future President Thabo Mbeki. Later, Gavin Relly of Anglo American commented that unless the ANC could come to terms with changing their static socialist (some said Marxist) ideological outlook into a direction which could accommodate capitalism, the ANC would find themselves outmanoeuvred and eclipsed as eventual rulers of South Africa. Having been sidelined for so long and having gone into exile bearing economic baggage packed during an era of socialist expansion, ANC economic policy was ripe for a radical re-think.

The world trend that was gathering momentum away from centralist socialism and rigorous capitalism to something in-between, something founded on pragmatism rather than ideology, had enormously important implications for South Africa's future. The timing of the changes, from the tentative beginnings under P. W. Botha to the first all-race democratic election in 1994, was propitious. Yes, it was heartbreaking for people living under apartheid to wait so long for liberation, but because Mr De Klerk and Mr Mandela were talking at the time the Berlin Wall collapsed, when democracy was enjoying a resurgence in some of the world's most oppressed societies, and when pragmatism was outdoing socialism, South Africa started her democratic life with a better chance of succeeding than any other country on the African continent.

Mr De Klerk coming into prominence, Mr Mandela's release from prison, the timing of the fall of communism: I sometimes wonder, do these things happen by chance?

I don't think so.

CHAPTER 22

Coming of Age

The question of expanding into South Africa's independent homelands had been discussed around Pick 'n Pay's boardroom table regularly. Towards the end of 1984 the discussions we had been holding with President Sebe of the Ciskei reached fruition and a new Pick 'n Pay supermarket was built in the Ciskei capital of Bisho.

The debate around whether it was moral or immoral to do business with the Nationalist-created independent black homelands was probably among the most emotive of South African issues. Many responsible, sincere people felt it was wrong to do business in the homelands because by doing so a degree of credence and respectability was given to one of the cornerstones of apartheid. I did not agree with supporting the half-measure system of 'border industries', which I felt was immoral. In that case, government lured industries with massive tax incentives to set up on the borders of independent homelands. The idea was that people obliged to live in the adjoining homeland would cross over to work in the South African-based industries, crossing back into the homeland at the end of the day. This was an attractive proposition to a government intent on entrenching separation. Profits generated from border industries stayed of course in South Africa. I thought this system was wrong because it exploited people living in the homelands and benefited no one other than the owners of border industries, able to employ cheap labour.

However, setting up properly in a homeland was an opportunity, from our point of view, to join homeland stores to our national network, hooking up to a superior distribution system and vast buying power so as to put low-cost goods efficiently on shelves. As for the Ciskei, negotiations with President Sebe had been protracted, but the bottom line was that they badly wanted to attract Pick 'n Pay into their country. Accordingly, we were offered a tax holiday – largess which the Ciskei government could afford because the South African government showered them with money, vainly hoping to prove grand apartheid viable.

As well as being exempted from paying sales tax to the Ciskei government for the first five trading years, our Bisho store was also granted a wine and malt licence. Although by this time we had managed to push through a few wine licences for South African Pick 'n Pay stores, we had been completely unable to break the stranglehold of the beer cartels, who blocked any effort to license supermarkets. There was no way they intended allowing beer to be discounted, so consumers continued to pay through the nose.

I am not trying to say that when we decided to open in Bisho, we did so wearing haloes and radiating philanthropic goodwill. We evaluated the project according to usual business principles and believed there would be profits for the company in the Ciskei. But for the people of Bisho there would also be a good selection of food, presented in a clean, ordered supermarket at much lower prices than they had previously paid. Not a bad trade-off, surely?

Opening day in Bisho – November 1984 – went off royally. Wendy and I were with President Sebe on a huge dais, from where both he and I delivered our speeches. In his address, the President said very nice things about us and a choir sang a song specially composed for the opening and dedicated to Pick 'n Pay. I had expected to find myself looking at an audience composed entirely of black faces, but it was soon apparent that the white citizens of towns over the border had flooded across to Bisho – border industries in reverse – in droves. Everything was cheaper in Bisho because we didn't have to charge sales tax, and that included beer, which the carnival crowds from both sides of the border bought by the case, thrilled with their bargain purchase. I am sure that no one who was at the Bisho opening in 1984 will ever forget the excitement, the celebration, the good vibes.

The honeymoon period of tax-free trading in Bisho was not to proceed smoothly for too long. Once we were established, the Ciskei government tried to backtrack on their concession. They implied that because their nation was poor and struggling they needed the big-brotherly love of Pick 'n Pay, which should help by paying sales tax – a blatant attempt at manipulation.

Still, many good things were happening. For one, in 1984 Pick 'n Pay was nominated for the Retailers' Hall of Fame in the United States for social responsibility work in retailing. Then, in 1985 I received a major award for Pick 'n Pay from the University of the Witwatersrand Business School and, in my personal capacity, an honorary Doctor of Law degree from Rhodes University in Grahamstown. The degree was conferred in April 1986 and on this occasion I dedicated my speech to the youth of South Africa because this was the university's main graduation ceremony. I spoke about the serious drain of talent South Africa was suffering as so many disillusioned young people saw no solution other than emigration, and about the responsibilities parents, academics, business people and politicians had to help create the kind of country young people would be proud to claim as their own. In 1986 there was also the arrival of a first grandson for Wendy and me – Nicholas Leigh Ackerman – born to Gareth and Mandy.

In the late 1980s, as the phenomenon called *change* picked up speed and gathered momentum, I decided to keep Pick 'n Pay on a steady path of expansion according to a careful plan of action. All the company's Australian interests had now been signed over to the Liberman family and so, free from external diversions, it was possible to concentrate on judicious additions to the existing countrywide network of 12 hypers and 81 supermarkets. At the same time, refurbishing existing stores and testing the black market through an acquired experimental cash and carry chain called Price Club went ahead.

In an effort to reduce my formidable workload, I appointed Hugh Herman to full MD, after he had shared this role jointly with me for the past three years. It was eleven years since Hugh had joined me at Pick 'n Pay, first as Property Director. His staunch support was vital to the smooth running of our ever-demanding enterprise, which now had a turnover approaching the R2 billion mark.

At this time, too, we continued expanding in the homelands: opening first one store in Mmabatho, capital of Bophuthatswana, then a second at Mabopane – a calculated risk since there had been a coup in the homeland between the two openings. Since Sol Kerzner set down his amazing flight of fancy, Sun City, on an unpromising Bophuthatswanan plain, the gambling and entertainment centre had made its host homeland the jewel in apartheid's crown. The hordes of well-heeled gamblers who made the trip to Sun City, just 25 minutes from Pretoria, to escape the confines of Calvinistic South Africa's anti-gaming laws, poured an enviable flow of revenue into the homeland's coffers. Being also one of the finest maize-growing areas in southern Africa, Bophuthatswana was the only homeland on the sunny side of viability.

One thing Bophuthatswana's elite did have in common with the other homelands was a propensity for pocketing profits. The coup which took place between the opening of our two stores was planned to oust President Lucas Mangope on the grounds of rampant corruption within his administration. The government of South Africa, however, thought otherwise; they refused to tolerate the popular uprising in the one homeland with a hopeful future. South African Defence Force and police contingents crushed the coup in a mere 14 hours, restoring President Mangope to power. In a show of solidarity, President Botha immediately paid a visit to Bophuthatswana, announcing firmly, 'We are back in control,' a revealing remark which he quickly amended to 'The President of Bophuthatswana is in full control'.

Each of the stores we set down in the independent homelands was plagued by problems – mostly related to labour. In the Ciskei capital of Bisho, union intransigence made the store there impossible to manage. I made a special journey to Bisho to address the union leaders and management, not least because there was an unbelievably serious shrinkage problem in the store. I told the unionists bluntly that if they were not prepared to work with Pick 'n Pay, to be loyal and honest, then the store would be closed down. I told them I was not prepared to have political matters brought in to ruin our company. The union leader stood up, shook hands, looking me straight in the eye as though our differences were resolved, then went straight off to declare a grievance and call for a strike.

I was totally disillusioned.

When Ciskei's President Sebe got to hear of the trouble in our Bisho store, he became angry because he had not known we were having trouble with the unions. He ordered us to sack the troublesome union leader and the Ciskei police to arrest him. The union across the border in South Africa immediately rallied behind their arrested brother, demanding his release and reinstatement at Pick 'n Pay in East London, the nearest size-able town across the border from Ciskei. Failing this, said the South African union, we might expect Pick 'n Pay stores to begin burning down.

Choosing to trade in the homelands – wistful creations of the Nationalist government – was certainly a whole lot harder than opting to steer clear of them!

* * *

In the midst of all this action, ordinary consumer issues continued to demand time and energy. I had to confront the powerful KWV, which regu-lated every aspect of wine distribution throughout South Africa. This cartel disallowed discounts and blocked licence applications from big chains such as Pick 'n Pay so as to discourage the supply of discounted wine to the public.

I told a gathering of wine farmers that Pick 'n Pay had only 36 wine licences between our 86 stores, cutting out 50 potentially profitable out-lets for their products. I advised the farmers to get on with the great job they were doing in producing wine and to take the marketing of their products away from the KWV cartel. This naturally enough did not endear me to the KWV or other organisations bent on controlling liquor sales in their own interests.

Then, I heard about legislation quietly slipping through Parliament to stop retail outlets from negotiating the same discount prices for fuel as big, bulk buyers, which had to be rapidly countered. On the fuel issue, we could never drop our vigilance.

In November 1985 a government edict arbitrarily outlawed a Pick 'n Pay petrol deal whereby the public received a rebate for serving themselves. This was yet another scheme we had devised to override anti-consumer laws against discounted petrol. The public reacted with outrage to the government ban on cheaper petrol, so much so that we were eventually granted the right to extend our scheme into February 1986, pending a major meeting between ourselves, the oil industry and government. The government and oil cartels simply never let up in their opposition, and we never let up in our resolve to defy them.

Government's crisp rejection of our proposals for deregulating the price of petrol in February 1986 constituted quite a heavy blow in the ongoing bout between us. However, I had no intention of letting them off without hitting back. I spoke to the press, telling reporters that with inflation running at 20 percent, with the South African currency firming, and the world barrel price of oil dropping, petrol prices should be coming down, not going up. Official silence in response was total. Even a planned television and radio debate on the issue between me and government spokesmen had to be cancelled, because no one from their side would make themselves available.

By this stage in the petrol price saga, I had learned enough to know that under cover of their silence, government would be mustering forces. Accordingly, I told the press that there would probably soon be a blanket ban on cutting the price of petrol but, when it happened, we at least intended to go down fighting. Sure enough, it wasn't long before government issued a directive requiring the oil companies to stop supplying Pick 'n Pay because of the rebel discounts we continued to offer. Four days before the specified cut-off date, we dropped our petrol price even lower as an act of justified defiance on behalf of consumers.

Another strategic lesson I had learned in the ongoing skirmish over petrol prices was the importance of staying a step or two ahead. Therefore, as soon as government judged us duly chastened and allowed the oil companies to resume supplies, a new scheme, pre-planned and ready to implement, was put in place. This was a petrol coupon scheme, which gave consumers grocery discount coupons with petrol purchases at our Boksburg hyper garage. Although it seemed impossible for government to argue that this harmless scheme constituted petrol price cutting, that is precisely what they tried to claim. But by now, I had had enough. We had been blocked at every single turn – even being forbidden to offer customers a free car wash at one time. I decided that we should take the petrol coupon scheme to court for a judgment because, win or lose, someone had to stand up to the oil barons and their backers.

The day judgment was due, I took my son Jonathan along with me to court. We listened to the judge's summing up for an hour and a half, at the end of which he ruled in our favour. The press immediately swarmed out of their gallery, surrounding Jon and me, asking for interviews, calling for comments. It was tremendously exciting, everyone was so thrilled and delighted. Sweet as the moment of victory was, I was sure the government would still go after us on appeal, but it didn't matter because we had made history that day and it was a great victory, worth winning, however short in duration.

Jerry Schuitema, a financial journalist and broadcaster with whom we always had a good relationship as a company, was one commentator who brought up the issue of retail self-interest after the petrol-coupon court triumph in 1986. As a corollary to all the high-profile consumer rights campaigns Pick 'n Pay was involved with over many years, motive has always come under scrutiny, as indeed it still does, because, of course, such campaigns inevitably attract greater numbers of customers into our stores, which in turn generates higher profits.

Following our successful court action against the government in 1986, it is absolutely true that our petrol sales soared. They soared because consumers wanted lower-priced petrol, and also because people wanted to back our efforts on their behalf. Fighting like mad for consumers, to which they respond by supporting you with their custom, is not a halo-lit form of retail philanthropy, but rather an exercise in enlightened self-interest in which everyone wins.

Again, in 1989, there was yet another increase in the price of fuel. Every time this happened we found ourselves in defiance of the

government because we refused to up the per-litre price of fuel already purchased, paid for and in our pumps. Why did a fuel price increase have to
be applied at midnight on the day decreed regardless of what stocks were
on hand? We could have netted millions in a bonanza of instant profit
when fuel price increases were announced if we had upped the price of the
500 000 litres of fuel in our pumps at any one time, as the government
decreed we should. But surely the term for that kind of practice is profiteering?

Towards the end of 1987, a diligent officer in the Board of Trade and
Industries latched on to the fact that Pick 'n Pay had imported six thousand modular television receivers from Taiwan and Hong Kong. At that
time, licences to assemble television sets were granted only to a very few
people, who accordingly held the market to ransom. Because there was no
competition, the price of television sets in South Africa was the highest in
the world – a fact unknown to most consumers.

But we had found a loophole in import laws, which allowed us to bring
in monitors and tuners as two separate units for local assembly. The resulting sets went on to the market at less than R1 000 each, about half the
standard selling price of a television set. The favoured few who held manufacturing licences and the public to ransom raised a mighty cry of outrage
when the public eagerly snapped up our realistically priced television sets.
They ran to the government, demanding protection. Their outraged representations easily persuaded the Board of Trade and Industries to impose
a large fine on us, which we refused to pay, preferring to challenge it in
court.

In the end we were not able to prevail against this particularly blatant
exploitation of consumers – the government imposed a ban which prevented us from importing the components from the East – but at least our
action highlighted how the public were being hoodwinked into believing
they had no choice but to pay exorbitantly high prices, which hit them
where it hurt most – in their pockets.

* * *

A set of triplets – two girls and a boy – born in 1988 to the wheelchair-bound dynamo Martin Rosen, General Manager of our Durban hypermarket, and his wife seemed an enormously symbolic, happy event, coming as it did just at the time of Pick 'n Pay's twenty-first birthday.

Martin Rosen, a symbol inasmuch as he represented thousands of young South African men whose lives were altered by the compulsory two-year military conscription, had fallen from a lorry and broken his back – cruelly, just an hour before his time in the army was up. Martin's career as a trainee Pick 'n Pay manager was on hold pending the completion of his national service at the time of the accident which paralysed him.

Wendy and I believed the best way we could help was by encouraging Martin to carry on with as normal a life as possible. Accordingly, he was first sent to America for the best medical treatment available, then welcomed back to pick up his training with the company where he left off. I consulted a top expert in the field of physical disability, himself disabled, and was advised to make no concessions to Martin's paralysis, but to treat him exactly the same as every other young trainee, which I did.

It felt very hard in the beginning but, just as the expert predicted, Martin conquered his difficulties because that was what he was expected to do at work. He went on to climb the corporate ladder, eventually controlling Pick 'n Pay's marketing endeavours on the company's main Board. At the time of Pick 'n Pay's twenty-first birthday celebrations, Martin was thriving as General Manager of the Durban hyper, and we had a characteristic in common with both his career and his family: all had shown phenomenal growth.

On the day Pick 'n Pay reached 21, a telegram went out to all managers everywhere in the country, telling them to forget about the trials of 1987 (detailed elsewhere) because, save for the results, it was over: 'Starting today, let our aisles be clear, our trolleys oiled and our baskets washed. Let's really make this our consumers' year.'

At the same time, a special twenty-first birthday card went to all retired staff with a token R21 cheque, inviting them to celebrate our birthday with us. Many special celebratory donations went to charities too – social

responsibility under Wendy's direction had matured into our most endur-
ing trademark.

The 21 trading years that had just skimmed by had been a phenomenal
success punctuated by odd setbacks. Then, as now, I believe setbacks in
business should be analysed to see what can be learned from them before
they are put where they belong: on dim archival shelves labelled 'Failed –
Over and Done With'. In 1988 the view looking back had its moments of
truth, but the view looking forward showed real promise, if you chose to
recognise it. In the present, our twenty-first year, working towards opening
the hundredth store – the Highgate hyper – presented the usual galaxy of
headaches associated with launching one of these super stars of retailing.
Back in the 1970s, we had not even been able to begin building the first
hyper at Boksburg because no one would lend us the money to buy a site.
Then, investors who weighed up the massive commitment necessary to
launch a hyper development – Boksburg was South Africa's first –
blanched at the magnitude of the risk. In the end we had no choice but to
go into a special partnership to buy the Boksburg site. This, in turn, more
or less forced us to develop a property portfolio. In our twenty-first birthday year, that portfolio had reached a market value of over R200 million.
Such is the virtue of necessity.

Another impressive number to emerge at our coming of age was a
turnover figure, confidently expected to double within four years, which
topped R3 billion. The stores offered a combined shopping area equal to
more than 45 rugby pitches, and space equivalent to five more was
planned for our twenty-first year. I enjoyed the analogy between shopping
space and rugby pitches: I was still a grocer with a passion for sport. I also
still believed that our strength lay in keeping our company to ourselves,
not falling at the feet of the banks, insurance companies and building societies, which by then controlled most other chain store groups.

* * *

In October 1988, Checkers Managing Director Clive Weil, who was flagging somewhat in his uphill efforts to turn round his ailing chain, began

launching scathing attacks in the press. He alleged, and was soon gleeful-
ly joined by the OK, that the system of confidential discounts negotiated
with suppliers amounted to commercial terrorism in the retail trade.
Leading the pack manipulating this unhealthy practice, alleged Mr Weil
and his co-accusers, were Pick 'n Pay buyers acting according to company
policy.

I have already explained where I stand on the question of confidential
discounts, which I prefer to call incentives. In the case of our company, I
refuted inferences, sometimes plain statements, that discounts negotiated
with suppliers went into our pockets as extra profits, which was and is not
the case. At the time of Clive Weil's diversionary campaign, I had figures
to prove that the extra discounts negotiated with our suppliers went
towards lowering prices for consumers. I pointed out that if the system of
incentives was abandoned, suppliers would have great cause for celebration, simply because no special discounts meant more money in their
pockets, which I did not think was fair or deserved. Undeniably, consumers would foot the bill for fatter supplier profits.

A fierce war of words erupted. I had my lawyers inform Clive Weil that
if he was not prepared to withdraw his allegations against Pick 'n Pay publicly he might have to do so in court. He refused to back down. The
impasse was broken by an invitation for Clive and me to appear on a live
televised debate to thrash out the issue. That TV debate became a case-
book study used by prominent business schools to demonstrate the
principles of handling damage control. For me, the key purpose of the
debate was to extract an apology from Clive in order to re-establish the
integrity of our people and the retail industry in general. In pursuit of this
end, the talk turned into a titanic clash, with the gloves off, until I got the
apology I wanted. However, although I succeeded in my primary aim, the
debate between Clive and me provoked intense reaction from both business and the public, some not favourable to me.

The issue was that Clive Weil had established a public persona as a
warm, friendly, unassuming guy, which indeed he was. He had invited the
public to glimpse his home life; Checkers TV commercials showed him
pushing shopping trolleys around his supermarkets, mingling with ordinary

shoppers with no airs or graces. He also took no offence when the press dubbed him Chubby Checkers on account of his not inconsiderable girth. Such attributes, in fact, endeared him to the public; so at the time of our live TV debate, viewers felt sorry for the unassuming boss of Checkers when I induced him – ruthlessly, some commentators said – to eat humble pie and apologise. The sympathisers, of course, ignored the fact that he had made his apology because he was wrong in the first place and admitted it. Reaction to the memorable Weil versus Ackerman clash interested me enormously. The debate proved that as a public figure, even when you were right you could end up wrong through misreading public sentiment.

Eventually, Clive Weil, dubbed 'Big Weil' by the press, moved on. He had smiled benignly and offered shoppers a decent, enjoyable shopping experience with good prices and warm, friendly staff, but his approach had not worked quite as well as his controlling company wanted it to. Being the warm heart of suburban shopping had not provided a buffer against the lean, mean, ruthless world of retail trading. In his early days at the helm of Checkers, Clive Weil had cautioned that it took time to turn a super-tanker round. Unfortunately the super-tanker that was Checkers had not succeeded in turning at all.

Whenever there was any change in the fortunes or ownership structures of a rival chain, there was always speculation about whether Pick 'n Pay would make moves to take it over. When Checkers did go broke in the early 1990s we weighed the situation up, then decided to continue striving to be the best rather than the biggest. Why should we want to take over other people's problems, after all? At that stage it was decided we should concentrate on renovating and upgrading existing Pick 'n Pay stores rather than buying out Checkers, which proved to be the right decision.

The policy argument against going around gobbling up all the opposition is well illustrated by the Shoprite take-over of both the OK and Checkers chains up to the early 1990s. The conglomeration of stores thus acquired gave Shoprite an overall market share of 42 percent against our 36 percent, but I wasn't too concerned, deciding to stick to our better-rather-than-bigger plan. As a result, our market share took care of itself in time. When Christo Wiese and Whitey Basson took on the Shoprite challenge I admired their courage and respected their ambitions, but I remained well pleased that the challenge of Checkers was theirs and not mine.

* * *

As 1988 wound down, a year that had begun at the high point of our twenty-first birthday celebrations ended on another high when our Brackenfell hyper set a world record for supermarket or hypermarket sales, taking a stunning R2,2 million in one day. Across the Atlantic, my mentor Professor W. Hutt, economist and visionary supreme, who had set my thinking on paths I would pursue all my business life, died in Dallas aged 88.

CHAPTER 23

Darkest Before Dawn

Once it started, the strike resulting from the breakdown of what had been protracted wage negotiations in Pick 'n Pay up to April 1986 spread like wildfire from store to store, town to town, city to city.

The mood of the unions turned ugly and their threats grew ever more militant. They planned to camp in stores, lie down and refuse to move. They also warned that any attempt to use police force to remove them would result in violence, which they knew perfectly well we could not risk, especially if members of the public were placed in danger. Once started, the strike rapidly spread from store to store. As the situation went from bad to worse, I felt real despair seeing union pressure turning Pick 'n Pay employees into enemies. These were some of the saddest, most difficult days of my career.

The irony of this confrontation – a forerunner of many more to come – was that the unions in this case had joined battle with the employer in the food industry who paid the highest wages and offered unprecedented benefits. Those were facts beyond dispute. Millions had been invested in staff housing schemes and millions in the educational bursary fund for the children of employees.

I was personally well known as an outspoken lobbyist for political change and human rights. Even as the ugly strike spread, my management had made it clear that the company was not fundamentally opposed to the cost of living increase the unions were demanding. We did not think the demand was unreasonable in the tough times of the day – but the threatening attitude adopted was.

What was obvious was this. If our 26 000 employees, who worked for a demonstrably enlightened employer, could strike, then other employers were going to ask whether it served their best interests to bother with social benefits and enlightened employment policies. In the meantime, our striking workforce forfeited wages they could ill afford to lose, while their union leaders continued to preach defiance.

It was also ironic that being the best payers made us the best target for union action. If Pick 'n Pay could be crippled, so could the entire food industry, and that was one of the aims of the unions. Under union orchestration in 1986, our people turned on us because we recorded high profits, yet it was these very same profits that made them the best-off food industry employees.

The dilemma we faced by the time the strike came to a painful end was one we shared with the mining houses in particular, and with most high-profile commerce in general. The fundamental problem came down to the fact that the tremendous wealth accruing to leading companies provided a convenient focus for highlighting inequalities in South African society, although such discrepancies were not necessarily related to commercial activity. But, to the workforce, the face of commercial success was unacceptable.

Of course, South Africa was not alone in having to grapple with this discrepancy but, here, the arrival of confrontation over such an issue added yet another layer to the complexities of our society.

In the aftermath of the 1986 work stoppage, our workers ended up worse off because the money they lost while out on strike cancelled the increase awarded. We had suffered a substantial loss in turnover and harm to our high-profile corporate image. Financial writers were soon wondering whether the wheels had come off for us as retail high-flyers after a savage re-rating by investors on the Johannesburg Stock Exchange sent our share price falling by more than 35 percent over the following three-month period.

In response, I told reporters that I saw tremendous growth ahead for Pick 'n Pay over the coming five years and that I was never concerned with ratings accorded to the company by the stock market. I just concentrated on running the company.

By far the worst result of the 1986 strike was the bitterness that followed in its wake, the loss of trust and understanding between management and employees, but some valuable lessons were also learned. Henceforth wage negotiations would be more flexible and we would work on the tactic of allowing future strikers to sit-in rather than forcing lock-outs because this had proved valuable in cooling situations down and preventing violence.

* * *

In spite of general economic uncertainty and the year's major strike, an upsurge in sales and an increase in profits and dividend followed for Pick 'n Pay. We put some of the profits into a R50 000 donation to the Mayor's Relief Fund to relieve the plight of Cape Town's unemployed, and I used the hand-over ceremony to make an impassioned plea to American business to stay in the country. Everyone in business was feeling edgy and uncertain when President Botha issued leading businessmen with another conference invitation. I was among those planning to attend who decided to use the occasion to demand the scrapping of the Group Areas Act.

It was increasingly apparent towards the end of the 1980s that central government were totally out of touch with the actual situation at the workface. This added a further complication to dealing with the unions in South Africa, which was anyway fraught enough in its own right. At one time, when we were being driven almost to despair by disparate influences, I asked the Minister of National Education, Mr F. W. de Klerk, because we fell into conversation about union activities at a business lunch, if he could speak to the government to explain that it was completely unrealistic to ask commerce, as they had, to award only an across-the-board 3 percent increase in wage negotiations. This was supposed to help curb inflation, but when I say that as a company we wanted to negotiate around the 20 to 24 percent level, it can be seen how far removed from reality the government was. On this occasion, the desperate efforts of the business fraternity to get government to face the impracticality of their approach produced the usual mutterings about companies sabotaging national financial policies and similar rubbish. In the late 1980s the government still liked to pretend they wore a velvet glove in dealing with business, but more often than not we felt the real iron fist within.

At the end of 1987, while there always seemed to be some issue boiling away between government and Pick 'n Pay, the unions were increasing their activities with the aim of squeezing business into submission. At a highly sensitive meeting, I was given the 'low-down' on the intentions of COSATU, which had laid plans to target companies such as Pick 'n Pay with the broader aim of creating havoc within the country. I have explained from the point of view of a businessman how unions, because of government repression, had become the only political outlet for black South Africans. Threats of strikes were in fact broader statements mustered under the banner of industrial action.

Union activism, on the march in the late 1980s, posed a significant threat to both our company and business at large. I knew I had to think deeply about the whole issue, particularly in view of increasing strife and almost daily confrontation between our staff and management.

It came as an unpleasant sign of the times when, while I was looking over our Milnerton store in Cape Town, I was verbally attacked by a 15-year-old casual worker. She furiously accused me of being in favour of apartheid, of the state of emergency, of detainees remaining in jail and so on. It was clear that she had gathered these erroneous facts from pamphlets being handed out by the UDF, a multi-racial umbrella group of anti-apartheid associations which was very active in the Cape. I was very, very angered by this unprovoked attack and barely managed to remain cool enough to tell my attacker that I would send material disproving her accusations. Anger and frustration suddenly seemed to be everywhere.

* * *

Wendy and I ended 1988 by going on an extended trip around the country. Between us we visited every store, shaking hands with hundreds of Pick 'n Pay employees. With ongoing labour confrontation and union problems in the company happening at the same time as political and civil unrest, I wanted to reaffirm a commitment to caring from the top. Even though one had to hold on hard to the belief that the fragmentation all around would eventually meld into an harmonious whole, for the time being I had an instinctive need to keep my hands around the company, to keep in touch and in control – on a very personal level.

Apart from good news in March 1989, when our company's results again surpassed every forecast, there was little else to feel cheerful about: a fresh bout of conflict with the unions over pay increases; a bomb scare – I believed linked to our union troubles – at our Claremont headquarters. At this time it was also disclosed that there was a massive lake of unsold wine accumulated from over-production against a declining export market. The obvious solution was to reduce the surplus through selling low-priced wine locally, but the industry cartel controllers had many sound reasons why a deteriorating surplus was better for the industry and better for the public when, of course, it was only better for them.

Soon, however, I had to turn my attention away from such issues because by April 1989 the possibility of a serious strike in Pick 'n Pay again came uncomfortably close. I wrote, 'When all this has settled down and I read this diary, words will never quite be able to express what I feel at this moment in time.' That was written at the end of an awful day – the day talks with the Conciliation Board began – the day we desperately tried to broker a settlement on the current wage dispute. There were exhausting exchanges between union leaders, the Conciliation Board, René de Wet, Hugh Herman and myself. The negotiations went back and forth, round and round, and as each minute ticked by, a strike loomed nearer.

As part of their pre-strike programme, the unions adopted the tactic of organising boycotts. Customers trying to shop at our stores in the worst affected areas had to run the gauntlet of threats. Intimidation was rife and workers didn't dare defy their union leaders even if they were not in favour of the mass action. I felt as though we were on the brink of something that could be disastrous for our company, because despite having negotiated with the unions in good faith, having been to mediation and offered, anyway, the best wage of any food chain in the country, something bordering on evil was out to ruin us.

The truth was that we were not being challenged and confronted merely on matters of union interest. We were being made into a figurehead against which political slings and arrows, long suppressed, long outlawed, were being loosed, while the marksmen sheltered behind the shield of a labour dispute. I was certain the true intention was to ruin our company so as to demonstrate union strength and reach, about which I had already been reliably warned. The trusting relationship built up over 21 years through fair management-to-staff practices had to be sabotaged, because a quiet workforce was not conducive to fomenting the civil disorder – the real agenda.

In our boardroom, we talked all this over for hours and concurred that we had to show firmness and not buckle under the pressure, even though it was already plain that we were sustaining heavy losses in reduced turnovers. I arranged to go on television to set out in an interview exactly what Pick 'n Pay staff stood to lose through the threatened strike action and through customers being kept from the stores. Staff needed to understand the logic: reduced company income impoverished their subsidised housing schemes and educational bursaries for their children, even threatened the very jobs that made such benefits possible.

By the narrowest margin of fortune, an all-out strike was averted in April 1989, but the respite was only temporary. According to warnings, the omens were there – we were firmly in union sights, and too good a target to miss.

* * *

With the immediate threat of a strike averted, the impending replacement of General Sales Tax by Value Added Tax (VAT) and the effect of the change-over on food prices again claimed time and attention. There was much public debate about the issue, but this in no way altered the fact that the public were not being properly informed about the new tax and the way it would impact on food prices. It never failed to amaze me how apparently reasoned theories from apparently well-meaning official spokesmen pulled the wool over the eyes of the purchasing public so thoroughly. In the midst of the VAT debate, Issy Goldberg, an economist, suggested in a public speech that I should be appointed Minister of Consumer Affairs by the government and put in charge of cutting into cartels and cutting down on the red tape hindering commerce. Once before, rather rashly, I had myself suggested starting a Consumers' Party. Great public support for the idea had thoroughly alarmed me at the time because I could barely cope with what was already on my plate, let alone take on another cause demanding a vast input of time if it was to be pursued with the passion it deserved.

Likewise, there was a very warm and approving public reaction to Mr Goldberg's idea. He envisaged a Minister of Consumer Affairs lobbying government on anything that affected the consumer, which would include aggressively fighting monopoly and cartel collusion and sharing technological knowledge between supermarket companies to improve efficiency. Mr Goldberg also envisaged his hypothetical Consumer Affairs person rallying the food industry to counter international disinvestment. While I was grateful that my name was suggested in this context, I was already doing all the things, in one way or another, that Mr Goldberg thought a Minister of Consumer Affairs should be doing, but I had by now crystallised my conviction that operating unfettered by any one political persuasion or title was most effective. Besides, I was no supporter of the Nationalist government, even if it was on its way out. Too many battles stood between us for a truce to be declared this late in the day.

I said much the same thing to a Reuters interviewer at that time, who asked the familiar question why I did not opt for an active political career. I repeated that I could not have been part of any Nationalist government because I opposed them and their policies. But, just as importantly, opposition of the type my company mounted – grassroots, nuts-and-bolts opposition on matters important to ordinary people – was a great deal more effective for being independent.

Perhaps things were about to change markedly with Mr De Klerk becoming President, as he surely would, because I believed through my own contacts with him that he would become the statesman South Africa sorely needed and would transform government into a more open and accessible process. I told the Reuters man that as a company we now also looked forward to having a more accessible Africa around us. Expanding an efficient food distribution system northwards would be good for us all, and we were already looking for the right opportunities. To thrive, we had to grow. If we missed expanding in the right area and in the right way, decline might follow.

Meanwhile, to the north the dim outline of a new market, peopled by African consumers who needed clean, efficient food stores selling well-priced goods, began to take shape like a mirage on the horizon.

CHAPTER 24

The Beginning of the Beginning

In November 1987, all South Africa was saddened by the tragedy of the *Helderberg*, the South African Airways jumbo jet which plunged into the sea near Mauritius after the pilot reported smoke on board. There were no survivors. Sinister aspects of the tragedy, which began to emerge almost immediately and which are today scheduled to come under scrutiny again in a fresh inquiry, hinged on a suspicious but as yet unproven connection between cargo the *Helderberg* carried and the quasi-government armaments manufacturer, Armscor.

The point is that the tragedy of the downed *Helderberg* was one example among many of how successfully the Nationalist government controlled information during the 1980s. In mid-1987 sweeping new curbs were put on the already heavily censored media. Any publication deemed responsible for inciting unrest could be censored or banned. Under the new regulations, government could caution any publication that it was exceeding 'permitted limits' and, if the warning was ignored, take action to close the publication without recourse to the courts. Therefore, with limpet mines exploding up and down the country, violent strikes and civil disobedience campaigns in progress, and bloody fighting continuing between Inkatha and UDF forces in Natal, the press had to operate under threat of summary closure if their reports displeased the government.

When the scope of actions carried out by government-affiliated agents and bodies finally began to surface in the 1990s, South Africans were shocked to discover how little we knew.

At one time, when I had been coming in for a considerable amount of 'official' criticism for so-called meddling in politics, I found out that the SABC hierarchy in charge of controlling news and programme content had received a directive to 'go easy' on me because someone in government – and I never knew precisely who – approved of my stand on peaceful change for South Africa.

I think I can best sum up the general climate of opinion in 1988 by saying that while there was an awareness that things were not going to change overnight, change was now an inescapable reality. Of course, many still believed the changes would be revolutionary rather than evolutionary, not least of all because political reform seemed to be anchored unproductively to rising opposition from the right. However, I personally believed that most whites who wanted to leave South Africa had now gone and that those who remained behind were here for the long haul, whether their politics were pro- or anti-reform.

Soon after Pick 'n Pay's twenty-first birthday celebrations subsided in a glow of goodwill, President Botha dampened things down in his inimitable style by launching a vicious attack on the company for awarding a percentage pay increase above the government request. Calm was definitely called for because it was maddeningly clear that government were trying to throw the blame for the serious inflationary trend in the country onto the private sector instead of placing the blame where it belonged – with themselves.

While this matter was being handled with all the calm we could muster, several people in the company received calls warning that poisoned goods had been introduced into our distribution system. Everyone was painfully aware of the havoc and loss of public confidence that could result from this especially dastardly form of cowardice. Police tapped phone lines in a desperate effort to identify the culprits while every item on every store and warehouse shelf was examined for signs of tampering – fortunately, negatively. The whole unhappy business was just a hoax, but protecting the public was the prime concern, no matter what it cost us.

Next, the government, still unnerved by the migration of whites to the right and hoping to appease hardliners who thought they had gone soft on apartheid, announced a severe crackdown to counter violations of the Group Areas Act. At the conference called by President Botha in October 1987 to address dissatisfaction among the business community, many of us had stood up to counsel against the insensitive enforcement of apartheid legislation, which would only serve to fan the deep resentment and anger prevalent among black South Africans. The President had seemed to listen to our representations, but now announced a 25-fold increase in fines for Group Areas Act violations. Increased police action was to back the compulsory eviction and blacklisting of those caught living or trading in areas not designated for their race group.

As it happened, the government never enforced this controversial legislation because, by the end of 1988, the tide had turned more strongly towards reconciliation, although it was not yet strong enough to prevent government from banning the UDF and many other, mostly black, opposition groups from participating in politics. COSATU also came under scrutiny, with restrictions imposed to prevent it from carrying on any political activities. Although industrial action was causing increasing problems for business and industry at this time, the government crackdown was an exercise in futility. The unions were on the march as events previously detailed have shown. It is a pity that many of the routes the unions chose slowed down the vehicle which could have carried a better deal to their members, but the differing perceptions of labour unions, their members and employers have been argued from every possible angle. I must say that in spite of the severe spate of strikes and disruptions experienced by Pick 'n Pay in the 1980s, I retained a respect for the principles of unionisation and for the aspirations of their members.

Meanwhile, the private business sector continued plugging away at grassroots problems. At an Urban Foundation lunch with Harry Oppenheimer, Gavin Relly, David Susman, Jan Steyn and others, I heard a frightening forecast of how many houses had to be built up to 2000 just to deal with the existing backlog of homeless and shack-dwelling people. The private sector was trying to do something about this most pressing of social problems but faced enormous difficulties around acquiring suitable land and persuading lending institutions to advance money for low-cost housing. The difficulties we faced then have still not been adequately resolved; indeed, the situation has worsened. No organisation, governmental or non-governmental, up to 2001 has come close to addressing how the thousands upon thousands of people pouring into urban centres can be housed.

As the housing problem, like the poor who needed them, was always with us in the 1980s, so was the division between pro- and anti-sanctions proponents. I started a fresh round of talks with Archbishop Tutu to discuss the evidence I had seen of the adverse effects sanctions visited on poor people, but found him still confirmed in his belief that hastening an end to apartheid justified any means, including the suffering of sanctions-induced poverty.

On the run-down to the beginning of South Africa's upcoming decade of democracy, Nelson Mandela, who had been in a Cape Town clinic recovering from a bout of tuberculosis, was moved to a half-way house on his discharge from hospital instead of being returned to prison. Although it was too early to interpret this as a sign of the government's willingness to begin negotiations with the ANC on the future of South Africa, it was rightly seen as the first step towards Mr Mandela's eventual freedom.

Then, on the day George Bush was elected to the White House, I went to see Mr F. W. de Klerk – now established as the front runner in the presidential race to succeed P. W. Botha – to discuss the role of business people in South Africa and start planning a Western Cape 'think-tank' at which businessmen could put forward their vision for peaceful change in anticipation of working with Mr De Klerk as the next President. It was clear to every observer that matters of massive import for the future of our country were gathering momentum. With the end of P. W. Botha's presidency now a question of when rather than if, his successes – such as reducing South Africa's isolation via ground-breaking visits to Mozambique, Malawi, Zaïre and the Ivory Coast, and seeing through independence for Namibia – did not impress his opponents. They clamoured for the release of Mr Mandela and the establishment of full democracy.

In this volatile climate, Mr De Klerk waited, biding his time, as the first pages of a breathtaking political thriller turned.

* * *

When 73-year-old President P. W. Botha finally announced his resignation as leader of the National Party in February 1989, he managed, characteristically, to irritate almost everyone. Rather than stepping down gracefully in Mr De Klerk's favour, as expected, he chose instead to retain his duties as State President.

The President's refusal to give way led to a situation of great confusion. For the first time in the history of South Africa, the head of government was not also the head of the ruling party. So who formulated policy? Who was now at the head of government – the leader of the party or the President? While this dilemma was being mulled over in political minds, there was at least a consensus between both progressive and conservative branches of the National Party: they had had enough of P. W. Botha's autocratic style of leadership.

I was as confused an observer as anyone else at this time but, in common with many like-minded people, thought the time was ripe for a coalition of moderates to jointly counter the strengthening forces on the right. There were particular calls for a coalition between the National Party and the newly constituted Democratic Party, under which the main liberal political groups were now grouped, but, for the time being, that gap was too wide to garner much support. The point is, political ground was shifting markedly as we moved into the 1990s. While white South Africans were still sorting themselves out into left- and right-wing affiliations, banned black leaders waited like arrows quivering in slings for the freedom to rally their supporters.

In July 1989 President P. W. Botha produced a diplomatic trump card which took almost everyone by surprise. He demonstrated the power he still had by holding an historic meeting with the still-jailed Mr Mandela at the official presidential residence in Cape Town. This unexpected encounter, which left most of us gasping, came as no surprise to

Mrs Thatcher in Britain, however. Her spokesman revealed that the British government had been kept informed about the meeting and warmly welcomed it – unlike Mrs Winnie Mandela, the ANC organisation, Archbishop Desmond Tutu and the South African government, all of whom were bewildered by the unexpected turn of events. Chief Buthelezi spoke memorably when he said the historic meeting was one of the last great gestures for which Mr P. W. Botha would always be remembered by black South Africa.

It was the beginning of the beginning.

As usual, a generous pinch of irony seasoned the meeting between Mr Botha and Mr Mandela. The meeting was testimony to the significance of Mr Mandela and the ANC as players in the South African situation. However, it had been illegal to photograph Mr Mandela for so long that the only photograph that could be found to accompany news of the meeting was one taken of him in the 1960s, nearly thirty years earlier. In 1989, the public still had no idea of how Mr Mandela looked.

Once the gasps of incredulity over Mr Botha's stunning display of statesmanship subsided, I found that an old adversary of ours – the banks – had grouped themselves together to get in the way of a national financial network we planned to set up. Since becoming the first retail chain to computerise our checkouts in 1976, we were always on the look-out for ways to serve our customers better. Now we planned a system that would link all 120 of our stores, supporting electronic fund transfers, scanning, cheque authorisation and other useful, time-saving services at points of sale. Called the Pay Net system, it added up to a great innovation in convenience for our consumers. The system had the potential to link in suppliers and possibly other retailers too, but the banks bristled at this upstart competition to their monopoly on financial services. They went out of their way to cause trouble and block us, as indeed banks were trying to do to retailers world-wide.

The Pay Net problem was a high-profile worry but only one of any number always on my mind. Sometimes, as I sat at my desk at the end of the 1980s, often engaged in furious phone calls trying to disentangle the dispute with the banks, or having talked intensely through some point of strategy with a colleague, I would look out of the window and see black-lettered billboards shouting news of more disruption. Teargas, rubber bullets, birdshot used to disperse mobs ... people dead and injured, buildings and shops destroyed. I wondered: could we really pull off a miracle, emerge from the mayhem and attain even a modicum of normality? On a personal level, was I doing the right thing encouraging my children to stay in South Africa? For the next five years at least, no firm answer one way or the other was to be forthcoming.

During the latter years of the 1980s, while many dramatic events were taking place within Pick 'n Pay and also while I was often travelling overseas giving speeches to try to keep the South African flag flying, I got close to Mr F. W. de Klerk, President-in-waiting. There was an occasion, before he assumed the presidency, when I asked him if I could go to America and say that when he became President he would do away with apartheid. He told me that I couldn't because that was not yet Nationalist policy, but we nevertheless spent two illuminating hours talking.

As a result of such contacts, Mr De Klerk told me he wanted to meet with various business people and asked me to set up some meetings for him. One big meeting, held at my offices in Cape Town, turned into an absolutely electrifying encounter. Mr De Klerk, pen poised over a yellow pad, looking like the lawyer he was, asked the gathered businessmen to tell him exactly what he should do when he took over from Mr Botha. We sat there for two hours, telling him the game was up, that apartheid had to go, that the world was squeezing us financially, which, combined with the cultural and sporting restrictions, was pushing us almost beyond the point of no return.

He sat listening while we told him that Mr Mandela had to be released, the Group Areas Act and separate education had to be abolished, as well as all the remaining Acts which had caused the odium of the world against us. At the end of the long, intense meeting, Mr De Klerk put down his pen and told us that he agreed with everything we had said, with the exception of ending separate education, which he did not believe the country was yet ready for.

If I think back to that particular meeting – because there were a number between Mr De Klerk and the business community before he assumed the presidency – I can still remember emerging so buoyed with hope. I really believed, at long, long last, that we were on the brink of a whole new beginning.

In mid-1989 the disunity in ruling National Party ranks erupted. Since Mr P. W. Botha had chosen to separate the role of State President, which he retained, from National Party leadership, now in the hands of Mr De Klerk, he felt progressively more isolated. Mr Botha was reported to have become obsessed with the idea that his ministers were ignoring him. When he heard on television news, in the same way as the general South African public, that Dr Kaunda of Zambia and Mr De Klerk were to have discussions in Lusaka, about which he knew nothing, it must have been painfully apparent that his suspicions were well founded.

When a furious Mr Botha confronted the Cabinet over the Kaunda issue, they countered, rallying behind the leadership of Mr De Klerk, suggesting that the State President should take sick leave, at least until after the pending general election, which was then scheduled to take place in three weeks' time. Mr Botha reportedly replied that he would rather resign than accept this – which the Cabinet chose to take as an offer, and accepted with alacrity.

P. W. Botha had been at the helm of South African government for slightly more than eleven years on his resignation. Under his leadership South African society had become increasingly violent, crime had increased markedly, and political unrest had reached such proportions that a state of emergency had been in force for the entire second half of his term of office. Incidents of arson, sabotage and terrorism had become everyday occurrences, which Mr Botha's government was only able to keep marginally under control through the imposition of draconian security laws and the curtailment of civil rights. On these counts alone it is no wonder that Afrikaner journalist Piet Muller was to describe the P. W. Botha era as 'the decade of shame'.

South Africa had also become far less prosperous under P. W. Botha. Most people were poorer, taxpayers' money had been wasted on a senseless war in Angola, foreign debt had increased alarmingly, and the value of the rand had dropped sharply against other currencies.

Yet, to P. W. Botha's credit, there was real progress towards restoring full citizenship rights to people other than whites during his term of office. In addition, many of the most offensive apartheid measures – pass laws, and bans on mixed marriages and sexual relationships across the colour line – were subject to reform under his government. He had also pulled off a piece of truly impressive statesmanship by holding the first significant meeting with Mr Mandela.

In the September 1989 election, three weeks after Mr De Klerk assumed the presidency, the ruling National Party took a major battering in its worst election performance in 35 years. There was a dramatic advance by the Democratic Party, offset by more gains for the Conservative Party on the right. The election made it crystal clear that unless the Nationalists under Mr De Klerk did something solid on the road to reform, they were going to lose out altogether. They seemed to absorb this lesson quickly and well because eight of South Africa's most prominent political prisoners, including the ANC's Walter Sisulu and four others sentenced to life imprisonment with Mr Mandela 25 years previously, were soon released. The first press conference addressed by ANC leadership in South Africa since the banning of the organisation in 1960 followed shortly.

In the history and reviews of the struggle to end apartheid in South Africa, I don't believe that the role which the South African business community played has received the credit it deserves. In the case I know best, that of my own company, we worked away at winning the winks and the nods that allowed us to chip away at the institution of apartheid – changing things *de facto* rather than *de jure*. And yes, we did prosper doing so. The business community as a whole worked persistently at peeling away apartheid. Major, dramatic events like the meeting businessmen held with the ANC were very important, but so was the slow erosion of apartheid through the influence of commerce. By establishing that pattern of steady change, working quietly and steadily, commerce was an unrecognised architect of change.

During a meeting I had with Mr Mandela soon after his release from prison, I told him many things which surprised him greatly about the role of business in dismantling apartheid. He said he had never realised the critical role business played until he heard what had happened and saw a pattern emerge. I don't think there is any other country in the world apart from South Africa where the efforts of the business community have been so instrumental in changing an institutionalised political system. I am extremely proud of my role, and grateful to have been part of such a fascinating, if maddening and taxing, process.

Meanwhile, as the decade of the 1980s wound down, I recorded that one of my resolutions for 1990 was to get my golf handicap back down to single figures.

Sometimes, after all, you have to take time to worry about the really important things in life.

PART FOUR

THE DECADE OF DEMOCRACY

'For how can you know colour in perpetual green, and what good is warmth without cold to give it sweetness?'
– John Steinbeck

CHAPTER 25

Against All Odds

As a nation, we were used to living on the edge.

At the time of President De Klerk's famous speech at the opening of Parliament in February 1990, decades of bad news, mayhem and isolation had fine-tuned us to expect the worst rather than the best. But when Mr De Klerk stood up in Parliament and announced the immediate curtailment of restrictions on the ANC and all major political organisations and, at long last, the imminent, unconditional release of Mr Mandela after 27 years of imprisonment, even those of us who expected announcements along these lines revelled in a rare surge of hope and optimism.

As a result of being part of business initiatives to promote change, I was not surprised by Mr De Klerk's announcements, but I was absolutely thrilled by the landscape of fresh hope he painted during his February 1990 speech to Parliament. Soon afterwards, I requested and was granted more interviews with Mr De Klerk because some unions and black political leaders had lost no time after his speech in calling for nationalisation of major businesses to fund a redistribution of wealth. While we could be eternally grateful that we were not hearing such calls during the era of socialist expansionism in Africa, some local leaders still clung to outdated ideas capable of killing the economy.

At our February 1990 meetings, Mr De Klerk told me he planned to travel to America and Europe later in the year on a sanctions-ending errand. The more his policies succeeded in opening up new avenues of opportunity, the easier it would be to divert disciples of nationalisation down them, he believed. In the mass euphoria following Mr De Klerk's irrevocable commitment to forging a new South Africa, there had been many enthusiastic predictions about how the South African economy would take off once sanctions were lifted. Taking a realistic view, I believed South Africa could achieve an annual growth rate of 7 percent once sanctions were lifted, which would double the wealth of the country in ten years – *if* a different attitude to productivity developed in tandem. A fair distribution of this hypothetical new wealth would show black leaders that economic equity could be achieved without damaging the economy, but labour had to play its part too.

Talking with Mr De Klerk in the early days of his presidency was a real departure from the past, when the white leadership on the whole gave time grudgingly and opinions other than their own short shrift. Within the constraints of the deluge of commitments that came with Mr De Klerk's celebrity after February 1990, following on our talks about ending sanctions we also discussed how the situation of free enterprise could be made more acceptable to black leaders. From my perspective, it was clear that employers needed to play their part through promoting on merit regardless of race, and through offering shares to employees. Labour, in turn, had to acknowledge that they had responsibilities as well as demands.

I thought that if state-owned enterprises such as the post office and transport services were privatised and if every penny raised went into social upliftment, we would stop hearing calls for nationalisation from the left and might also appease vociferous right-wingers – who believed that Mr De Klerk was a traitor to the Afrikaner nation – if the economy could come right.

The honeymoon of unclouded hope was, however, short-lived. I wrote in my diary in February 1990: 'We could be on the threshold of a Golden Age.' But by September I was writing, '… the situation on the ground is really very, very frightening'. Mr De Klerk had officially declared the 'season of violence' ended but the ferocity which marked the beginning of the era of reconciliation had South Africans shuddering.

This was the grand era of marches, mass action and organised protest. Consumer boycotts became a terrible bugbear. Sometimes they turned very nasty. On one occasion, people were shot dead in a township on the outskirts of Welkom after mass meetings promoting a consumer boycott against businesses in the town centre got out of hand. By mid-1990, we calculated that consumer boycotts and stayaways had cost Pick 'n Pay R5 million, cheap compared to the whopping R25 million loss due to similar causes chalked up at Checkers.

Up and down the country, the forces of violence gathered and dug in for a long campaign of terror. At our Randpark Ridge store in the Transvaal, Pick 'n Pay staff, incited by outside troublemakers, turned on the store's manager and attacked him severely. It was an awful episode. Then, two of our employees were shot dead in Johannesburg by an AK-47-wielding madman who fired indiscriminately into crowds of commuters innocently making their way home.

The savage conflict between ANC and Inkatha factions escalated, causing the deaths of 381 people in one night alone. Our nerves were not soothed at all either by the appearance of the AWB leader, Eugene Terre'Blanche, who came to Cape Town for talks with Minister of Law and Order Adriaan Vlok flanked by a booted, khaki-clad escort of grim-faced right-wingers, openly sporting pistols on their hips.

I wrote of 'really churning' at that time, being very tense, yet trying always to keep a cool head. Retrospectively, I'm not sure if it was just myself I was trying to cheer up when I put into a May 1990 diary, 'there is always light at the end of the tunnel, there is always good news with bad. That is how it has always been and I have learnt to take them both on the chin.'

Also in May 1990 Mr De Klerk and Mr Mandela, backed by their own high-powered teams of negotiators, met for a first round of talks to determine the future of South Africa. World attention focused on these talks, described as the most crucial in the history of South Africa. In the prevailing climate of violence it was particularly hoped that the ANC would at least discuss the thorny issue of their armed struggle, still being actively pursued.

Disappointment and dismay had been rife among white South Africans on hearing Mr Mandela calling for an intensification of the struggle, including armed resistance, defiance and the international isolation of the apartheid regime, mere hours after his emotional release from prison on Sunday 12 February 1990, when he addressed an ecstatic crowd numbering thousands on Cape Town's Grand Parade.

What was meant to have been a triumphant return to public life for Mr Mandela was marred by bloody clashes between police and youths, which left parts of Cape Town looking like a battleground. Although Mr Mandela struck a conciliatory note acknowledging Mr De Klerk's role in normalising the situation in South Africa, and also called on 'our white compatriots' to join blacks in shaping a new South Africa, audiences world-wide had, in fact, witnessed the opening skirmishes in a vicious four-year-long season of civil strife.

My understanding of Mr Mandela's post-prison performance was that he clearly had to use his speech to appease radically differing elements among his following. Throughout the later years of his imprisonment, the major issue standing in the way of his release had been his refusal to denounce the ANC's armed struggle outright. Mr De Klerk often spoke to me about how the two of them talked and talked around this issue. In the end, Mr De Klerk decided to release the long-incarcerated leader unconditionally, before he forswore armed struggle, because Mr Mandela had declared himself willing to make a constructive contribution to a process of peaceful political change. For the time being, that had to be enough. Exactly as Mr De Klerk had to consider the conservative elements in his party in order to push through reforms, so Mr Mandela had to be mindful of radical elements among his supporters. Both leaders trod a precarious path.

* * *

I did not rush to establish contact with Mr Mandela as soon as he came out of prison – as so many did – but in time I came to know him well, and indeed still do. After his release, we spoke at length about the issue of sanctions – my long-held belief that they most hurt the people they were supposed to help, and his that they were a crucial bargaining tool in the liberation process.

I remained deeply involved with the ongoing campaign to bring sanctions against us to an end. Of course, the game plan had changed a lot since Mr De Klerk's tenure as President. It was no longer a case of a few lonely leaders such as Chief Buthelezi and the business community speaking out against sanctions and apartheid from the wilderness. But there is no doubt that the work we did to keep the debate – and some doors – open made a positive contribution to Mr De Klerk's campaign. He went to the United Kingdom and spoke to British Labour leader Neil Kinnock and to Prime Minister John Major. I spoke to the British Directors' Association to keep in touch as trading and sporting doors were opened, and met a high-powered trade delegation from China with Anton Rupert. Being accepted again was a heady feeling.

As Mr De Klerk progressed through Europe and America on his early 1990s sanctions-ending quest, Mr Mandela followed closely in his wake, still giving a counter-story. But the doors Mr De Klerk was opening did not seem likely to slam shut again for the time being. At the same time, I had been trying to organise Mr Mandela's attendance at one of our business people's 'think-tank' meetings, still regularly held, for the express purpose of drawing him out on his continued support for sanctions. He was, however, reluctant to make firm commitments at that time, being increasingly preoccupied with a painful domestic crisis with his wife Winnie, which was fast coming to a head.

A few months later, however, Mr Mandela and I did discuss the burning topic of sanctions. At that time I was very surprised, in view of his frequent statements against the dropping of sanctions, to hear that he no longer personally favoured this form of coercion, but that he had his party's policy to consider. We also talked about Pick 'n Pay's social responsibility policies and he asked me if I would organise a dinner in Cape Town with various business people so he could talk to them about the ANC's future plans, which I readily agreed to do.

During the course of that meeting in Johannesburg we were interrupted three times – once by a call from the United Nations, and once each with calls from Mr De Klerk and the Transkei Premier. I could see the strain Mr Mandela was under and, indeed, he told me he was being pulled from pillar to post. Talks with Mr De Klerk were scheduled for the following day and he was to make a major address at the United Nations the following week. Mr Mandela looked tired, worn out by conflicting pressures.

The time allotted for our meeting flew past, but before leaving I stressed how strongly I felt about the damaging effects of sanctions and the importance of a free economy if the private sector was to produce money for social upliftment.

On other occasions Mr Mandela and I spoke about the grace of his ability to forgive a people who had put him behind bars for 27 of what should have been the most productive years of his life. He explained that being imprisoned for so long had given him abundant time to read and reflect. Starting with Socrates, he had worked through all the notable philosophers, a task which had brought him to the conviction that he had to learn how to forgive. He told me he couldn't leave prison as a bitter man, because then he wouldn't be a good leader.

One particularly beautiful day in Cape Town, when Mr Mandela was in my office, I looked out at the brilliant blue sky above Table Mountain, framed in my window, and remarked how lovely the mountain appeared. Mr Mandela replied – wryly – that it was pleasant to look at the mountain from this angle and as a free man, because the only view he had had for twenty-odd years was the one from across the water on Robben Island. I could have kicked myself for being so insensitive, but in Mr Mandela's typically gracious way he laughed to ease my discomfort.

Mr Mandela is the most natural, unaffected, charming and friendly person of stature I have ever been privileged to know. His memory for names and faces is astonishing, his ability to put everyone at their ease is legendary. Like the late Princess Diana, Nelson Mandela, from his earliest days wearing the mantle of an icon, made everyone he spoke to feel important and interesting.

He also adores children. One day, after his inauguration as President, Gareth and I were invited to breakfast with Mr Mandela at the house he occupied on Groote Schuur Estate, having graciously allowed Mr De Klerk to continue to reside at Groote Schuur itself. When I got there I was surprised to find that Gareth had not arrived at the appointed time. Mr Mandela and I nevertheless settled down to breakfast in the meantime and soon the door burst open to admit a flurried Gareth, delayed in traffic, leading his small daughter Emma by the hand. I was surprised to see my granddaughter there and asked Gareth why he had brought her. He said Emma had refused to be left at school that morning, begging to be allowed to come with her father to meet Mr Mandela. She had been so persistent, he hadn't known how to refuse.

Before I had a chance to apologise for this unexpected small guest, Mr Mandela got up, wreathed in smiles, to hold out a chair for Emma at the table. The little girl sat silently listening to proceedings; then, as our breakfast meeting wound up, presented Mr Mandela with the gift of a bookmark she had brought along specially for the occasion and asked Mr Mandela, in a very small voice, if she might have his autograph in her book. 'Absolutely not,' he answered, smiling into her crestfallen face, 'not, that is, until you've given me yours.' Then he took her by the hand and lifted her up to the leather-bound visitors' book, insisting that she sign her name there before he put his autograph into her book.

On many later occasions when I met Mr Mandela, sometimes to talk about serious, critical situations, he would ask at some juncture after Emma. He told me several times that he used the bookmark she had given him nearly every day. He never forgot people's names, whether they were mighty or humble, and he never forgot the context in which he had met them.

* * *

In June 1991, Mr De Klerk took his next giant leap forward. He declared the new South Africa officially on the march as Parliament relegated apartheid once and for all to the past, voting overwhelmingly to scrap the Population Registration Act. Through that racially based piece of legislation the lives of every South African had been affected in the minutest detail.

Unfortunately, violence continued unabated. Armed men continued to rampage through urban townships killing and maiming residents. South Africans started to wonder with dread whether this was the true face of the new South Africa. Mr De Klerk, stunned by a crushing local election defeat to the Conservative Party, reached a new moment of truth. He decided to put his political future on the line by calling for a snap whites-only referendum in which voters would be asked to indicate with a 'yes' or a 'no' whether they supported his government's initiatives towards democratising South Africa.

Shares on the Johannesburg Stock Exchange tumbled following Mr De Klerk's announcement, but this was no time for the faint of heart. I immediately called meetings to allocate funds for promoting a 'yes' vote under the auspices of the Private Sector Fund launched for this purpose.

Around the time of Mr De Klerk's make-or-break referendum I had agreed to make the keynote address at a major conference in Johannesburg called to inform potential overseas investors of prospects in South Africa. I decided there was no alternative but to be upbeat in approach and told the audience that everyone supporting the referendum process needed to unite to ensure that Mr De Klerk achieved a convincing and resounding victory. Thinking to divert delegates' thoughts away from the tumultuous state of the country, I also spoke about the complex divisions governing our economy.

At the end of the apartheid era, South Africa's per capita gross national product (GNP) was on a par with poor countries such as Poland, Yugoslavia and Mexico, owing to business having been sandwiched between a suspicious black community and an interventionist government. Yet, having the world's largest deposits of minerals and largest mining industry outside the Soviet Union, we had developed the only modern economy in Africa. While ours was an economy displaying paradox aplenty, it also offered opportunity aplenty. Without foreign capital, the South African economy stood no chance of growing sufficiently to provide, not only opportunities, but the basic necessities of life such as clean water, sanitation, housing and education, which millions lacked but now eagerly anticipated.

Later that day, I met with the Governor of the Bank of England and with the Rothschilds – in South Africa to discuss the latest situation as it related to their investments here. They thought there had been a very positive reaction to what I had said and a willingness to understand our special economic problems. Next day in my office, however, I took quite a number of abusive calls from aggressive right-wingers who said I had no right to put the case for a reformed South Africa.

As ever, you could never please everyone, but there were at least some causes for celebration in the midst of the massive eruption we were living through. In company with every other sports fanatic, I had been incredibly excited to see South Africa walk onto the cricket pitch in Australia to pulverise the Aussies in a World Cup match. Our cricketers were there because of reforms, and their stunning victory over the World Cup favourites sparked emotional responses unprecedented in South Africa's history. The ANC chief of sport, Steve Tshwete, broke down and cried in the South African dressing room after the team's nine-wicket triumph – providing a powerful image of sport's capacity to unify.

The day before Mr De Klerk's March 1992 referendum, our cricketers hit another high, beating India to secure a place in the World Cup semifinals. The interesting point about this is that those backing a 'yes' vote in the next day's referendum rejoiced over the cricket victory because it bolstered white confidence and encouraged optimism. The power of the South African passion for sport began to be recognised for its massive potential as a unifying force.

On referendum day, white South Africans flocked to the polls and finally broke with the past, handing the 'yes' alliance a massive mandate to negotiate an end to minority rule. A jubilant President De Klerk described the landslide victory as the final death-knell of apartheid and the real birth of the new South Africa. I had worried a great deal about the outcome of the referendum, because our whole future hinged on support for Mr De Klerk; so I found the positive outcome immensely cheering.

There was also quiet confidence in South Africa that talks between all interested parties on the mechanism for adopting a new South African Constitution would bear fruit. Though talks were often deadlocked and fearfully difficult, there was some progress by mid-1992. I heard from a highly placed source that the country would have an interim government within the coming six weeks, which appeared a substantial prospect after Parliament was recalled to deal with the huge amount of legislation flowing out of the negotiations.

* * *

Just when there seemed to be real political progress, Boipatong, a Vaal Triangle township, was the scene of a ghastly massacre, when Inkatha-affiliated members of township hostels attacked and killed ANC-supporting township residents. As a result, the ANC walked out of the constitutional negotiation talks, blaming the government for, at worst, instigating violence and, at best, for failing to control it.

As another result of the ANC walk-out, Archbishop Desmond Tutu and the ANC threatened to advise international sporting bodies to sever recently re-established relationships with South Africa and to bar us from participating in the pending Barcelona Olympics. It was an alarming turn of events. I sent a very crisp and firm fax to Mr Tshwete of the ANC regarding their threats, appealing to him not to kill hope in this country. I told him that I acknowledged the enormity of the Boipatong tragedy but also recognised the importance of holding on to anything which promoted unity.

In reaction to the terrible events at Boipatong, one of the largest strikes in the history of South Africa was called; millions of workers up and down the country stayed away. On day two of the strike, fifteen thousand protesters marched on Cape Town's city centre, burning and looting. A furious mob arrived at the headquarters of Pick 'n Pay, toyi-toyi-ing – as the national protest dance of the new South Africa was called – and refusing to move on until a delegation from the company accepted a memorandum regarding ANC demands. Again, there was no separating business from politics.

Also at this time, in the Cape coastal town of Fish Hoek, leaders of the right-wing Conservative Party told a rowdy meeting not to buy from Pick 'n Pay because we supported the ANC. The slur was entirely erroneous – my company did not support any political party. Contributions we later made, which I will explain in context, were spread among the main parties contending the first democratic election in 1994.

Towards the end of 1992, a year we would retrospectively see as one of the most painful transition years, serious cracks appeared to be affecting the relationship between the two principal players in the production – Mr De Klerk and Mr Mandela. Nevertheless, they still shared a resolve to see the process they had started through to the end, thanks largely to the real breakthrough that veteran communist Joe Slovo had introduced into negotiations, offering Mr De Klerk's existing government a period of five years of joint rule – the saving 'Sunset Clause'.

Then, on 10 April 1993, just days after the parties making up the constitutional negotiating teams had at last agreed to resume multi-party talks, the revolutionary-turned-peacemaker and Communist Party leader, Chris Hani, was gunned down outside his Johannesburg home. Next day a right-wing Polish immigrant Janusz Walus was arrested in connection with the assassination, followed a few days later by the arrest on the same charge of Clive Derby-Lewis.

The cold-blooded assassination of Mr Hani was an event loaded with menace. In the prevailing climate of fear, with distrust between the races rife and violence barely contained, the assassination of the popular people's leader had the capacity to tip the balance towards utter chaos. As political leaders of all persuasions called desperately for calm, ordinary citizens held their breath.

As a company, we decided that in view of the emotions raised, we would make a contribution towards the cost of Mr Hani's funeral, as businesses had been called on to do, and would not enforce our usual 'no work, no pay' policy against people staying away to attend the funeral.

Throughout the country, people stayed away from work and joined seething marches protesting against the assassination. In Cape Town, furious mobs again converged on the city, smashing and looting in a disgusting display of pure hooliganism. I witnessed some of these awful acts myself and felt a knot in my stomach at the sight of such unrestrained fury.

Mr De Klerk and Mr Mandela stuck to their commitment to peace in the ensuing turbulence, but their credibility and authority were dented. For Mr De Klerk, the implications of the assassination were particularly grave, suggesting that his government's grip on an armed and dangerous white right-wing was tenuous. Then, as Nelson Mandela addressed crowds at Mr Hani's funeral, tens of thousands of left-wing radicals walked out in protest against his pleas that reason should prevail. Even though he also slammed the National Party as corrupt, illegitimate and unfit to govern, the crowd were not mollified. Their mood was ugly and vengeful. On the painful march to democracy, we had reached one of the lowest points.

Negotiators locked in exhausting talks around the constitutional table recognised how close the country had come to total anarchy and at last, after a marathon day's long session, announced a firm date for the country's first democratic election – 27 April 1994. As I travelled up to Johannesburg to celebrate Nelson Mandela's seventy-fifth birthday, just after the election date announcement, I reflected how even that outing showed the changing nature of life in South Africa. We *were* going through such tumultuous times, yet things that were outlawed a few years previously were now common practice. What we needed now were cool heads, steady hands and stout hearts to pick our way safely through the minefields of transition and change.

In September 1993, reeling from shock after violent shock – the St James massacre, the murder of American student Amy Biehl, the Heidelberg attack – Capetonians had joined millions of people throughout the country in a demonstration to mark National Peace Day. As the traditional noon gun sounded in Cape Town, people across the city joined hands and observed a minute's silence, praying for peace. Joint winners of that year's Nobel Peace Prize, Mr De Klerk and Mr Mandela, both denounced the violence ripping South Africa apart and pledged themselves to peace.

To ordinary South African citizens, however, peace pledges tasted of bitter irony at that time. How was peace possible when violence between Inkatha and ANC factions ground horribly on? At the end of 1993, Chief Buthelezi still refused to allow the Inkatha Freedom Party to participate in the April 1994 election hurtling towards us, although Mr De Klerk made it perfectly clear that the election would go ahead with or without their participation. Personally, I had always admired Mr Buthelezi for his stand against sanctions and apartheid in times when it was definitely unfashionable for a black leader to do so. But his intransigence over the 1994 elections tempered my admiration with concern about the possible effects of his decisions.

In December 1993 whites-only politics in South Africa came to an end. The House of Assembly, where Hendrik Verwoerd had unveiled his master plan for apartheid and had later been assassinated, where the laws of apartheid had been forged and fought, met for the last time. As the Speaker announced the 237 to 45 vote that sounded the death-knell of white rule, ANC-aligned members leapt triumphantly to their feet shouting '*Amandla awethu*' ('Power is ours'). From the gallery above, one hysterical white right-winger screamed down at government ministers: 'You are busy with treason – I hope your punishment is not as great as your crime.'

It was a fitting conclusion to a terrible year of division, darkness, bitterness and dissent.

* * *

Only weeks away from the April election, Bophuthatswana went up in flames. Mayhem reigned as thousands of people took to the streets claiming to have toppled the government of President Lucas Mangope. The Mmabatho Pick 'n Pay store was looted and our other store in the homeland, at Mabopane, was burnt to the ground. Four days into the battle of Mmabatho, journalists filmed the horrific execution of three white right-wingers attempting to surrender to Bop police.

In Johannesburg, sniper fire tore into a thousands-strong crowd of Zulu marchers outside the ANC's Shell House headquarters. South Africa's commercial heartland turned into a bloody battleground as ANC security guards, who claimed to have come under attack from the marchers, opened fire on the marchers, prompting answering fire from police. In the aftermath of the carnage, the government announced emergency measures and called an urgent summit with the ANC and Inkatha. Again, South Africa held its breath.

Days before the election, CNN devoted an extraordinary ninety minutes' broadcast time to coverage of the first live debate between President De Klerk and Mr Mandela. Millions of viewers across the world watched the debate, which ended, over a handshake, with the message 'Yes, there is hope'.

In the last tense days prior to the election, we told every Pick 'n Pay manager to call on anyone in authority, including myself, at any hour of the day or night, if they needed advice or just someone to talk to. Such was the climate of apprehension prevailing.

At the eleventh hour – election-wise – Chief Buthelezi's IFP agreed to take part, boosting hopes that the election would be peaceful. Interviewed by a French journalist, present in South Africa along with hundreds of foreign press correspondents to cover the election, I said that the most important issue during the coming five years was how to encourage economic development. We simply could not let the forces of disruption and violence ruin the future of our country. I told the journalist he could assure his readers that Nelson Mandela had no intention of turning the country into a banana republic. This he had personally told me.

Intent on spreading panic among whites on the eve of elections, right-wing elements set a rumour campaign in motion, whispering of chaos, food shortages, black-outs and after-election anarchy. The rumours had the effect of galvanising already jittery people into action. After frenzied sweeps through supermarket shelves, trolley-load after trolley-load of tinned food, pet food, milk powder and candles flew out of stores.

But the forces of darkness – electrical or otherwise – did not prevail in the end. On 27 April 1994, the miracle South Africans of goodwill had longed for, happened. Confounding every prediction, millions went peacefully to the polls. As we all remember, it was a day of particular joy for black people. No matter how old or infirm – a poignant picture showed an ancient black lady being trundled to a rural polling station in a wheelbarrow – no matter how long the queues or how hot the sun, people got there, waited, and cast their votes.

The April 1994 landslide victory for the ANC, which ushered in a Government of National Unity, is part of our history now. At the time I wrote in my diary: 'A really very exciting time. A near miracle with the wonderful peace that seems to be pervading everyone after the election. The outstanding statesmanship shown by Mr Mandela and Mr De Klerk in their speeches to their parties, Mr Mandela accepting victory and Mr De Klerk conceding defeat. It was not defeat, however, as without him there would never have been a coalition government and a peaceful hand-over of power.'

A few days later, on the eve of Mr Mandela's presidential inauguration, I took the opportunity to talk to the Duke of Edinburgh, in South Africa for the occasion, about Cape Town's Olympic 2004 bid. He was very interested, very supportive, echoing the common sentiment: Nelson Mandela's forgiveness and South Africa's taking on democracy without the revolution the world had predicted provided a shining example which the whole world saluted. Our Rainbow Nation – so christened by Archbishop Desmond Tutu – was the darling of the world. As the Duke said, it was an incomparably wonderful time to be bidding for an Olympic meeting.

CHAPTER 26

Birth of a Dream

In mid-1990, I prepared for a trip to Europe, where I was to make two important speeches – one for the CIES in West Germany, the other an address to Manchester University's School of Business in the north of England.

Just before I left South Africa, I was touched to receive a Scopus Award, a coveted award initiated by the American Friends of the Hebrew University to honour, according to the citation, 'individuals of vision and understanding'. It was both humbling and amusing to join a list of past recipients which included Artur Rubinstein, Itzhak Perlman, ex-President Gerald Ford, Jeane Kirkpatrick – and Frank Sinatra.

The speech I gave to a fifteen-hundred-strong audience at the CIES conference in West Germany was delivered in a city still captivated by the coming down of the Berlin Wall in November 1989. My speech to the CIES – an organisation of top retailers and suppliers from all around the world – gave a real-life account of how the power of subjugated people could still be acknowledged and advanced through enlightened management and marketing philosophies. Retailing, and manufacturing too for that matter, did not operate in a vacuum in South Africa, because political and social realities permeated every part of our marketplace. As I was to discover in conversation with delegates afterwards, this was the first time they had considered the implications of trying to run an ethical enterprise, or indeed any enterprise, in an unethical system, as many South African businesses did during the apartheid era.

That group of hard-headed business people were captivated to hear of the particular challenges South African business had faced on a daily basis for decades. Leaving aside the bureaucratic bungles of apartheid government as they impacted on businesses, problems relating to isolation, sanctions, conscription and violence might all crop up on an average day in the life of a South African trader. Furthermore, an organisation's actions could be construed as too left- or right-wing, pro-white or anti-black, pro-Jewish, anti-Semitic, anti-Muslim, and many other variations at any given time. It was virtually impossible not to alienate *some* section of the buying public.

As though all this was not challenge enough, in South Africa we traded with one foot in the First World and the other in the Third World. Where else might a manager bargain one day with union representatives acting according to international labour law, and the next with a sangoma, a traditional African healer? The eclectic mix of races, cultures and religions making up the public of South Africa forms a highly complex body of consumers for marketers to target accurately, not least because of the eleven official languages spoken. There is extreme sophistication – the South African retail industry, for instance, has sometimes been far ahead of the USA's in innovation – alongside unsophistication belonging to centuries long past.

The South African business community has navigated this complicated sea of contradictions unusually well, often brilliantly, but up to the present time, seven years into democracy, has still not been properly credited, in my opinion, for its ingenuity and guts.

Following my address to the electrically-charged CIES conference in West Germany, I set off almost immediately for the United Kingdom, where I was scheduled to speak at Manchester University's School of Business to mark its twinning with the University of Cape Town. I was expecting nothing more than the passing of a pleasant couple of days in Manchester, during which I might test the waters for attitudes towards

South Africa since Mr Mandela's release, and make a good impression on behalf of my company. In the event, Manchester University's Business School became the setting for the first act of an episode that would take me to some of the highest and lowest points of my life.

At dinner, I found myself seated next to the man who had worked as deputy to Bob Scott, head of the City of Manchester's Olympic Bid Committee and one or two of his Committee members. This Committee had just had the misfortune to lose their quest to host the 1996 games to the winning city, Atlanta. The Manchester bid team had made a determined and spirited bid to host the 1996 games, so I asked the deputy whether, this being their second unsuccessful attempt, they were going to try again? His answer changed my life.

Speaking with the knowledge of one who had been involved in two Olympic bids, the deputy told me that Manchester was then seriously considering its options as a candidate city because Australia was considered such a strong contender for the 2000 games due to be awarded in 1993, and the International Olympic Committee (IOC) would love to see South Africa take the honours for the 2004 summer games, which meant it would be many years before Manchester believed they would have a real chance to win. This information, this revelation, went off in my head like a giant firework. At that stage, no one in the world had spoken to the IOC about South Africa hosting an Olympic Games, but they were apparently so taken with the symbolism of Nelson Mandela's release and South Africa's brave moves towards democracy that they had themselves concluded that South Africa could be a shining candidate to host an Olympic meeting.

I could see that Wendy, who had been listening intently to my conversation with Bob Scott's deputy from her place across the table, was similarly captivated by what he had to say. A spark jumped between us as though we were plugged into a joint power point. The first intimation in 1990 that South Africa could aspire to hosting an Olympic Games was made more amazing when one recalled how recently we had begun to be accepted back into the fold of international sport. Our national athletes had not appeared at an Olympic meeting since 1960, thirty years previously. Images of what an Olympic meeting in our country could bring us in terms of fortune and what it could do to unify South Africa were flashing around my brain, as I guessed – correctly – they were in Wendy's mind too.

It was the birth of a dream.

I have in my office today a small silver tray, engraved with the thanks of Manchester University's School of Business to commemorate the speech I gave there in 1990. To me, the tray has always signified the beginning of our Olympic odyssey, the start of the dream at first shared only with Wendy, who had felt the spark and grasped the possibility with hope and enthusiasm equal to my own.

* * *

Very shortly after my return from Manchester I met with Gordon Oliver, Mayor of Cape Town, to tell him what I had heard. We sat in the mayoral parlour on a day of dazzling Cape sunshine and brilliant blue skies, talking about the possibility of this gem of an opportunity for our city. Gordon Oliver was from the start incredibly enthusiastic. He called in a town planner, the late Neville Riley, to join us and both caught the mood magnificently, saying they would start at once to talk to members of the City Council to muster full support for the project, even though it was at that stage only a dream.

In view of later events, it is crucial to record that the City Council's early, enthusiastic involvement and backing for what became Cape Town's 2004 Olympic bid conclusively proves that all of us – the City Council, myself and my future committee – always saw the project as Cape Town's bid on behalf of South Africa and Africa. The bid was never an I-am-great-Raymond-Ackerman thing. Until disharmony rent the relationship, there was harmony and cooperation, enthusiasm and joint commitment to Cape Town's 2004 bid between the City Council and myself. The Mayor, councillors and other officials had a high profile in the bid – we stood together at numerous functions and news briefings, presenting one face as the partners we were.

As a typical South African in my passion for sport, I had experienced the same frustration as thousands of fellow citizens forced in following international sport, from which our teams were banned. Many a time I felt like hurling some missile through the television screen while watching teams we could challenge, competing without us. Following fast on the heels of the first spark in Manchester – the first tentative realisation that we might aspire to host an Olympic meeting – a gut feeling of *rightness* had been with me. If we were to try for the 2004 summer games, there would be enough time to sort ourselves out politically. The hope of achieving a peaceful, democratic dispensation under Nelson Mandela was the light at the end of our political tunnel.

And if we did manage to pull off this miracle, surely we would become the best-placed country on the face of the earth to stage an event built on the principles of universal brotherhood? I imagined Africa's first Olympics staged beneath Table Mountain in Cape Town, the Mother City, the oldest town in South Africa. Ours was the city Nelson Mandela had looked at from Robben Island during his imprisonment. It was inspiring to imagine a flotilla of lighted ships, one bearing the Olympic flame, sailing from Robben Island to Cape Town, symbolising the triumph of statesmanship over chaos. In keeping with the spirit of our continent, we could turn away from flashiness and ostentation in our Olympic event, go back to grassroots and simplicity to recapture core values.

As a businessman, I was of course also aware that staging a successful Olympic meeting in Cape Town would benefit Pick 'n Pay enormously. But the Olympic spin-off would spread over the whole of South Africa – not only in terms of commercial gain but in creating employment, promoting tourism, boosting the economy in so many positive ways. At the beginning of the 1990s it was true to say that violence and crime were increasingly causes of grave concern. I believe that if South Africa had been able to grasp the opportunities an Olympic meeting offered, crime levels in Cape Town would have dropped in direct relationship to increased prosperity and fuller employment. The 2004 Olympics spelt prosperity for South Africa, in both the short and the long term, and this was the core motivation driving those of us working towards presenting a successful bid at the beginning of the campaign.

So, by mid-1991 I was convinced that Cape Town could stage a creditable Olympic meeting from every logistical point of view. Wendy flew to

Geneva to meet IOC director François Carrard, deputy to IOC President Juan Antonio Samaranch, to discuss Cape Town becoming a candidate city, although of course the possibility was still only a dream. Mr Carrard, with whom we developed a very good relationship, was excited and enthusiastic and offered his special guidance should a South African bid come about.

I met with Mr De Klerk, who was cautiously enthusiastic because of the magnitude of taking on an Olympic bid but who nevertheless backed us on behalf of national government, although, as the City Council had already done, he pointed out that funds could not be committed at this early stage. I also met Mr Steve Tshwete, then the ANC chief of sport and head of South Africa's National Sports Council (NSC), who was similarly enthusiastic. He promised to get clearance from Mr Mandela and the ANC Executive because their blessing would help any future representations to the IOC enormously.

With support mustered from the Mayor and City Council of Cape Town, national government and the ANC, I now crucially needed the support of Sam Ramsamy, who had recently returned to South Africa from exile in London, where he had done excellent work leading the South African Non-Racial Olympic Committee there. Although Sam Ramsamy had been against South Africa gaining readmittance to the Olympic movement before there was meaningful transformation at home, his work in exile had kept the Olympic flame alive for South Africa. On his return home, Sam had formed a National Olympic Committee of South Africa (NOCSA), after consultations with Nelson Mandela and IOC President Samaranch, with the help of Johan du Plessis, who had for years tried to keep the Olympic flame alive in South Africa just as Sam had done in exile. As President of the newly formed NOCSA, Sam was handling the difficult task of bringing a whole host of sporting bodies together and, as such, had quite a nightmare of diverse interests to unify. He was also at that time concentrating on securing South African participation in the upcoming 1992 Barcelona Olympics.

The first meeting between Sam Ramsamy, Johan du Plessis and me took place in Johannesburg. Given the immense differences between us at the time of that first contact – I was a wealthy white businessman fired up with enthusiasm for my Olympic dream; he was a previously exiled black sports administrator handling a highly complicated role – the meeting went surprisingly well. The tone was formal but friendly. For my part, I had come to learn whatever I could because Sam Ramsamy knew the Olympic movement from the inside and I did not.

I explained my dream of Cape Town having the games and passed on what I had heard through my international contacts, which was received with interest. Then, notebook and pen poised, I asked Sam to talk me through the whole process of choosing a candidate city. He told me that there could also be groups in Durban and Johannesburg that were keen to pursue an Olympic bid, so it would be necessary to hold a national competition to nominate one city to stand for South Africa. That done, the nominated city would have to address the IOC triangle, comprising the IOC at the top and international sports federations and national Olympic committees at either corner.

I sat scribbling away, taking down page after page of notes, as is my custom. After all this valuable information had been given, Sam said that although he did not discount the possible validity of my dream – to me by now more an obsession – he thought it was premature because the main focus for South Africa at that time was to secure participation in the 1992 Barcelona Olympics. He suggested that we should leave my ideas in abeyance for the time being, but I had another plan.

I told him that while I understood his present preoccupation with the Barcelona games, I thought it made good sense for me to make an immediate start at forming a committee in Cape Town because, all being new at this game, the sooner we started the more we could gain. He concurred without further discussion, other than to reaffirm that nothing could be done about starting committees in Durban and Johannesburg, the real first step in the process, until after Barcelona.

And so, this was the course of action we settled on, agreeing to meet for review as soon as the Barcelona issue was resolved. In the event, South Africa was readmitted to the Olympic family on 10 July 1991 and cleared to participate in the Barcelona Olympics.

As soon as Sam Ramsamy had agreed that I could gather a committee to start working towards entering Cape Town into a national competition to choose a South African Olympic candidate city, I came home, formed a committee and set off in search of seed money. Although the Mayor and City Council of Cape Town, the ANC and Mr De Klerk for the national government had all applauded the idea of the Olympic dream, enthusiasm was all they could offer at that early stage by way of support. None had funds they could commit, so I went knocking on various corporate doors, asking contacts in the business world to share the dream. Peninsula Beverages (Coca-Cola), Shell and BP immediately caught the mood and each pledged R250 000. In the case of the oil companies, I was particularly grateful, considering how often we had been at loggerheads over the price of fuel. I solemnly promised that if Cape Town's quest ultimately succeeded, the names of their companies would be engraved in stone on the steps leading up to the City Hall or on the Grand Parade, and indeed I would have done just this.

Generous as the pledges by Coca-Cola, Shell and BP were, there remained a considerable shortfall between the total pledged and what it would cost to cover the first phase – preparing to present Cape Town's case against national co-contenders Durban and Johannesburg, neither of which had yet made any start on presentations. We still had to await Sam Ramsamy's return from the Barcelona Olympics before NOCSA would decide whether there would be a South African bid at all, let alone get Durban and Johannesburg started in readiness for a competition between the three cities. But, since we had taken the decision to start Cape Town's planning, the question of funding had to be addressed.

It was at this stage, after consulting with my family, that I offered to put in the difference between pledged money and what was actually needed – between R5 million and R6 million, I thought – as an interest-free loan on condition that the capital would be repaid if Cape Town won the national competition. When I told the city officials and the Minister of Finance this, they thanked me profusely for the generosity and promised, in the case of the City Council in minutes of a Council meeting, that every penny spent would be reimbursed from Council funds, government funds, sponsorships or whatever. Making our loan interest-free was my family's special contribution to Cape Town's quest.

At the time we started work on Cape Town's Olympic planning, the amazing success of the 1984 Los Angeles summer Olympics had unwittingly put a whole new spin on the process of bidding to become a host city. Before Los Angeles, interest in staging Olympic meetings was lacklustre and dwindling. The 1976 Montreal Games had lost money. The 1980 Moscow Olympics, boycotted by the USA, didn't make a rouble. Then, for the 1984 Los Angeles Games along came ex-advertising man Peter Ueberroth, who master-minded a penny-squeezing, television-friendly event that netted a cool US$220 million. Only two cities had asked for the 1984 Olympic Games, but a dozen begged for the 1992 winter Olympics and six for the summer events.

The organisation Juan Antonio Samaranch acquired when he took on the IOC presidency in 1981 was almost bankrupt and very small. After the dazzling financial success of the Los Angeles Games, the floodgates opened on hopeful bidders, and the number of IOC officials charged with travelling the world to establish bona fides and check the suitability and readiness of host city hopefuls mushroomed to over a hundred. Of course there were, and still are, moral, upright, decent people committed to the real values of the Olympic movement among their number, but keeping close surveillance and overall control of so many widely dispersed IOC officials proved problematic. Incidents of excessive gift-giving spiralled out of control until the IOC, no longer able to dismiss expensive solicitation as 'rumour', put a $150 limit on gifts, among other constraints, which did little to stem the flow of largess, as revelations around bidding for the 2002 Salt Lake City winter Olympics later showed.

It was against this backdrop that we resolved within the first Cape Town Olympic Bid Committee to compete fair and square on behalf of Cape Town – if we got the chance to do so. Later, when Cape Town had become South Africa's official candidate city for the 2004 Olympics, I asked the IOC President's deputy, François Carrard, outright whether our chances would be helped or hampered by sticking strictly within the rules laid down by the IOC. He replied that conducting a moral bid based on getting to know voting IOC officials personally and gaining, not buying, their respect would definitely stand in Cape Town's favour.

Acting accordingly, from 1992 – well before the national South African competition had happened – I started synchronising regular business trips abroad to include meetings on Olympic matters. Wendy and I networked away like mad. In company with Ngconde Balfour we attended various important networking international conferences. Ngconde is an affable, likeable man – later, Minister of Sport and Recreation in Mr Mbeki's administration – who was at this time a personality from the world of black sports, a man who had been on Robben Island and who was introduced to our Cape Town Olympic committee by our Public Relations consultant, Kevin Kevany. Quietly, in this first and as yet unofficial stage of Cape Town's campaign, we began to gain confidence that our policy would put us on the right track.

* * *

Wendy and I travelled to Spain to be part of the thrilling, exhilarating Olympic experience in 1992. As a result of the Boipatong tragedy it had been touch and go as to whether we would be allowed to participate, but South Africa did march in company with all the world's Olympic athletes at the opening of the Barcelona Games. In Barcelona, I caught sight of Sam Ramsamy across a hotel room and he gave me a desultory wave. He had undertaken to see that I was invited to various functions around the Barcelona Games at which he would introduce me to members of the Olympic family, but this did not happen. So, left mainly alone, we made use of the time to look, listen and learn. In spite of being frantically busy, the Chairman of the Barcelona organising committee gave generously of the sparse time he had, providing valuable insights into the bidding process and other practicalities laced with the wisdom of immediacy.

Following the hand-over of the Olympic flame by Barcelona to Atlanta, the next city to host the summer Olympics, in 1996, I returned home eagerly anticipating the next stage in my own Olympic dream – the national competition Sam Ramsamy had promised to put in place after Barcelona.

Games of a less companionable nature had been in play over the timing of the national competition between Cape Town, Durban and Johannesburg that would elect an official Olympics 2004 candidate city for South Africa. I had spoken to Sam Ramsamy in February 1993 after his return from the Barcelona Games and received the unexpected and unpleasant news that NOCSA had not really made a decision on when they intended organising the voting between the three cities. Voting would not, after all, take place in April or May 1993 as previously declared. Still, after two and a half years of intensive, behind-the-scenes work, we went ahead with the official launch of a Cape Town Olympic Games Committee, constituted firstly to coordinate a bid for Cape Town in the national competition. I chaired the committee jointly with Ngconde Balfour.

Ngconde and I made a good team; what he lacked in experience he made up for in charm. In 1993 he freely admitted that he lacked experience at executive level and preferred to let me take the lead in contacts with the media and meetings with high-powered personalities.

One of the first tasks the Cape Town Olympic Committee took on was going out to tender to find a team of the very best people to prepare our national presentation, which would form the framework for a possible future bid to the IOC. Preparing a presentation to the standard we demanded would be time-consuming, requiring skilled assessments of every angle of feasibility, professional costing and a workable time-frame. Crucially, our plan had to be an equitable one, drawing in rich and poor areas, advantaged and disadvantaged people. To achieve a finished presentation in the detail and to the standards we envisaged relied on harnessing top talents in the fields of law, architecture, engineering, accountancy, public relations and an array of allied disciplines.

When we went out to tender, calling for applications, we knew we wanted the best and we knew we had to pay accordingly. A crack team for Cape Town would not come cheap. Responses flooded in, causing my committee, the Mayor and city councillors to sit down for days on end sifting through the mountain of replies, interviewing and finally appointing a very fine team. Incidentally, the fact that consultants for Cape Town's bid were selected in a joint process between my committee and city officials entirely refutes later accusations that plum positions went to my friends and colleagues. We chose consultants Ove Arup as civil engineers and Price Waterhouse as accountants because they are known to be among the top in their field world-wide. Arthur Andersen – later accountants to the Cape Town bid – were selected because they had worked on other Olympic bids and were therefore best qualified to help us. Similarly, all the consultants eventually appointed after tenders had been called for and awarded in consultation with succeeding Mayors and various councillors were chosen completely objectively as the best.

At any rate, the team immediately started work on the intricate and meticulous planning which would ultimately result in a series of thick books comprising comprehensive feasibility studies that mapped Cape Town's plans to host an Olympic meeting. The dream edged a little closer to reality.

Investigations soon concluded that 50 percent of the infrastructure necessary for hosting such a meeting – road systems, public transport and other amenities – was already in place. Remember, we were not looking at eventually hosting a grand, extravagant Olympics, but a no-frills affair, one with an African flavour. As for funding the bid, our committee had worked out ways from the beginning to draw in private-sector sponsorships which would shoulder all costs. The ratepayers of Cape Town were not to be asked for a single cent towards funding a Cape Town Olympic bid, even though the city stood to score a bonanza if we succeeded.

After quite a bit of prodding, NOCSA at last proposed a selection process to put a designated candidate city for a South African Olympic bid to the vote. Taking a sensible and fair route towards this process, Sam Ramsamy proposed calling in three independent judges who would visit the competing cities of Cape Town, Durban and Johannesburg, then make recommendations to the Executive Committee of NOCSA.

A meeting was called in Johannesburg to brief bidding teams from the three competing cities, and I attended with members of our Cape Town committee. We went to that meeting resolved to come away with absolute clarity on the procedures to be followed, and accordingly went armed with a long list of points to raise. As the meeting proceeded, it soon became clear that what I saw as legitimate questions, put with the intention of reaching clarity on the bid process, were being interpreted by Sam Ramsamy as unnecessary interventions. His responses became more and more irritable and inappropriate, his attitude more and more aggressive. Durban and Johannesburg teams watched all this with barely concealed glee – it didn't take a genius to know they were thinking that with such animosity existing between Raymond Ackerman and Sam Ramsamy, Cape Town's chances of winning the national competition were considerably diminished.

With hindsight, I am now able to say that Sam Ramsamy's antagonism towards me at the Johannesburg briefing meeting was the first time – and the first of many later times – when he simply could not contain his annoyance at being forced to compete with someone of my standing in the community. Various commentators have since suggested that his antagonism built up because he could not stand my approach, which he saw as pushy, arrogant and over-enthusiastic. I will be the first to say that Sam Ramsamy was not in an easy overall position with regard to controlling and forming the activities of NOCSA in 1993, but I will also say straight out that he harboured a huge jealousy towards me from the very start of what became a monumental clash between us. I was stung by the humiliating way he chose to take me on in front of my own team and those from Durban and Johannesburg at the briefing meeting, but was aware that he chose to do so out of an anger that actually had nothing to do with the way I was putting questions and conducting myself. The campaign to undermine me as the figurehead for Cape Town's Olympic bid started to roll as Sam furiously faced me at the Johannesburg briefing meeting.

Battering as the experience had been, our team returned to Cape Town fortified by the firm date of January 1994 for the national competition. We were already far down the track with our city's presentation, while Durban and Johannesburg were just starting on theirs. We greatly looked forward to showing our plans to the three IOC personalities chosen to evaluate the three South African contending cities.

These three Olympic luminaries – John Coates from Australia, Charlie Battle, a brilliant organiser and co-architect of Atlanta's winning bid, and

Spaniard Miguel Abad, leader of the Barcelona Organising Committee – chose to start their tour of the three candidate cities in Cape Town after their arrival in South Africa.

Confident, primed and prepared as we were in Cape Town to show off our ability to become an Olympic host, the various violent events that had occurred recently in the country in the run-up to the 1994 election did not create a particularly favourable climate when John Coates, Charlie Battle and Miguel Abad came to call. However, the really interesting point about those early IOC evaluations is this: in spite of the chaos prevailing in the last few months before the first democratic election, in spite of being caught in a whirling twister of crime and violence, we were still seen as a country working on sorting out the problems – a country with the kind of future conducive to playing host to the Olympics.

* * *

When Cape Town won the nomination to bid on behalf of South Africa for the 2004 summer Olympics, it wasn't really fair.

For a start, how does a rival compete with a city universally acknowledged to be among the world's most beautiful? Then, as the oldest city in South Africa, the Mother City gained enormous additional recognition after 1990 for having Robben Island, the little bit of land the world sees as a symbol of reconciliation, just off the city's Table Bay shoreline. Add sophistication and an ordered infrastructure to the scenic glories and symbolism of Cape Town, and you have a city uniquely positioned to host the Olympic meeting that the IOC wanted to see in South Africa. Durban and Johannesburg are both wonderful cities with their own unique attributes but they couldn't begin to compete with the overwhelmingly advantaged Cape Town in the bid to host the 2004 summer Olympics.

Nevertheless, when we gathered in Johannesburg on Saturday 29 January 1994 to hear the verdict, we all brought butterflies with us. Up and down the country, well-known watering holes were packed with people eagerly awaiting the televised announcement of which city had won. Sam Ramsamy finally stood up to say the magic words that we held our breath to hear. 'The winner', he said, 'is … Cape Town.' Our team jumped up to hug one another in a show of sheer exuberance. Across Cape Town a huge cheer went up. This was one of the great moments of my life.

Straight after receiving the nomination, elated beyond words, I went into a meeting with Sam Ramsamy and the three IOC officials. The IOC trio then proceeded to outline the bare bones of what we now had to do. Even in skeleton form, it was formidable. There was an enormous amount to do in the four years available before the 1997 vote on a venue for the 2004 summer Olympics.

By the time of the national presentation we had already compiled several heavy books of blueprints for Cape Town's bid as an Olympic candidate city, so much of the spadework was already done. Our planning was so far down the track, I felt quietly confident we could achieve what we had to in time for the 1997 IOC vote.

The real challenge now lay not only in completing the details of our bid but in winning over the IOC members, one by one, around the world. That was the priority, the real game plan, the prime goal. I had by now consulted widely with major players in Olympic bids across the world and they all gave one overriding piece of advice – work at winning support for your bid as a unified team with one voice representing all interests so as to win the confidence and approval of the IOC voting bloc.

Now, on Cape Town's nomination, John Coates wisely reiterated the importance of getting our public relations campaign going and starting to meet IOC members in their own countries. It was all about developing relationships. Having achieved a high international profile as a successful businessman was seen as a mighty plus in favour of my leadership of a Cape Town bid, as I was told then and on numerous occasions afterwards. The IOC attach great importance to successful track records of the business kind, because people who can run large businesses smoothly and at a profit can usually be relied upon to do the same for an Olympic event.

With all this good advice in the forefront of my mind, a handshake from Sam Ramsamy and the good wishes of the IOC officials ringing in my ears, I flew home to Cape Town in the late afternoon of 29 January with the rest of our bidding team, in triumph.

If any confirmation was needed that hosting the Olympics could raise spirits and unify people in the midst of severe tribulation, we got it in surfeit on our arrival back in Cape Town. People had flooded out to the little private airport where our chartered plane landed to greet us in a spontaneous display of delight. We had toasted our success in champagne on the way home, expecting to disperse and go quietly home on our return. Instead, an ecstatic crowd greeted us like conquering heroes bearing a valued trophy. We were whisked off to face a barrage of cameras and microphones and to party away the remainder of a thrilling day.

CHAPTER 27

Without the Yeast, There Will Be No Cake

I decided in March 1990 to appoint my elder son, Gareth, to a new full line direction on the Board of Pick 'n Pay. At the time of his appointment Gareth had been the director in charge of the group's superstores in Johannesburg. Now, at the age of 33, he was to represent our family on the Board. The financial press made much of Gareth's relative youth, which he countered by pointing out that I had been General Manager of Checkers before my thirtieth birthday.

My decision to place Gareth fully on the Board, with Hugh Herman remaining as Managing Director, was part of the plans I had for the future. There was much speculation that I was planning to hang up my boots and hand over the CEO reins to my son at the time of his appointment to the Board, but this was not my intention. The factor of family in Pick 'n Pay was always in the forefront of my mind. At the same time, I realised that the sheer complexity of the company, with its R5 billion turnover, before-tax profits of R131 million and 26 000-strong staff complement, demanded clear direction, both in the interests of our family and of the company. This was of particular importance in 1990, when conditions in the food-retailing industry were in overall decline.

Up until 1994 and the aftermath of that year's crippling industrial action, I was constantly amazed by Pick 'n Pay's ability to ride out recessions, remaining buoyant as swells and eddies of market difficulty swamped competitors. In 1990 we did it again, recording record profits in March, and again we remained consistent in ploughing hefty hunks of profit back. At that time we launched a R1 million campaign with a Pick 'n Pay cheque for R100 000 to resuscitate Groote Schuur's cash-strapped Cardiology Department, where Professor Chris Barnard had carried out the world's first heart transplant in the 1960s.

Bursaries, under Wendy's direction, now had a multi-million rand annual budget, while the company's commitment to staff and social uplift-ment schemes, poverty relief and a whole host of other causes far outstripped commitments from any other South African retail group or, for that matter, comparable overseas groups. Financial analysts remained puzzled by our poli-cies of social commitment, often pointing out that cutting back this form of expenditure would instantly raise our bottom-line profit several percent-age points. But our table would never have been properly balanced unless our strong and crucial 'social responsibility' leg was firmly on the ground.

If we had long since established an overall direction for our policy of social commitment, events in South Africa after 1990 demanded a fresh look at destinations. As the barriers of apartheid started to come down, vistas of even more alarming division emerged, and among the greatest of these were educational inequalities. So it was that later that year Pick 'n Pay and a family trust belonging to Wendy and me donated a million rand to the University of Cape Town's Bridging Department to help disadvan-taged black students.

The UCT donation attracted two types of response. The first and by far the largest batch of comment applauded the spirit of giving to a cause so vital to the new South Africa. The second said that in view of the sparkling profits achieved by Pick 'n Pay we had only done what we ought. Prominent among this group were union spokesmen. In response, I point-ed out that according to my judgement the profit motive should always remain dominant, especially in a time of transition, when calls for redirection of funds came incessantly. Redistribution at the expense of building profit was a recipe for disaster, because it had always been profit that generated growth in the economy.

As these differing responses show, at the beginning of South Africa's decade of democracy it was as impossible as ever to stay on the right side of everyone.

* * *

In the month before my sixtieth birthday, as an indication of how endlessly eventful my life always seemed to be, this list of events cropped up on one day alone. First, I was invited to become South Africa's representative on an international committee tasked with advising an upcoming United Nations conference on the environment – a huge breakthrough, since we had been barred from all environmental bodies in the world. Second, the government at last responded, in a minor way, to our ongoing lobby against the imposition of VAT on basic foodstuffs by zero-rating brown bread and mealie meal. Third, I met with the International Olympic Committee, in South Africa on a fact-finding mission. Finally, I tried to figure out a weird situation which had arisen in one of our stores in the Eastern Transvaal town of Nelspruit.

Seven black Pick 'n Pay employees at the Nelspruit store had been identified as witches after a sangoma, a traditional healer – one Myonyane Mpapane – had been paid R5 000 by the workforce to get to the bottom of a series of mishaps. The sangoma, who wore a most impressive jackal skin headdress for consultations, and drove a BMW motor car (according to a newspaper report of the time), 'sniffed out' the seven Pick 'n Pay employees. The remainder of the workforce immediately demanded that the store manager should suspend the seven, on full pay for two months – a handy modern version of punishment, no doubt replacing banishment from the village – failing which the non-witches would call a strike.

The store manager was naturally perplexed. He had a curious dilemma on his hands, not only on account of the cross-cultural clash between established labour practice and traditional beliefs, but also because the accused witches soon presented an angle of their own. They said that they had been singled out, not because they were witches, but because they had been promoted into positions in Pick 'n Pay that the witch-hunters had their eyes on. Their colleagues, they reported, hated them. One woman said the real reason why she had been singled out was that she held a plum job as cashier at the cigarette counter – a much-coveted position. 'A lot of people want our jobs,' she said darkly.

A twentieth-century labour dispute, South African-style. No wonder stress levels ran so high among those unfortunate individuals whose job it was to mediate in such disputes.

The influences of what everyone now called 'the new South Africa' were creeping into a lot of company decisions I had to make. At this stage, these mainly related to such matters as whether or not to sponsor advertisements in party political supplements to newspapers, for example. I mostly directed that such requests be turned down on the grounds that as a company we had never supported any political party. Later, funds we donated specifically for voter education were deliberately misinterpreted as political gestures, but that issue belongs to later pages.

During 1991, as a company we identified and stared for the first time full into the fearful face of the greatest misfortune ever visited on Africa: the HIV virus and AIDS. An AIDS consultant was called in to help formulate an AIDS awareness campaign and, most importantly, teach us how we could best help our own afflicted employees. I made the point that as a humane company we recognised the seriousness of the AIDS scourge, and would work hard to counter the fear and ignorance causing ostracism of AIDS victims in the workplace. Infected people would never be summarily dismissed on the grounds of their illness. We began to look earnestly into treatment options and the best ways of helping infected people, both within the company and through wider social-welfare programmes.

In whatever time I could find, I kept up the campaign to get government to zero-rate staple foodstuffs for VAT and continued to warn against 'add in' as opposed to 'add on' VAT on foodstuffs. The 'add on' system would allow consumers to see at once how much tax was included in the price of an item, whereas the 'add in' system was just a loophole for mischief, which many would use to hike the price of food. When government did finally zero-rate many staple foods in September 1991, it was great news for us and a great relief to the poorest people.

* * *

On a wet and very sad day in August 1991 we buried my sister Moyra Fine, who had succumbed to cancer. Accolades for her dedicated work keeping the independent theatre alive through the worst days of apartheid flooded in, giving great comfort to her grieving husband, Issy, and three children, Nicholas, Andrea and Derrick. As always, after something awful came something bright. In September, Wendy and I celebrated our thirty-fifth wedding anniversary, which our children marked beautifully with a delivery of 35 roses from Constantia, the valley at the heart of our family.

Storing the sadness of Moyra's passing and shrugging off the irritation of the latest simmering dispute between union and management in the Western Cape, I headed for the USA to present a paper as South Africa's representative on an international committee working on issues of sustainable development in readiness for the next major United Nations world conference on the global environment. Perhaps there is just something about being a South African, whether our country is cast in the role of polecat or pet, which naturally attracts controversy. When the topic at the USA conference turned to Third World debt relief, a Nigerian delegate aggressively declared that all African countries should be released from their debts and paid reparations, because the Western world had grown rich on African minerals.

They picked on me, of course, to respond: convenient figurehead for Africa's supposed exploiters, if I am to be unkind; representative of a country straddling the First and Third Worlds, if kind. I had, however, been highly annoyed by the Nigerian's outburst. In my reply, studiously ignoring the apprehensive white faces around the debating chamber, I said that the Nigerian's statement was absolute nonsense because all countries had to work hard and not look for handouts to build their countries. As for South Africa, we wanted investment from the West, not handouts. I admitted that South Africa had been undemocratic and slow to adopt policies of human rights – but then so had most African countries with their one-party states. Why should reparations be paid to despotic, autocratic leaders; surely that would be wrong? The effect of my response was something akin to putting a stick into an ant nest and stirring.

A BBC crew, filming proceedings for a documentary, immediately sent over a request for an interview, which I gave. I talked to them for more than 15 minutes on South Africa's need for investment instead of hand-outs. Then, a sub-committee of the conference requested a case study on the growth of Pick 'n Pay, with special reference to the 'four legs of the table' principle, including social responsibility.

Skirmishes and all, I spent an amazing few days at that USA conference, far better than I had expected. But now, in March 1992, it was time to concentrate fully on the upcoming twenty-fifth anniversary of Pick 'n Pay at a time when worsening labour relations and endless tension threatened to drown out any celebratory cheers on the company front. To keep our spirits up, we settled on the theme *Part of Your Life, Part of Your Future* for the anniversary celebrations, hoping such optimism would stand firm in the face of a mounting tide of pessimism.

However, along with fellow retailers, we were on the rack in 1992, with union demands and lowered growth expectations keeping me awake at night. Pick 'n Pay had a wage offer on the negotiating table that was considerably above food-industry averages at the time, but it still did not satisfy the union, which continued to demand more. Some of our staff started behaving in an outrageous and stupid way, hampering trade, obstructing and threatening shoppers, convening unconstitutional and noisy meetings in store-trading areas.

The question of how to get profits right, our life-blood after all, in this climate of confrontation became an urgent and all-consuming issue for me. How could the diverse interests of the company and the consumer be best served in that atmosphere of simmering hostility? An ominous, anonymous phone call warned me that a mass strike, strongly favoured by the ANC Youth League, was in the offing but I decided to ignore the information.

On the eve of our quarter-century celebrations, I flew up to Johannesburg in a last-ditch effort to avert the crippling strike towards which we seemed to be hurtling headlong. It was an extremely sensitive situation: we refused to budge from the offer we had put on the table, because the offer was completely fair, while the union continued to insist that it wasn't. I spoke to a gathering of shop stewards and unhappy-looking staff, asking them to take into account the importance of our twenty-fifth year and to consider the whole history of the company. I pulled out everything I could think of; it was all very emotional, touch and go. I could sense that many among the listeners were struggling between their union affiliations and a real loyalty to the company, which, after all, made much more than mere wages available to them through the joint and equally important efforts of all our people.

Eventually, the shop stewards withdrew to discuss matters amongst themselves. If they rejected conciliation, a debilitating strike would follow as sure as night follows day. However, as soon as the union spokesman stood up after their consultations, I could sense they had basically decided to accept our offer, which came as a great relief – for the time being. I felt in my very bones that the company was still on the relatively calm outer edges of a massive storm brewing. When we reached the eye in 1994 and came out the other side, nothing would ever be the same again.

* * *

Nothing prepared me for the shock of Hugh Herman's resignation, coming as it did in a time of unprecedented turmoil. Hugh, my Managing Director, the man whose contribution to the building and the success of Pick 'n Pay since the 1970s had been of immeasurable worth, had stood beside me through trials of fire.

I understood, of course – who better? – that running an enterprise comprising 121 supermarkets, superstores and hypermarkets with a staff of 26 000 took a heavy toll. Executives in Pick 'n Pay had an especially exacting time because the company had to be run the way I wanted, with open doors and our hands around every aspect of the business. Adding to the load, constant uncertainties about South Africa's future, labour unrest fanned and fomented by hostile unions flexing their muscles in a new-found form of political expression, and a sluggish economy, all tested the mettle of the toughest executive.

Although I understood Hugh's decision, and we have remained friends, I have to say that I was anguished by his resignation. But the die was cast, and the next priority was to decide on replacements. Hugh and I spent hours analysing Sean Summers's very strong motivation to move into the MD role. Since Sean had burst into our company consciousness during the 1960s he had worked through every facet of the business, but always chafed to move onwards and upwards. He worked incredibly hard and his formidable abilities were beyond question, but I did not think he was quite ready to take over as MD at that time. In the end, I felt it was in the company's best interests if he retained his Food Director portfolio for the time being, in readiness for the next phase of moves, which would surely happen in four to five years' time.

After analysing the situation from every angle, I decided to appoint my son Gareth, then 35 years old, and my lifelong associate René de Wet, then 49 years old, as joint MDs. I saw the new management team as a competent combination of youth and experience. Sean was appointed deputy MD. The new appointments naturally caused some bitterness – some real stalwarts inevitably felt overlooked. But perhaps people would have felt less envious of Gareth's and René's appointments had they known the degree of turmoil awaiting them.

Food manufacturers, retailers and wholesalers found themselves in competition for the shrinking spending power of hard-pressed consumers. I wrote that in 37 years of retailing, I had not seen tougher trading conditions. As violence piled misfortune on misfortune – two of our workers were shot dead in one of the hundreds of armed robberies cursing the country – a sense of grimness pervaded South Africa.

Rounds of talks between Pick 'n Pay and the unions always seemed to be in progress somewhere or other, although progress was not a word easily associated with labour relations at this time. Talk was increasingly acrimonious and attitudes towards finding solutions unhelpful. Staff were more militant than ever, and had to be warned that if they persisted with parading on shop floors, hampering trade and intimidating shoppers, only one warning to disperse would be given before the police were called in.

We were not alone in suffering the tribulations of labour crises. Checkers, subjected to a purposeless but crippling strike, began closing stores and retrenching staff. As some 2 500 jobs were lost, strikers resolved to picket the homes of Checkers' directors in Johannesburg. The OK, caught up in dramas of their own, chose this time to introduce a clause into their worker contracts recognising traditional healers as part of their medical-aid package – a sign of how hard employers were working at trying to bridge gaps and foster understanding.

The dark clouds of hostility between Pick 'n Pay and union negotiators built up inexorably, layer after layer. Soon I was working tense 18-hour days, keeping constantly in touch with our team of negotiators. This time there was no eleventh-hour reprieve. Every offer, every compromise put forward was rejected, until the union abandoned talks altogether.

The ferocity displayed by some employees during the first ten days of the strike shocked me to my core. Jane Campbell, a customer at the Milnerton store which my son Jon managed, wrote to a newspaper: 'I have never witnessed such savagery as that displayed by the toyi-toyi-ing strikers in Pick 'n Pay Milnerton. Taunting customers is not what striking is about.'

The *Washington Post* reported on the simmering racial tension accompanying the Pick 'n Pay strike in South Africa, after some two hundred rioting strikers had been injured when police, called in by the government, fired rubber bullets into one mob who were threatening the lives of store managers and shoppers.

Night after night, terrible pictures of incidents like this flashed onto news bulletins, showing baying mobs of strikers smashing windows and insulting shoppers. I felt ill, helpless, totally disillusioned while watching the image of Pick 'n Pay staff as courteous, helpful individuals – an image I had worked so hard to establish – being systematically smashed to smithereens.

President Mandela called me to offer the services of his Minister of Labour, Tito Mboweni, as an independent mediator in the savage strike which crippled Pick 'n Pay. The President's offer of assistance – which I accepted with grateful thanks – was made because he disapproved of a union targeting a benevolent employer, which happened to have been the first retail food chain to back the rights of employees to unionise.

As the strike raged on into a third week of near-anarchy, Wendy and I narrowly escaped being attacked by a screaming mob of roving picketers looking for more trouble in downtown Cape Town. Another mob, wearing Pick 'n Pay uniforms, gathered outside a Cape Town Jewish old-age home and shouted anti-Semitic remarks. I was absolutely appalled. Strike leaders were quick to deny the suggestion that the strike could be linked to anti-Semitism.

Meanwhile, I began to dread picking up my office telephone because I had started receiving death threats. It wasn't the first time in my life I had been threatened, but this time the callers sounded particularly sinister – people who meant business. Wendy, thoroughly alarmed by the threats and unsure where to turn, decided to consult the visionary sangoma Credo Mutwa to see if he could cast any light on the identity of the death-threat callers. Credo Mutwa had been a controversial person since his books – *Indaba My Children* and a sequel, *Africa Is My Witness* – had set out, in his words, to explain his 'much despised race to the world'. Much of what he has said remains controversial, but up to now he still commands respect among disciples of the alternative.

I know it will seem strange that Wendy and I should give credence to predictions, horoscopes, visions, feelings – those nebulous unexplainables – but we do because of all the times their accuracy has shocked us. How do I explain away hearing the voice of my father reverberating from Table Mountain just after his death, telling me I was to return to Cape Town, just before I was fired from my job in Johannesburg, and having to do precisely that?

Credo Mutwa's meditations on what was going on around me produced an image which, at the time, made no sense whatsoever. He told Wendy that I should beware of a small Oriental gentleman. A small Oriental gentleman? Because of the obvious connection between the death threats and the 1994 strike, I immediately ran a checklist of union adversaries through my mind but there didn't seem to be anyone who fitted the bill.

For the time being, it was a mystery. When I later stumbled on the truth, obvious enough all along, I could not believe I had been so blind. But by then it was too late, the harm had been done.

As ugliness and intimidation continued unabated on our strike front, both company and workers began taking serious strain. Nevertheless, we refused to give in to terrorist tactics. When I replayed video reports and went through press cuttings, some of the strikers' behaviour was beyond belief. But despite the best efforts of the union bullies, Pick 'n Pay customers were not easily intimidated. During the strike, tons of letters came in from consumers, pledging their support, backing and continued loyalty.

Those letters warmed my heart, which was otherwise devastated. I began to wonder whether everything I had worked to build was going to come crashing down, become a wasteland created of hostility. Even if the company did continue after the strike, would anything ever be the same again? Illusions were shattered, trust was in tatters. It was sad beyond belief.

Meanwhile, we all hurt. A promising joint-venture scheme involving Pick 'n Pay and an overseas company was cancelled. Small traders who shared premises with our stores in shopping centres suffered tragically. They were caught in the crossfire, helpless in the face of a situation not of their making. Paradoxically, as the strike slashed net profits, so it became increasingly difficult to know how the union's unreasonably high wage demands could be funded anyway. The strikers, too, were battling to keep their heads above water. They had not been paid since the beginning of the strike, which went into its fourth week at the end of July 1994. Dire difficulty afflicted the families of sole breadwinners. Union funds did not pay school fees or put bread on bare tables.

It was a hopeless confusion of conflicting interests. Union leaders challenged President Mandela on remarks he made about the strike harming reconstruction. Mr De Klerk told me that he and the government wanted us to remain absolutely firm as the country just could not tolerate riotous behaviour and unreasonable demands.

At this low point in the conflict, a man from a union unrelated to ours told me that COSATU had jointly decided to target big, figurehead companies for industrial action, to show Mr Mandela how much power they had, how many voters heeded their calls and danced to their tune. Pick 'n Pay, sadly, was one of the targets. The fact that we had been an enlightened employer for nearly thirty years counted for nothing. What did count was that we were big, high-profile employers – perfect prey.

Early in August, the strike was at last settled. All involved emerged bloodied, battered and chastened. Financial commentators declared that Pick 'n Pay had inflicted the greatest single defeat that any union had suffered in South Africa, because we had held out and refused to be bullied into an unreasonable agreement. Many believed this would strike a blow for better union relationships in the future. Be that as it may, the salient fact was that at the end of the strike both the company and our workers were worse off than before.

In spite of 'attitude clauses' built into our agreement with the union, workers returned to the stores sullen, angry and confused because the increase the union had finally agreed upon did not compensate them for wages lost in terms of 'no work, no pay' provisions. And, for the first time in the history of our company, profits took a severe beating. Earnings plunged, share prices fell.

At the end of the bleak 1994 strike period, all concerned had paid an unconscionably high price for something utterly senseless. But, senseless or not, the strike had brought Pick 'n Pay to a watershed. To go forward, we had to change into a new mode, we had to find ways to heal the hurt and return to running a business for consumers with courtesy, warmth and efficiency.

The ink was barely dry on comments I made in an August 1994 diary about not letting the strike get me down, not letting events affect the marvellous opportunity South Africa had of getting the Olympics, when an absolutely astonishing news cutting came to my notice. Under the headline 'Confusion over bid for 2004 Olympics', it was reported that Sam Ramsamy, speaking at the Commonwealth Games, had declared Cape Town's bid for the 2004 Olympics might be withdrawn in favour of South Africa hosting the Commonwealth Games in 2002.

Without consultation, without regard for consequences, those comments from Sam – later repeated in a local television interview – demonstrated the degree of division underpinning Cape Town's Olympic bid.

CHAPTER 28

A Silent End

As the euphoria following Cape Town's nomination began translating into an intensification of pace in our bid, NOCSA summoned Kevin Kevany, Ngconde Balfour and me to a meeting in Johannesburg. We arrived at the NOCSA offices on time – to be kept waiting a full three hours. Although the waiting time extended over lunch, we were not offered anything to eat. Finally someone produced three cans of cooldrink, and I will leave you to imagine how insult piled on injury when I found mine bore a Checkers label.

When we were finally admitted into the presence of Sam Ramsamy and members of his NOCSA Committee, we were a tired and irritated trio. However, without apology for this ignominious beginning to our official relationship, Sam fired his first broadside: he didn't like our consultants, who had, by anyone's book I would have thought, done a magnificent job. I was having none of this, and stuck calmly with my assertion that we had the best team and they were doing a great job. With the issue of the consultants put aside for the time being, Sam lined up his next missile. He and his committee, he declared imperiously, objected to Wendy being on mine. This really was a monumental cheek, not only because Wendy had been sparking the whole Olympic fire with me years before anyone else had even thought about it, but also because Helga Ramsamy worked alongside her husband in NOCSA. I pointed this out very plainly, telling him that as his wife was working actively on the Olympics with him, so my wife would work with me.

Suddenly, antagonism reigned supreme. I could see that the NOCSA Committee members were very uncomfortable and that they did not agree with the unjust fare being dished out. I protested coldly that I refused to be treated in such a way, whereupon the NOCSA men, dismayed and uncomfortable, asked me to step outside for a brief while. They wanted words with Sam Ramsamy alone.

When next he appeared, Sam was a contrite man. He told me he was sorry about his behaviour, that his committee had told him he was wrong. He hugged and even kissed me, saying how we were going to work together from then on. For the first of hundreds of upcoming times, I reminded myself that there was a common goal here. Cape Town hosting the 2004 Olympics on behalf of all the people of South Africa was what mattered above any other petty consideration. Accordingly, the ill-starred meeting between our respective committees recommenced.

To place the various sporting bodies concerned in Cape Town's 2004 bid correctly, imagine a triangle representing the IOC hierarchy. At the apex is the International Olympic Committee in Lausanne. At one corner in each participating country is a National Olympic Committee and at the other national sports councils. Thus NOCSA was the National Olympic Committee for South Africa, funded by the national councils representing various local sports, all under the umbrella of the International Olympic Committee.

The main task of national Olympic committees such as NOCSA is to get two teams of athletes ready – one for the summer and one for the winter Olympic Games if their country is participating. In addition to funding from sport councils, national committees also receive sponsorship funds for the purpose of training athletes and nurturing budding talent – their primary reason for being. The International Olympic Committee deal only through their own local representative at national level. Sam Ramsamy became South Africa's IOC representative, as he remains to this day, which is a role separate from his presidency of NOCSA. I do wish to record here that both Mr Mandela and Mr Carrard of the IOC spoke to me on separate occasions when a decision was pending on who to appoint as local IOC representative for South Africa. I expressed my support for the appointment of Sam Ramsamy to both men, emphasising the good and positive work he had done for many years in the cause of keeping the Olympic spirit alive during South Africa's sporting isolation.

Where the bidding process is concerned, the role of the national Olympic representative is to guide the bid through his ties with the IOC, introduce bid chairpersons and committee members to IOC voting officials, and generally to ensure that the bid committee chairperson and his or her team are doing a good job. Unfortunately for us all in South Africa, Sam placed a different interpretation on his job description, but we are far from being the only country to grapple with conflicts of interest around Olympic bids.

After the débâcle of our first meeting with NOCSA in Johannesburg, I was alarmed at how rapidly the relationship between Sam Ramsamy and myself as the figurehead for our city's bid had deteriorated after Cape Town's nomination. Worse, however, was soon to follow. Events at the Johannesburg meeting proved to be merely preliminary skirmishes, after which battle proper commenced. At the first full meeting between NOCSA and my committee in Cape Town, Sam turned to me, in the full hearing of the committee members present, to tell me that I must stop being naïve over the Olympic bid. Now, as a businessman who could claim a good degree of success, I hardly thought myself naïve, but Sam Ramsamy soon made it clear why *he* thought I was. In order to impress the right people, he maintained that funds had to be available to provide whatever he might think necessary in future, over and above the rules of the IOC. My immediate task, he insisted, was to set about creating a war chest for this purpose. Once I had stocked the war chest with funds, he – Sam Ramsamy – would take charge of administering it.

Dismayed, I reminded him of the IOC's clear rules setting out what could be given as presents. Indeed, he had himself given me IOC books to read which set out those rules. As I have mentioned, I had already asked the IOC's François Carrard outright whether it would help or hinder us as a potential bid city to stick strictly to rules laid down by the IOC, and had been told plainly and unequivocally that sticking to the rules would stand any future bidder in better stead. The IOC were serious in their intent to clean up their tarnished image.

As Sam Ramsamy continued to insist that he needed this war chest, I started to worry equally about the emphasis Sam was placing on handling IOC people himself. During his years in exile, he had acquired an insider's knowledge of the Olympic movement – that was indisputable. For my part, I acknowledged that he knew more about the inside workings of the IOC than I at first did, which was the reason I had asked for his advice and guidance from the beginning. But a chasm of misunderstanding was opening up between us. I kept insisting that we should build on strengthening ties with contacts already established to woo IOC votes according to the IOC rules; he continued to insist this was naïve.

So there it was, the real beginning of what I suspect was still then an unconscious campaign to undermine the Cape Town 2004 bid because of my position at its head. In this early disagreement between my committee and NOCSA, a precedent was set that would eventually grow into the rot of disunity set to rob a city, a country, a continent, of a golden opportunity that would never again be quite so accessible.

Sam Ramsamy's position over who was and who was not allowed to approach IOC officials developed into a huge headache in time. As Cape Town's bid committee chairman, I took several delegations of committee members to international IOC meetings. Such visits are a requirement in the process of an Olympic bid. The IOC recognises them as opportunities for bid committee chairpersons and members to woo votes through meeting IOC officials, fostering goodwill and respect. As South Africa's official IOC representative, it was Sam Ramsamy's job to introduce me and my committee to members of the IOC voting bloc, but we would be left to stand around like fools, decked out in our smart Cape Town bid blazers, unintroduced. These breaches of etiquette always obliged me to walk around introducing myself and my accompanying committee members, which looked absolutely dreadful.

At one very important meeting in Paris, I organised a special dinner for members of the African IOC voting bloc because their knowledge and opinion of us as fellow Africans was crucial to our bid. The dinner was, incidentally, well within IOC rules. Sam Ramsamy arrived late with his wife and sat down at the end of the long, jovial table to sulk silently. I was absolutely mortified, especially noticing the puzzled glances our guests were exchanging. Warm ties were formed at that dinner, despite the angry presence fuming darkly at the end of the table. When I later tackled him about his behaviour he flung out furiously that it was *his* job to woo the IOC, not mine, which was of course procedurally wrong. It was all so unnecessary. What did it matter who issued the invitation to the African bloc, since all of us were supposed to be pursuing a common goal?

* * *

Over time it seemed as though my co-Chair, Ngconde Balfour, the man who should have been concentrating on channelling his talents and qualities into his leadership position within the bid, was being made part of what increasingly seemed a conscious effort to undermine Cape Town's quest. This concerted effort to undermine the morale of my committee diluted the thrust of our real purpose. When my leadership again came in for criticism from Ngconde Balfour, I had to point out to him that it was impossible to have two or three driving a train. It was apparent that key interests in Cape Town's 2004 bid were pulling in different directions, and this worried me enormously.

From the time we had secured Cape Town's nomination as South Africa's Olympic 2004 candidate city, I never intended running the bid in the role of CEO. Running Pick 'n Pay at full tilt was already a massive undertaking, but I knew I could function very adequately as Chairman of the bid if a CEO handled day-to-day affairs. It is important to reiterate that it was never my intention to run Cape Town's Olympic bid as CEO because of later accusations that I hankered after autocratic and absolute power. In fact, around the time events between Sam Ramsamy and me turned nasty, Wendy and I had already compiled a shortlist of prospective CEO candidates for the Cape Town bid, after travelling the world interviewing prospective candidates. It is also worth mentioning that Chris Ball's name appeared on our shortlist.

When I talked to Sam Ramsamy about appointing a CEO, he suggested I should approach his NOCSA deputy, Russell Macmillan, then CEO of M-Net Supersport as well as secretary-general of NOCSA, which sounded like a brilliant plan. Not only were Russell Macmillan's credentials impeccable for the role, but appointing him to work full-time for the bid could create a vital bridge over the troubled waters between NOCSA on one bank and me and the Cape Town bid team on the other. However, after deep negotiations, Russell Macmillan finally declined the offer to join the Cape Town bid, electing, wisely as it turned out for him, to stay with M-Net.

While these various machinations were in progress, the real work of the Olympic bid had to go on. I flew around from meeting to meeting, talking to big business about sponsorship. Now that Cape Town was officially in the race for the 2004 Olympics, it was easier to extract sponsorship pledges, and that side of planning began to look rosy. Some of South Africa's top financial brains were pressed into service on central funding issues. Our committee then worked out that a contribution of R60 million would be needed from central government, while a further R70 million would be raised from private sponsors. The ratepayers of Cape Town were not to be asked to shoulder any financial burden on account of the city's Olympic bid, even though a fantastic financial windfall would be theirs should it succeed.

Towards the end of June 1994, I went to see Mr Mandela and had a very pleasant lunch with him. We talked about the Olympics – specifically around getting China to move their bid to the year 2008. On an information-gathering trip to Atlanta a couple of years before, I had met members of the Chinese Olympic Committee, in Atlanta on a similar errand to mine, under the leadership of a charming, Oxford-educated man. This man told me that they were seriously considering moving Beijing's bid forward to 2008, because 2004 was not an auspicious year in the Chinese calendar.

In mid-1994, hearing further speculation that China might wish to move to 2008, I telephoned my original Chinese contact, who confirmed that China *was* hesitating about the 2004 bid on two counts: first, 2004 was unlucky and, second, since hearing that Cape Town was a co-bidder for 2004, they believed our challenge, with Nelson Mandela at our head, was almost insurmountable.

The Chinese official suggested that Mr Mandela should phone the Chinese Premier to offer the support of the African bloc for a 2008 Beijing bid, should China decide to withdraw from the 2004 competition. I told Mr Mandela I had heard from several well-placed sources that if he were to phone as suggested, there was a good chance China would withdraw. Always a staunch supporter of Cape Town's cause – his exact words at this time were that he was 100 percent behind Cape Town's bid – Mr Mandela immediately agreed to do so.

So it was that Mr Mandela called the Chinese Deputy Premier – the Premier was ill – who liked the idea of having African support for a 2008 Beijing bid. He promised to discuss the matter with the Chinese Olympic Committee. Before long, they confirmed their withdrawal from the 2004 competition, expressing themselves happier with the prospect of a 2008 bid. One of Cape Town's major competitors for the 2004 games fell away.

I can also reveal that in informal discussions with the bid committees of rival cities Athens and Rome, I received verbal agreements that they would withdraw from the contest for the 2004 summer Games. Although nothing was written down, I am certain they were serious. Of course, pledges are not the same thing as votes actually cast, and no one can say with certainty that the governments of Greece and Italy would have been prepared to allow their bid committees to withdraw from the 2004 Olympic contest. I can only say from my personal participation in events that the organisers of Athens's and Rome's 2004 bids believed there was no real point in challenging Cape Town because we were so favoured to win.

* * *

In September 1994, a joint NOCSA and Bid Committee delegation received Cabinet approval for Cape Town's Olympic bid. Central government approval opened the way for a potential bonanza of gross economic benefits to the City of Cape Town and the country as a whole. Sponsorship pledges were coming along nicely, and all should have been action, verve and optimism around our bid. Instead, suspicion, division and hostility ruled supreme in our Olympic roost.

During September, at a banquet in honour of visiting British Prime Minister John Major, I went from table to table lobbying for the Olympics. By now, Wendy and I were well on our way to achieving our final tally of having visited 75 out of a total of 102 IOC members around the world before the Cape Town bid was taken out of my hands. This had been a tiring but incredibly worthwhile exercise. Wherever we went, we were always very well received, and I am convinced that the passion I had for Cape Town's cause, coming from a businessman of standing, was infectious. I am absolutely certain that up to the time the disunity finally ruined our chances, between 35 and 40 IOC votes for Cape Town had been secured. Again, it is never possible to guarantee that votes would be cast in any one direction, but I do know that important voters whom Wendy and I came to know so well, respected our efforts and looked favourably on Cape Town as an Olympic venue.

Meanwhile, back home, a campaign was being fomented against my leadership of the Cape Town bid. The campaign to destroy the relationship existing between my Bid Committee and the City of Cape Town was especially sad because, until those orchestrating disharmony started working to destroy it, the relationship between us had been strong and constructive.

Harmony within the bid was further hampered when the press started referring to me as 'Mr Olympics'. Sam Ramsamy ticked me off angrily about hogging the limelight, as he saw it. If it hadn't been so sad, I suppose it was funny. I didn't need to seek publicity – it usually sought me and, again, what did it *matter*? By this time I had already received several warnings from people overseas, who told me to watch out for the back-stabbing and jealousy around the Cape Town bid.

According to popular belief, the core issue around which Cape Town's Olympic bid fell into disarray came to the surface in the shape of a dispute over which delegated authority would enter into a contract with NOCSA to process the bid to the IOC Committee in Switzerland on behalf of Cape Town. NOCSA refused to sign a contract – in fact a marketing agreement without which sponsorship funds could not be released – on the basis that the Bid Committee I headed 'could provide no satisfactory proof that it was the authorised representative of the city'. Communications flew between myself on behalf of my committee and NOCSA in Johannesburg. Early in the dispute, important papers pertaining to the contract issue, which NOCSA requested, were sent to their offices, after which they apparently disappeared into thin air.

The supposed dispute over the validity or otherwise of my Bid Committee's authority to run the bid on behalf of Cape Town masked the real bones of contention contained in the contract NOCSA presented for signature. The real problem was that Sam Ramsamy wanted what I believed to be a completely unreasonable allocation of funds for NOCSA activities and expenses. At this time I urgently needed to access sponsorship agreements already negotiated with three major South African companies to keep the Cape Town bid going. I had already poured nearly R10 million of my own money into the bid. The R10 million that each of the three major sponsors had agreed to put in would have taken me over half-way towards the total budget requirement we had now put on the bid – R65 million. However, the sponsors would not release money until a contract with NOCSA was signed, and I refused to sign a contract which allowed NOCSA to use funds in a way I considered extravagant and unnecessary.

At this stage, I tried to negotiate an interim agreement with NOCSA which would at least have released some funds the bid urgently needed, but NOCSA declined to do so.

In the midst of this unseemly feud, IOC President Juan Antonio Samaranch paid a call on Cape Town. While Sam had been enthusiastic about having the IOC President in South Africa, he insisted that the visit should be at the expense of the Cape Town Bid Committee – which, at this stage, meant at my cost. I had therefore signed a pile of cheques to pay for the de luxe visit we planned for Mr Samaranch.

This being the case, I was nonplussed when, just prior to the arrival of the IOC contingent in Cape Town, Sam ordered that members of my Bid

Committee, Ngconde Balfour and myself were to keep strictly away. We were not to meet the Samaranch contingent formally at the airport, nor were we to speak at any meeting.

Once I had choked down my anger at this attempt to exclude us from something I had engineered and paid for in its entirety, I made up my mind that Ngconde and I would make our own way to the airport to meet Mr Samaranch. At a later reception I ignored Sam's pathetic interpretation of protocol and introduced my team personally to the IOC visitors. It was at a lunch function in honour of Mr Samaranch that Mr Mandela, probably unwittingly, pushed the relationship between Sam Ramsamy and me beyond the point of no return. In his address to the guests, Mr Mandela pointed me out as the man who was 'going to bring the Olympics to Cape Town. There is Mr Olympics.' Sam was lividly angry.

On a nicer note, Mr Mandela received an IOC award at the lunch and was hailed not as the man of the decade, but as the man of the century, by an admiring Mr Samaranch. It should all have been wonderful cement and, but for the cracks, it would have been.

The visit of Mr Samaranch to South Africa was an absolute triumph, except that the IOC visitors had plainly seen the depths of disunity plaguing our efforts. Mr Samaranch, particularly, sensed the mood of simmering hostility. When a discreet opportunity presented itself, he gave me his private telephone number, asking that Wendy and I should meet him privately at the IOC headquarters in Lausanne. That meeting did take place, and Mr Samaranch spoke plainly when he said that Cape Town's case remained strong and favourable to host the 2004 meeting, but that we had to resolve our differences within the bid or else we would lose.

But all my best attempts to resolve these differences were to no avail. Towards the end of 1994 I recorded having one of my tensest mornings ever, during which Sam refused to sign any agreement with my Bid Committee, still on the grounds that my committee was 'not legal'. It was clear that a high degree of connivance was happening, when suddenly a similar line started to come from the City Council. City officials engineered a threat to issue a court order forbidding my committee to sign agreements with NOCSA. Sam, bland as butter, wondered why we had not previously cleared this dispute with the City Council. Later, I had a flaming row with him, which, again, I erroneously thought cleared the air.

* * *

In the opening weeks of 1995, I began to wonder whether it would be in the greater interests of the Cape Town bid if I resigned from the bid. Apart from the ongoing hostilities with Sam, I continued to sign various Olympic accounts, even though I had no money other than my own with which to do so. Shouldering the bid finance while taking knives in my back was a frightening experience, but whenever things got particularly bad, I still told myself that the goal of getting the Olympics would make all the trials insignificant.

When four top City of Cape Town employees left to meet with IOC officials in Lausanne after having agreed to form a new bid body, they confirmed they were travelling at the behest of NOCSA. This immediately attracted the attention of the press. 'Olympic Row Erupts' and other such statements exploded into banner headlines, forcing a response. I told the press that the City Council people had gone to Europe without the blessing of our committee and that the increasing tussle was a tragedy because the bid had reached a point where we were probably going to win in 1997. But if the bid continued to be undermined by deceit and disunity, we could not win.

At this point, my frustration at the negative pettiness dragging Cape Town's bid down was becoming intolerable. In February 1995, I spoke to Minister Kader Asmal, telling him clearly that a guarantee from central government for R5 million was required to keep the bid going until sponsor money could be released. I suggested that NOCSA should be obliged to issue a letter or an agreement along interim lines in order to have some R70 million of sponsorship money released. If NOCSA failed to do this, the game was over for us all.

I hated the situation in which I found myself and, had I not been fighting for Cape Town and for the continued employment of all the people involved thus far with the bid, I would have abandoned the whole mess.

Then, real drama struck. NOCSA suddenly presented the City Council with a new draft contract to sign which, to the horror of some of the councillors, asked for funding vastly in excess of the amount my committee had negotiated. The extra millions, furthermore, were to come from the pockets of ratepayers, whereas the plan we had worked on relied solely on sponsorship money – much already pledged. Councillor Arthur Wienburg protested that the contract gave dictatorial powers and a virtual blank cheque to NOCSA. They wanted funding for plush offices and parking in Cape Town until the year 2004, plus money to whisk them and their entourages off around the world, to stay in luxury accommodation, as they saw fit. Quizzical councillors and, later, a sardonic public wondered in particular about the contract's call for millions to be spent on sending only a handful of entrants, the NOCSA President and his entourage to the 1994 winter Games.

When President Mandela got to hear about all this, he was alarmed and soon on the phone, calling me to an emergency dinner meeting with himself and Minister of Sport Steve Tshwete. Over dinner Mr Mandela earnestly requested me to remain positive and to concentrate on the future rather than the present crisis. Within a few days the dispute over the bid set up such a clamour that the issue came before Parliament. There, Mr Mandela told the House that he was calling for a meeting between all opposing parties to resolve the crisis.

At that precise time, with Mr Mandela earnestly working at resolving the situation, former Mayor and Exco Chairman Clive Keegan went on the radio to say that the Cape Town City Council had taken over my Bid Committee. Later, despite evidence on tape, Mr Keegan was to deny making any such statement.

Lower depths still remained to be plumbed. An evening meeting – convened to try to resolve differences, as Mr Mandela had requested – turned into one of the most awful I have ever attended. In front of everyone, I was accused by NOCSA of being a liar. Minister Tshwete, also at the meeting, immediately jumped to his feet, demanding that NOCSA withdraw those disparaging remarks. To me the worst thing was that the insults had been read from a prepared statement. They were not accusations made in the heat of a moment, but planned, written out, rehearsed. Somehow, and I really don't know how, I remained aloof. When it was my turn to speak I only mentioned the future, exactly as Mr Mandela had asked me to do. I did not refer once to any problems with the City Council or NOCSA.

By mid-morning next day I had taken calls from Mrs Adelaide Tambo and Mr Mandela, expressing great distress at the behaviour of NOCSA. Wendy, who was furious at the injustice of what I had had to endure and desperately upset for my hurt, expressed her disgust personally to Mr Tshwete, who also later telephoned me to apologise for the behaviour of NOCSA. Later, Mr Tshwete even maintained that he 'would not allow anyone to take me out of being the leader, or my team' after the City Council put on a presentation, unmentioned to my committee and to which we were not invited, that outlined their plan for conducting a Cape Town 2004 bid. Their plan changed the entire philosophy of the bid. In so doing it also represented a full frontal attack on the integrity of myself and my committee.

Next time I faced Steve Tshwete and Sam Ramsamy at a meeting in Johannesburg, both refused to listen to my repeated requests that an agreement should be signed with my committee to protect the bid money situation. With my requests went my undertaking that all money put into the Cape Town bid from whatever source would be rigorously controlled.

It was a dreadful situation. The press had got wind of this make-or-break meeting. Reporters crowded the corridor outside our conference room. Every time one of us went outside, microphones were thrust at us.

At a press conference later that evening, I listened in amazement to a statement prepared by Steve Tshwete and Sam Ramsamy to which I was supposed to have agreed. I had done no such thing and could hardly credit such blatant misrepresentation. Suddenly, in the midst of this awful, unseemly bun fight, I made up my mind.

I stood up to say that I agreed entirely with remarks the press had made – it was, as they suggested, utterly unseemly for three responsible people to go on with a fracas like this. In all probability our chance to win the 2004 Olympics for Cape Town might already have been lost anyway, because we were being perceived, not only by the local press but by the IOC too, as a bunch of squabbling amateurs unable to reach even preliminary agreement amongst ourselves. I said that the best thing for me to do was to resign, leaving Steve Tshwete and Sam Ramsamy to pick another team and get on with it.

With that, I turned my back and walked out.

* * *

When it finally happened, my resignation from the Cape Town bid was greeted with much dismay. All along there had been a strong lobby of citizens who did not back the Cape Town bid. They had valid concerns that had to be addressed, but among both the supporters and the detractors of the bid there was consensus that it had its best chance of succeeding and was being best run in the hands of the original Bid Committee I had formed. Although some people worried that Cape Town would not cope, they did not worry about how the bid would be conducted if it had gone ahead. After my first resignation from the bid, there were several attempts at brokering a reconciliation that would have allowed my continued involvement with the campaign. President Mandela himself called a meeting to try to elicit an agreement between NOCSA and my committee, and in deference to him I agreed to return if four specific conditions relating to the precise future conduct of the bid were applied.

The reconciliation lasted barely a month. Then came the final break-up. In that short time, NOCSA had reneged on all four agreed conditions.

A very flawed agreement, one which had been bulldozed through, was eventually signed between NOCSA and the Cape Town City Council at a ceremony to which my committee were not even invited. It has since been suggested that the City Council gained their Olympic bid inheritance reluctantly, but I believe that is nonsense.

On Thursday 11 May 1995, I had an elegant letter delivered in which I resigned completely from the Olympics. To say that it was a very, very sad day – as I wrote at the time – was a massive understatement. I was heartbroken. The dream Wendy and I had nurtured for four and a half years fell cruelly apart, but I could no longer be party to what the Cape Town bid had become. I telephoned Wendy, who was in America, to tell her of my final resignation. I could hear her crying on the end of the line. She, the stalwart and passionate supporter and innovator who had worked so hard and diligently to support me in my dream, was devastated. I wrote on the day of my final resignation that those responsible had a lot to answer for. They had sabotaged something that would have given people hope that our country could make it over the coming difficult years. I found it incomprehensible that people could get away with something so despicable.

Ironically, in the month of my final resignation from the Olympics, South Africa celebrated a sporting extravaganza which showed better than a million words what we could have gained from winning the 2004 summer Olympic Games. Between 25 May and 24 June, we hosted the 1995 Rugby World Cup. When South Africa played contest favourites, Australia, in the opening match of the tournament, the entire country came to a standstill. Between then and the afternoon of pure magic when President Mandela donned Springbok Captain François Pienaar's No. 6 jersey to shake hands with the home team and the All Blacks prior to the final, the whole of South Africa watched, listened, cheered, hoped and dreamed of a South African victory with a unity of purpose hitherto utterly unknown. After a stunning Springbok victory, the champions were fêted in a ticker-tape victory parade through Johannesburg streets packed with ecstatic, all-race crowds.

Although I had resigned from the Olympic bid, I had no intention whatsoever of writing off the debt owed to me personally for money I had lent to keep the bid functioning. Furthermore, consultants who had worked with my committee were owed money they had legitimately and efficiently earned. Soon after Chris Ball was appointed to run the bid in my place, I offered to share the knowledge gained over my five-year association with the Olympics, for which he thanked me. I also stressed that there was a moral duty to pay back money I had lent, then standing at around R15 million, and to pay the consultants.

By the end of 1996, there was nothing constructive left in my dialogue with the usurpers of Cape Town's Olympic bid. On my return from attending the Atlanta Games, matters regarding the repayment of monies owed to consultants and to myself seemed to have nowhere to go other than a court of law. Then, a situation occurred which allowed me some leverage.

Chris Ball, already in the midst of massive problems of his own with Mr Ramsamy and NOCSA, called to ask for a R7,5 million Pick 'n Pay donation towards an Olympic sports development fund. I was very pleased to tell him that he would not see a single cent until the consultants who had not been retained by the new order received their money in full. The ploy worked perfectly because the long-suffering people, who had put in so much excellent work, were at long last nearly paid in full. I too received the assurance that I would be paid in full, although over a six-month period.

I eventually recovered about R7,5 million of the R15 million I was owed, but money was the smallest part of the heartbreaking loss I shared with the whole of South Africa.

* * *

In the early evening of 5 September 1997 Cape Town fell silent.

Since early that afternoon people had packed into sports bars and clubs. They had gathered in droves on the Grand Parade and at the Waterfront, confident that a night of unprecedented celebration lay ahead. With millions of TV sets tuned and big screens focused, the moment came. People watched breathlessly as IOC President Samaranch mounted a podium in Lausanne, Switzerland, opened a sealed white envelope, paused to read, then announced: 'And the winner is … Athens.'

Instead of a great triumphant cheer going up across South Africa, there was the baffled quiet of disbelief. Cape Town had lost the bid for the 2004 Olympics? Surely not – how could that be when President Mandela had himself stood before the IOC Committee to tell them why it had to be Cape Town for the 2004 choice? But even his earnest request, that Cape Town should be awarded the first Olympic Games of the new century to give impetus to Africa's march towards the new future it deserved, had not swayed the IOC Committee.

I watched the award of the 2004 Games ceremony at home in Constantia with Wendy and the rest of my family, feeling like someone sitting outside his own daughter's wedding, not allowed in. Some members of the press had asked me if they could be present when news of the award came through and, although Wendy had not been too pleased by it, I agreed. I did so as a small mark of my appreciation for the support the press had shown for Cape Town's bid.

Although in the end I had had severe misgivings about Cape Town's chance of winning, I was terribly sad when the axe finally fell.

The day after the final announcement from Lausanne, Pick 'n Pay ran full-page newspaper adverts saying that although we hadn't pulled it off, we were still proud to have been part of the bid. It had been a valuable experience. In so far as Sam Ramsamy's behaviour is concerned, I have firm evidence to support my contention that he orchestrated a campaign to undermine my authority and to cast doubt on the authority of my leadership. It was at the behest of Sam Ramsamy's NOCSA that three members of the Cape Town City Council travelled to Lausanne to see the IOC in a prelude to the signing of the contract between NOCSA and the City Council. NOCSA stalled the well-documented attempts on my part to sign a tripartite contract with them and the City Council on behalf of my Cape Town bid – the contract which would have given us access to the sponsorship funds we had to have in order to remain viable – as an important part of a deliberate campaign to remove me, the Bid Committee I led and the consultants working with us from further involvement with Cape Town's 2004 bid.

After the events relating to my involvement with the Cape Town 2004 Bid, I became aware that I had been an unwitting part of a broader political picture. The advent of democracy took black South Africans off the sidelines and into full participation in all aspects of our emerging new dispensation. Cape Town's Olympic bid was an effort belonging to the entire nation, and while I always accepted this as being the case, there were those who believed it was unthinkable that such a high-profile, internationally focused quest should be orchestrated and managed by a private capitalist businessman who also happened to be white.

Two years after the failed Cape Town bid, Ngconde Balfour, now Minister of Sport, came to see me in my office and spoke to me about how political issues had impacted on our doomed bid. He told me that there was now a broad consensus that the Bid had had its best chance of success in the hands of my committee and that it was considered unfortunate that I had been obliged to resign my role.

I was deeply grateful that Ngconde Balfour had come to see me and had cleared up several perplexing questions with his summary of events. Between us, the air was finally cleared.

Since my long-held and dearly cherished Olympic dream ended, a number of versions of what really happened have been written and spoken about. On one occasion in 1998, when I decided during an interview with Derek Watts of M-Net's *Carte Blanche* television programme to give the first full account of events, I discovered that even though distanced by a few years, there are still those who prefer not to have such an account aired. I had been having a fairly cursory interview with Derek Watts when he became very excited by what he was hearing for the first time about events around the Olympics. He hurried away to organise a better recording, after which we sat down and did an extensive interview, which was destined to be flighted in full on an upcoming edition of *Carte Blanche*, giving the first real account of events. What actually appeared was a bland few minutes of material out of which all controversy and contention had been cut. Derek Watts later explained what had happened when word got out that the *Carte Blanche* team had filmed a controversial interview with me about the Olympics. Russell Macmillan, M-Net executive and an associate of Sam Ramsamy's, had insisted on seeing the material prior to screening. It was apparently at his insistence that all contentious issues relating to NOCSA were cut.

To Wendy, in particular, who had worked all her life promoting the cause of free speech, this naked form of censorship was absolutely abhorrent. She wrote to Derek Watts, protesting that a body blow had been dealt to freedom of expression, particularly as *Carte Blanche* journalists were rightly esteemed for their fearless investigations and exposés. However, in this case it seemed intolerable pressure had been brought to bear, scoring a resurgent triumph for all those forces which had for decades decided what the South African public might or might not hear.

To me, the *Carte Blanche* incident just confirmed the accuracy of an old adage – the truth hurts.

* * *

As I watched, viewing a ceremony as slick and sensational as all that had gone before it, a huge lump came into my throat. The triumphant Sydney 2000 Olympics closed with the handing over of the torch to the next summer Olympics hosts, Athens – and it should have been handed to us.

But, in the midst of the inevitable emotion I felt at the close of the Sydney Olympics, I changed focus to the future, thinking about lessons South Africa should learn from having lost the 2004 Olympics to Athens. It is my habit to focus on the future rather than on the past. Notwithstanding all that had happened to me, it is a matter of record that after I was ousted from the Cape Town bid, I continued to support it with money, expertise and my heart because to do so was to the greater good.

But, and this is a vital but, if South Africa chooses to bid for a future Olympic meeting, we will be embarking on an exercise in pure futility unless those involved have the guts to assess honestly the reasons for the 2004 failure before going ahead. If this is not done, and behind this statement I place my entire conviction, history will simply, drearily repeat itself.

The key to putting together a successful Olympic bid, as I have said time and again, is unity of purpose. Soon after Sydney won the 2000 summer Olympics, an Olympic Minister was appointed to concentrate solely on the Australian effort. Everyone connected to a bid has to stand with, fully support and trust their bid committee chairperson.

Since Sydney, I have frequently been asked whether, in view of that superb effort, I still believe South Africa and Cape Town could have pulled off the 2004 summer Olympics. My answer is an unequivocal yes. We did not anyway have our eyes on a presentation on the scale of a Sydney – our Olympics were to have an authentic African flavour representing the realities of our continent. In the right hands, I am certain we can compete with anyone in the world when it comes to organisation, planning and financial management.

The other question I am often asked is whether I would choose to be involved with a future bid. In answer to that, the first reality is that I am over a decade older than when I first embarked on my dream to bring the Olympics to Cape Town. Therefore, I would certainly not take on such a task in the demanding role of CEO. Even more emphatically, I would not do so at all unless all the ignominious in-fighting ended once and for all. Under a management I could work with and on clear terms of reference, I would be prepared to act as Chairman of a future bid, because I do have plenty to bring to any such party, and I have never wavered in my conviction that Cape Town could bring the Olympic Games home to Africa.

CHAPTER 29

The New South Africa

In mid-1994, watching Pick 'n Pay slip almost helplessly towards a national strike and with sniping and backbiting dogging my every Olympic move, I have to say I experienced a dash of alarm along with a rush of pride when I heard I had been elected to the Chairmanship of CIES, the international organisation of food and food-related retailers with which I had been associated for decades.

In 1994 the Paris-based CIES operated in 41 countries. The combined retail volume obtained by members was then in excess of $750 billion. It was truly a great honour they had bestowed on me, but how could I find the time to honour the commitment as it deserved? Still, I knew I had to accept. Apart from the honour of being elected Chairman, the CIES board had bent over backwards during the years of apartheid isolation to accommodate me as a representative from pariah South Africa. They once had relocated an entire conference because the first choice of venue refused to admit South Africans. Now, as Chairman, I could make a meaningful contribution to the organisation as a way of expressing my thanks.

Just when it seemed the spotlight fixed remorselessly on Pick 'n Pay during all the ugly weeks of the strike might turn elsewhere, Mr Mandela, who was in the USA, unwittingly loosed a controversial cat from its bag.

After he disclosed in a speech there how he had approached twenty titans of corporate South Africa and asked each for at least R1 million to build up his party and finance the ANC's campaign for the April 1994 election, a report found its way into the South African press naming me as not only one who made the requested donation, but one of the few who had given double the amount requested. The donation I had made on behalf of Pick 'n Pay was cited as the reason the raucous strike we had just suffered rankled Mr Mandela so. This was entirely untrue.

At the time the Board of Pick 'n Pay decided to donate money to the ANC, we also voted funds for Mr De Klerk's National Party and Mr Buthelezi's IFP. These donations represented a complete divergence from usual policy, which was not to support any political party. The April 1994 election was, however, without precedent in the history of South Africa and therefore demanded an unprecedented approach.

Since there was no South African law requiring that political gifts be disclosed, and since it was anyway no one's business but ours and our shareholders' how we spent company money, we saw no reason at the time of the donations to make them public. Equally, we also took no steps to conceal the donations. I remember saying to our Board that disclosure of the donations was almost inevitable. Such matters always surface at some stage. When it did so towards the end of 1994, I followed my usual policy of being open and frank with the press. I had taken lessons to heart watching Nixon crumble years before, because he had been devious to the press and the public about Watergate.

Before the donations were handed over, all three recipient leaders undertook to use the money exclusively for voter education – a huge necessity among an electorate who in the vast majority had never participated in a modern electoral process. A greater amount had gone to the ANC because they had the most voters to educate. Since Pick 'n Pay had been only one among several companies making donations to political parties prior to the 1994 election, it was not our financial contribution to the ANC which prompted Mr Mandela's concern over our devastating strike. It was instead a genuine dismay on his part that a company with a demonstrably high profile as enlightened employers, campaigners against apartheid on a practical level, should have been targeted. He was also worried about the ramifications of union militancy in the economy and for employment.

* * *

On the morning of President Mandela's inauguration – 10 May 1994 – Wendy and I assembled with other invited guests at 6 a.m. to be taken by bus through to Pretoria, which was the scene of the celebrations. The atmosphere in Pretoria was absolutely wonderful, indescribably exciting. Just being present at such a momentous event was incredibly emotional. Even now, I hardly have words to express the feelings I had that shining day, a day I will remember in minute detail for ever. Newly inaugurated, President Mandela stood in the spotlight of the world. His address was stirring, often lyrical. He committed his government to renewal and the preservation of liberty. He reached out to all South Africans to join him, to work together 'as a united people, for national reconciliation, for nation building, for the birth of a new world'. However, when the new President raised Mr De Klerk's arm, the body language of the ex-President conveyed the tenseness that had developed between the two leaders. Still, for the time being Mr De Klerk was sworn in as co-Deputy President with Thabo Mbeki.

Restructuring in the 'rainbow nation' settled itself within a formal framework when South Africa's brand-new Constitution was introduced by President Mandela and Deputy President De Klerk. The Constitution adopted on 10 May 1996 was the country's first democratic Constitution drawn up by a multi-racial assembly. Details of the new Constitution had been hammered out by legislators coming from vastly differing perspectives and with often ill-assorted aspirations for their own groups, so the final, shiny new document was another triumph that our contrary country could chalk up to reconciliation and compromise.

Relationships within the Government of National Unity – in place since the April 1994 election – were not, however, heading for harmony. By mid-1996 Mr De Klerk was talking around the possibility of pulling his

NNP party out of the alliance to form an opposition to the ruling ANC. I had the opportunity to discuss this with Mr De Klerk a number of times, but particularly at a large meeting at Groote Schuur.

Mr De Klerk described his dilemma over whether to stay within the Government of National Unity or pull out to form an official opposition, as one based on effectiveness. In view of the many differences between himself and Mr Mandela, would he not better serve the interests of his electorate and good governance within the country by speaking as the voice of opposition rather than coalition? My opinion – the consensus – was that Mr De Klerk could still be most effective playing a part in the unity structure. His role in bringing the country to the point where we had such a government, as a result of a stunning process of reconciliation and democratic election, was absolutely fundamental and of immeasurable worth. Within the unified structure, we felt, lay the best opportunities for directing national affairs according to Mr De Klerk's principles. Outside, there was always the possibility of being sidelined to the massive ANC majority in central government – which indeed did happen after Mr De Klerk decided to follow his inclination and take his party into opposition.

After his going into opposition, I received a gracious letter from Mr De Klerk thanking me for the constructive relationship we had maintained during his years as a minister, President and Deputy President. He wrote, 'As leader of the Opposition from 1st July 1996, this will become even more important … I should appreciate it if you would also feel free to contact me whenever you might think it advisable.'

Mr De Klerk took his party into opposition at the time when another new, and some said equally misguided, initiative was putting the embattled psyche of South Africa under excruciating scrutiny. In testimony before hearings of the Truth and Reconciliation Commission (TRC), Eugene de Kock detailed a hitherto unknown history of hit squads and other horrors. His revelations were just some among the awful litany which poured out of the TRC hearings. I was among a number of well- known people interviewed for my opinion on Eugene de Kock's evidence. Each of us interviewed indicated that the degree of brutality which had apparently been commonly practised came as a revelation and a shock, but I also said

I believed both sides should come clean and bear responsibility for the terrorism that had occurred.

In response to my answer, a Mrs Shapiro wrote a furious letter to the *Cape Times*, castigating me for daring to suggest that there was a wider guilt to take into account. I was upset by this reaction and the inference that I sat in some kind of ivory tower, surrounded by the trappings of wealth and power, and knew nothing of ordinary lives. In fact, I had been made particularly sensitive to the real, day-to-day horror of life in the violence-racked townships since a friend of our family died by the unspeakable method of necklacing. I had also called at the homes of some of Pick 'n Pay's employees to commiserate after members of their families had died in a similarly awful manner. Arguments around all the implications of the TRC have now been bouncing back and forth for years – and have yet to come to any undivided conclusions. No wonder South Africans living abroad say they suffocate in the bland, uncontroversial political climates that blanket the safe shores of their new homes.

* * *

Another new chapter opened in South African politics with the dawn of the Mbeki era in May 1999. South Africans again confounded the critics by turning out in their millions to vote for the second time in a peaceful, patient, if not perfect election. I waited with interest to see how Mr Mbeki would do as a savvy, hands-on political manager. I felt sure he realised that if the priority of the ANC's first term had been to achieve stability and to bed down democracy, the second had to be about delivery, fuelled by economic growth and the creation of jobs.

Over seven years into democracy, it is already a miracle that the ANC government have stayed within the bounds of a free economy with such admirable commitment. Many ANC leaders were indoctrinated by the ideals of socialism, just as white leaders of the past were indoctrinated by apartheid. Now, if the ruling ANC will take the bold steps necessary to create the economic climate in which employers can hire and fire, work intelligently with the unions to trim workforces, if necessary, in order to channel those people into newly created opportunities, and increase the tax-paying base, then an era of golden opportunity awaits.

I predict that some time into the first ten years of the twenty-first century, the ANC will split into a left and a right faction. To the left will go the present communist and union affiliates, while the remainder of the party will attract a far greater percentage of white and black supporters – those voters who are unable to accept the present affiliations within the party. I am sure that a future ANC, more centrally positioned, will decide what they have to do for the economy, and do it. In these predictions for a future stronger, rightist form of government, there also has to be allowance for a welfare underbelly to take care of the needy.

The point is that, given an economy which works, there will be money to provide a social net through which no citizen will be allowed to fall. I must also say that I am not, and never have been, against unionisation. Pick 'n Pay was the first major food retail organisation to accept union representation and I know we have learned salient lessons from these representatives. For the future, though, unions in South Africa must learn to recognise the economic forces that ultimately work in their favour.

As for the twin monster curses of twenty-first-century South Africa, yes, we do face the catastrophe of the AIDS scourge and, yes, we are a society cursed by crime. But I do not believe that those before us and we ourselves have come through all the trials of the past only to be defeated by a viral and a social disease. I have faith that a cure for AIDS will be found and that a cure for crime will come about as a natural result of harnessing the awesome potential of South Africans into an economy kind to all.

Considered geographically, South Africa is perfectly placed to become the technological powerhouse of the southern hemisphere, just as the Republic of Ireland has become in the north. For centuries past, Ireland's best export was her people. Countless thousands of Irish migrants flooded into England and America, fleeing the abject poverty and economic despair at home. Recently, however, the tables have turned magnificently. Identifying the massive advantage of their geographical position right between America and Europe, the government of Ireland began enticing technological businesses into their country with tax breaks and a whole host of clever incentives. The result is an economy booming to such an extent that Irish recruitment agencies now scour the world – South Africa included – to fill the two thousand new jobs being created weekly at home.

If Ireland has been so clever, why can't South Africa cash in on our geographical advantage too? Poised as we are between South America, Australia and South-East Asia, we have a geographical position unparalleled for opportunity. If our government would emulate the smart government of Ireland by introducing incentives and demonstrating clearly that this country will never follow the foolishness to our north, we could be at the beginning of an era of opportunity unsurpassed at any other time in our history. Imagine if our well-trained, valuable human resources did not dream of taking their skills elsewhere because life was so good here. Imagine full employment and a massively boosted middle class. Imagine us enticing immigrants because there were just too many jobs to fill.

There is no reason why those dreams could not be our reality. We have the position, we have the experience and the nerve, the intelligence and the will to prove everyone wrong. There is a part of Africa that could have the rest of the world gasping in admiration for its achievements – and all we South Africans live there.

I have persuaded my children to stay in South Africa because I believe in the dream of this country as the powerhouse of the southern hemisphere.

CHAPTER 30

The Crown is No Heirloom

I now see that my release from an obligation to the Olympic bid, heart-breaking and counter-productive as it was, freed me to take the new look and the bold steps necessary to put Pick 'n Pay back on track. If events had turned out differently, I would have had to embark on the three most strenuous years of our effort towards the 1997 final vote at precisely the time Pick 'n Pay needed undivided attention to restructure and redirect.

Restructuring and Vuselela ('rebirth'), the two concepts on which we picked ourselves up to forge forward with new confidence, would not have received the undivided attention they demanded if the bid process had continued making huge demands of its own. At the end of one particularly harrowing day in the Cape Town Olympics saga I wrote, 'I know tomorrow is another day, but sometimes I just don't see it.' If it took my ignominious ousting from one of the dearest-held dreams of my life to show me where my tomorrows lay, I gained much more than I lost.

The 1994 strike had forced me to recognise that things had gone fundamentally wrong with the way Pick 'n Pay was working. Clearing my mind as best I could, I sat back and did some hard thinking and thought about how I had run Pick 'n Pay for thirty years, mostly using my own judgement and gut feelings. But, not only had the strike given us our first-ever drop in profit, it had knocked down the morale of the company and damaged our reputation. Growth since 1991 had anyway been pedestrian, margins had fallen and profitability, measured by return on assets, had also dipped.

Because I always believed in the virtue of listening to advice, hearing other opinions and consulting experts, I concluded that the time was ripe to call in outside consultants to take a really critical look at the status and well-being of the company. What was needed was a corporate health check run by specialists.

The specialists I picked to run our health check were Australian consultants Bain & Company. They came in for six months and did a magnificent job. Tim Simms, in particular, really helped me to see how I had to rejig the company. The questions I posed were: Do we have a future as we are today? And, as a public company reliant on growth, *can* we grow? I also needed a clear succession plan – the time had come to throw all the nebulous premises of the past away.

After six months of intensive analysis, the consultants came back to tell me that I had a wonderful company, that we would get over the strike but that we would have to find creative ways to do so. With their fresh professional ears and eyes, they pointed out that the twinning of René de Wet and my son Gareth as joint MDs had not worked well, not because of any fault on the part of either, but simply because they were too similar. The fault was mine for not recognising the impracticality of putting such similar men together. When this flaw was identified by outside eyes, I saw immediately how right they were.

The reconstruction Tim Simms recommended called for splitting the company into two divisions, each with its own main board and management team, with the objectives of accelerating moves into the mass market while continuing to nurture and grow the company's traditional middle-class market. One division, Pick 'n Pay Retailers, was to be headed up by Sean Summers, to oversee the running of our core supermarket and hypermarket chain. The other, Pick 'n Pay Group Enterprises, was placed under Gareth to focus on the enterprise side of the business. Under Gareth's wing fell the Score Supermarket chain, which we had acquired the previous year, franchising operations, homeware chain Boardmans, cash-and-carry chain Price Club, and new developments outside South Africa – a wide and complex portfolio to manage.

These were bold moves, the greatest departure from accepted practice within the company since its inception, but I had high hopes for what I saw as a brilliant plan. This restructuring was a response to two sets of problems that had dogged the company for too long – one to do with market position and the other with leadership.

When details of the restructuring were released there was inevitable speculation that Gareth's new post was a demotion bred of dissatisfaction because the joint managing directorship between himself and René de Wet had not proved viable and had not worked well during the 1994 strike. However, I made it perfectly clear that Gareth was being groomed to take over from me. I told the press that although I would only jump when I hit top speed, it was time to make way for the younger generation in the greater interests of the company. I said to Rene, now my Deputy Chairman, that we had to be careful not to 'ring fence' our involvement. By this I meant that we should not interfere with the teams of Sean and Gareth; we had to act as a conduit to help them and give guidance when they wanted it.

* * *

Vuselela. As a concept, it was a triumph; as a catalyst for rebuilding morale, it proved magical. Vuselela, an African word for rebirth, swept away the sullen vestiges of hostility left lurking behind the 1994 strike. Because of it, the company changed forever, in one way going forward towards one united dream, yet in another going back to what we had once been. Sean Summers, powering away in the Retail Division he now headed, and our marketing dynamo, Martin Rosen, came up with the concept of Vuselela, and it was absolutely brilliant.

Under the Vuselela programme, loyalty events and courtesy events identified those of our employees – from the humblest shelf-packer to the highest manager – who were projecting the image of a retail organisation which really, genuinely cared for the consumer. Winners went on all-expenses-paid trips to Disneyland to experience a concept built on the fun of serving customers brilliantly. At Disneyland, our winners watched the ultimate professionals at work, then brought their knowledge and enthusiasm home after having the holiday of a lifetime.

Part of the Vuselela thrust involved looking more closely at the make-up of the thousands we employed. Did we, as management, really know our employees, really know their difficulties and dreams? I had spent close on thirty years travelling around the country, shaking hands with thousands of people in stores, listening to what they had to say, yet I was shocked to find out that over 40 percent of our employees were either functionally or totally illiterate. Accordingly, countrywide literacy and numeracy programmes were introduced. We started a whole new concept of graduation ceremonies, making a real fuss of the people who had successfully completed their courses. The graduates put on the same gowns and mortarboards they would have worn at any university graduation, to receive their certificates. These programmes have become critical parts of our personnel structure; graduating with a certificate of literacy is a highly prized experience for people of all ages. For them, the spirit of Vuselela translates into access to opportunities the developed world took for granted centuries ago.

Franchising, another Vuselela sapling grown into a many-branched tree, started as a way of empowering people to share the success of the Pick 'n Pay formula for their own account. On my travels overseas I had seen franchising working in Holland and France, where big chains allowed franchised stores of their own names as a way of helping small traders. Retailing is among the toughest and most cut-throat of all businesses. Food retailing in particular, since it had become mainly the province of big chains in South Africa, was almost impossible to challenge from the position of the small shopkeeper. But I began to think along the lines of what I had seen working in Europe and thought about franchising Pick 'n Pay instead of controlling it entirely as a company store. When I first broached this idea, my Board mostly thought I was mad. I was a minority of one, but very determined and convinced. The franchised stores eventually launched were called Pick 'n Pay Family Stores. The first of these to open was in Westville, KwaZulu-Natal, in the hands of a General Manager of ours from the region who was so excited by the prospect that he didn't mind being the guinea pig. In time, the franchising concept succeeded so well, we began to worry that too many top people were being wooed away, but as a Vuselela tool for empowerment, we are well pleased that this should be the case. In 1995 Gareth took the new franchising drive under the wing of his Group Enterprises division, where it continues to thrive today.

* * *

The end of my Olympic dream, which freed me up to channel more much-needed energy into the affairs of Pick 'n Pay, also gave me more time to concentrate on the fortunes of my family. At this time, everyone in the family was on edge over my daughter Kathy, who was due to have a second baby after losing her firstborn to a heart defect. We all breathed more easily after the beautifully named Arielle Sapphire, our sixth grandchild, was born. Before I had much time to savour that delightful event, I became embroiled in an ugly situation over my daughter Suzanne's divorce, which teetered on the brink of becoming a courtroom confrontation. Then I had to mourn the loss of Arnold Galombik, my friend for fifty years, who died of a massive heart attack. We lost five beloved family members in a short, dark space of time – Kathy and David's firstborn, David's father, and Wendy's father, mother and sister Pamela: a sombre roll-call. On the side of family resurgence, though, Jon had become engaged to Samantha Drummond-Hay. Samantha walked into a party at our home on the arm of someone else and came face-to-face with Jon, similarly attached. That, for both of them, was that. It was love at first sight.

I hadn't changed much since the days when I acquired the first four Pick 'n Pay stores. Even though there were now stores dotted all around the country, I still liked to visit them personally to shake hands and look people in the eye to see what made our employees tick.

A taste for a simple life and simple pleasures was also not much changed. I still voted raw Jungle Oats, boerewors sausages and peanut butter my favourite foods. I liked to eat out in simple restaurants that served plain food quickly, rather than the elegant variety that kept you waiting hungry between courses. When Wendy was away and unable to scrutinise the cholesterol content I consumed, I liked nothing better than to indulge in a special treat – a plate of boerewors and chips. When a newspaper survey asked some 'celebrities' to define what made a woman attractive, I picked Miss Piggy as my ideal on the grounds that she was fun and had spunk and guts.

For over 26 years, I have played snooker at home on Monday evenings with a small group of special friends, as I do to this day. Monday snooker with Ryno Greenwall, Hilly Nachman, Howard Symon and Tony Ashberg is my relaxation, my battery re-charge, my weekly oasis.

In September 1997 I was still sports-mad and out on the golf course at every possible opportunity. One Saturday, going round the Clovelly course with my friends Tony Ashberg, Ryno Greenwall and Ian Levine, I got a hole in one. This mild achievement excited me enormously, not least because the last time it had happened to me at Clovelly I had been 18 years old, practising on 1 April on my own without even a caddy to witness the triumph. I remember rushing home to tell my father – who coolly wondered why I thought he would be stupid enough to fall for such a silly April Fool's Day joke. No amount of persuasion ever made him change his mind on that score, even though a lone Clovelly groundsman came forward to say he could confirm the coup.

* * *

In the office, I was often aggravated by petty but vexing problems between Gareth and Sean, testing their new roles. My reaction to this friction was to encourage both of them to concentrate on the success of the overall restructuring, and on the triumph of Vuselela. It had taken my farewell trip to Europe as CIES Chairman to clarify my thoughts about the proper purpose of restructuring, to companies in general and ours in particular. During my year in the CIES chair, I had travelled widely, spoken at numerous conferences and with very many world-respected retailers. As a result, I had come to an alarming conclusion: the guts were going out of retailing.

Retailers everywhere were devoting so much time and energy to thinking themselves forward, plotting strategies around global pricing and electronic shopping, they were forgetting to look after their customers. They were forgetting to take a holistic view of the shopping experience. Old-style concepts – such as creating in-store excitement with promotional activity and atmosphere – were in danger of becoming forgotten arts.

Home buying and what that meant for retailers was on everyone's lips. I believed the intelligent approach to home buying, which will certainly be a favourite method of shopping for many, was to treat the concept as another in-store department. Even as increasing numbers were pointing a mouse to choose goods, stores still had to remain lovely places in which to shop, places where attention to detail, innovation and promotion were never orphaned to the 'electronic department'. When I voiced these opinions as outgoing CIES Chairman, some delegates were not very happy – particularly when I went on to point out that retailers were also tending to lose contact with each other. It was no longer so usual to visit one another to monitor at first hand what was happening around the stores of the world, which was a pity.

As for restructuring, whether it was done for the purposes of introducing electronic shopping or, as we had done, for other reasons, the aim was not to restructure to do business as usual. Neither was it about the figures coming out of an overhaul. No, the key point about restructuring was to make positive changes to the attitudes of people right through the business and, on that score, I could thankfully report that the restructuring of Pick 'n Pay and the introduction of the Vuselela programmes were succeeding magnificently, so much so that Vuselela Phase Two, with a R1,5 billion budget aimed at fresh development, was about to be launched.

Innovative share incentive schemes had involved people at nearly every level in the company. It was not only top executives and management who participated through these schemes in a company that was in great shape despite the fluctuating fortunes of South Africa's volatile economy. In our thirtieth year our people, now numbering over 30 000, pulled off the biggest-ever day in our history when till points registered a stunning R56 723 million worth of takings.

The Vuselela initiative kept perfect time with changes in the new South Africa. In many important ways we had come of age, although not to become static but rather poised to take our place in the next century, only a couple of years away. With franchising operations going so very well, I was again looking around for ways to go global, pursuing a possible retail franchising deal with Shell in the Philippines. On this errand, I set off on a fact-finding mission to the capital of Manila hoping to put a feasibility study in place. The population of Manila was then close on seven million people, making it one of the biggest cities in the world. Like South Africa it had huge poverty and affluence living cheek-by-jowl, although the Filipino people far outstripped South Africans in levels of literacy, the Philippines being a 93-percent-literate nation.

As always in South Africa, it was impossible to keep on the right side of everyone. Even the very successful Business Against Crime initiative launched in an attempt to mobilise the resources of business against horrendous crime levels attracted detractors. There were some, President Mandela included, who worried that focusing on crime reflected unnecessarily negatively on the image of the country. On this score, I differed. Although we had come so far so fast, foreign investors still held back in large numbers because of rampant crime. Any initiative aimed at reducing crime had to be applauded. There was simply no point in pretending that crime did not exist at such a horrifying level. However, it was also important to keep problems in perspective, an exercise we were not too good at as a nation.

At the 1998 CIES conference I had been staggered by the number of quality people still expressing an interest in investing in South Africa, one way or another. When these business people raised concerns about crime levels or about what would happen to South Africa after President Mandela retired, I pointed out that, difficult as times were, they did not approach the difficult times business had faced ten years before.

Meanwhile, just in case I thought that the recent changes I had made to the structure of Pick 'n Pay excused me from difficulties for the time being, I received a few rude new awakenings.

* * *

Consumers, finding their bank accounts ravaged by house-bond repayments that had shot up by as much as 50 percent, caused retail stocks to take a huge walloping as sales figures wavered. In addition, the merger which had taken place between Shoprite, Checkers and the OK had for the first time presented us with one large competitor as opposed to the several smaller ones we had become accustomed to challenging. Armed with firm new management plans aimed at countering the retail slump, the newly consolidated army of our opposition had marched forth confidently. Clearly, this was a time to keep a cool head.

Within our ranks, more change was the order of the day. Although I had been entirely happy with improvements since the company had been split into two distinct divisions under Sean Summers and my son Gareth, they had been agitating for a reshuffle of executive structure. It was accordingly decided that René de Wet, my trusted lieutenant, should retire, making way for Gareth in the role of Deputy Chairman with responsibility for off-shore operations. Sean was appointed Group Managing Director in charge of the core Retail Division – the engine room of Pick 'n Pay – as well as Group Enterprises. I experienced much pressure over this latest realignment, and quietly worried whether it was really for the best. The new structure would certainly help to maintain clarity and simplicity because it had become clear that it was necessary to have one Managing Director responsible for performance while retaining the identity and focus of each division.

At the same time, I was becoming aware that Gareth needed some kind of a mid-career sabbatical. He was not clear about his direction, not sure whether he really wanted to live his life at the pressurised intensity I lived mine as hands-on Chairman of the company. Soon after the executive reshuffle had been put in place, I therefore persuaded Gareth to take his family off to London where, apart from gaining time apart to think where he wanted to go, he could usefully take care of the still-unresolved Philippines investment proposition. All round, it seemed a sound idea.

The last quarter of 1998 – during which I began to worry very much yet still very quietly about the necessity of putting a proper succession plan in place, working on the family coming together to back whoever was to be my successor – was marked by a shower of sad and bad, good and joyful events. On the good side I became professionally acquainted with the marvellous Genus Resources consultants, with whom all my family were to work on our joint futures. Even better, my son Jon and his wife Sam gave Wendy and me another lovely grandchild – Joshua Marcus, a brother for Gabriella. Then, after an extremely difficult pregnancy, my daughter Suzanne, who had married Paul Berman the previous year, gave birth to Robert, a brother for Natasha and Nikita, in November 1998. On his eightieth birthday, President Mandela married the much admired Graça Machel.

To the score of sad and bad events went an attack at one of our Johannesburg stores in which four men burst in and sprayed our staff with AK-47 bullets – the kind of occurrence that had become wretchedly familiar to businesses up and down the country. Then, one night when the Planet Hollywood restaurant at Cape Town's Waterfront was packed with people, a powerful explosion ripped through the restaurant leaving two people dead and more than twenty injured. It seemed we were ever-doomed items on a never-ending agenda of terror. To those of us trying to promote South Africa as a destination for tourists and for investment funds, the blast shattered our efforts again.

On the final year's countdown to the new millennium, I had some hard and serious consolidation of my own to do. I set myself to face a journey down the most complex, sensitive and emotional road I had yet travelled.

* * *

Watching the calm professionalism that Genus Resources consultants Tom Davidow and Richard Narva brought to the raw-nerve discussion around my succession, I realised that I felt like a pressure cooker building up steam, while all around me pots bearing the contending interests of my family and Pick 'n Pay bubbled away, needing to be stirred and seasoned and set at the right temperature to bring out their best flavours.

Although I had voluntarily taken the initiative to put long-term planning in place so as to structure the interests of my family and company into the future, the process – being something akin to taking out your own innards to examine them – was painful, sensitive, complicated and potentially dangerous. Once started, there was no knowing where we might all end up.

The planning which I retained the Genus consultancy to help us with happened at a time when a global revolution in the management and ownership of family businesses was in process. We were far from alone in finding ourselves at the crossroads. Despite the complex difficulties family-owned businesses experience in the modern business world, they nevertheless do retain inherent strengths. In terms of volume alone, family-owned businesses make up about 80 percent of South African business and comprise 60 percent of companies listed on the Johannesburg Stock Exchange. Around the world, family enterprises dominate, accounting for 80 to 90 percent of all business.

From the time I had first insisted on a share structure in the newly public Pick 'n Pay, which secured the controlling interest in the hands of my family, I had never deviated from my conviction – more like a paranoia – that this was always to be the case. However, nearing the end of the twentieth century, global trends in family-owned businesses were impacting strongly on my thinking. In the case of Sainsburys, the family-owned food chain that had become a British institution, when Sir John Sainsbury – a man I greatly admired and from whom I had learned so much – retired, younger members of the family found themselves facing a dilemma. Retailing in Britain was going through a difficult period of transition. But the company the younger Sainsbury family inherited had not put in place a division between the family interests and the day-to-day running of the company. Younger members of the family became disillusioned when rival chains out-performed a Sainsburys struggling in the difficult trading climate. At one time, rather than waiting for a recovery, some of the young guard decided, metaphorically speaking, to head for the checkout. Today, a sizeable proportion of the company remains in family hands. I know Sainsburys very well, and I know they went through a difficult time regaining family control while keeping the day-to-day running of the company in the right managerial hands.

An opposite scenario unfolded around the future of the legendary Ford company of the USA because, in that case, proper planning was in place. When William Clay Ford, Junior, fourth-generation heir to the Ford family fortune, took on the role of Chairman he persuaded the company's talented CEO-in-waiting, Jacques Nasser, that an arrangement of shared power could be mutually beneficial and rewarding. In combination, William Ford offered the Ford shareholders two precious commodities – stability and profitability – while Jacques Nasser, a results-at-all-costs executive, brought a decisiveness to the day-to-day running of the company that had Wall Street watchers swooning in admiration.

The division of Chairman from Chief Executive at Ford offered a case-book study of what such an arrangement, properly managed, could do to take a thriving family enterprise forward into the new millennium with confidence and competence. With the proviso that roles must be clearly defined and undisputed, there can be a formidable working relationship between a Chairman whose fortunes, and those of his family, are tied to the company and a Chief Executive whose track record promises success.

Krister Ahlström of the mighty Swedish Ahlström Corporation high-lighted a common failing in family-structured businesses. He pointed out that while, through caring deeply, family members can pursue an emotional involvement with management, they might not be on top of business realities. In the first generation, the ownership and the management of the company are wrapped up in one person – the founder. In the second and third generations a gap forms and gradually widens. Owners become more removed and less able to see what is happening in the business, although they still retain control. This is when it becomes crucial that a company should be run on professional, not family, terms.

Such wisdom was in the forefront of my mind during the intricate planning process I embarked on with the Genus consultancy. Through a deeply introspective, intellectual process there is now a laid-down Corporate Governance for Pick 'n Pay, which ensures that there will be a Board of Directors of sufficient strength to ensure that the management of the company continues on an ethical basis. One of the cardinal indicators of business in the new millennium is the absolute importance of ethics.

Young people the world over want to see the strength and development of ethics in business – they look to the business as well as the political world to set such values. The green revolution of the twentieth century bears witness to the heartfelt international reach towards ethics in all our structures.

We have also structured a Family Council with various arms, which I believe to be one of the most carefully conceived of its kind. Through this democratic forum, all future decisions concerning the unity of the family and the company are made within the council of the entire family. I have not set up this Family Council so that I can one day continue to rule from the grave, but so that my family can retain control of the company when I am gone, should they wish to do so. Of course they might one day decide to sell, but at least such a decision would have to be made democratically.

Although I had also been working for some time on a succession plan for Pick 'n Pay, and had indeed published a 'Structure for Sustainable Growth' in 1998 when Gareth was appointed Deputy Chairman in an executive capacity, my work became more assiduous in the latter part of the 1990s as my elder son wondered whether to retain this executive role in the company.

During the time Gareth had been in London on his sabbatical year he had thought long and hard about the 20–25 working years ahead of him. He had by then spent almost his entire working life within Pick 'n Pay and he had watched since childhood the stresses and strains I shouldered in running the business. I now believe that I should have given more time to being a father to my children and less to being father of Pick 'n Pay. Gareth bravely decided not to wait until he might one day make the same statement. He wanted to do other things with his life, spend more time with his family. Accordingly he started meeting with the Genus consultancy while he was still in London, to map a course.

Of course, the simplicity with which it is possible to write this retrospectively masks the fact that this was a time of terrible heart-searching and tension. It was no secret that I had been grooming Gareth as my successor. The fact that he might not be an active participant in the management of the company at precisely the time that René de Wet – who had

fielded so much for me, supported me and understood my mode of working – stepped down, made me feel almost faint at the prospect of how
much I would have to continue to shoulder in my sixty-eighth year.
Wendy and I cast around with the consultants in search of solutions. We
both suffered: as parents concerned about the well-being of our elder son,
and in our positions heading up a retail giant responsible to thousands of
staff and shareholders. I felt deeply for Wendy at this time, remembering
how she had not always been sure it was best for her children to enter the
family business at all. Indeed, as the children were growing up she often
tried to persuade them to find some other career.

When Gareth finally decided to get out of the executive running of the
company, there was a sense of relief simply because a firm decision was
made. However, I would not be honest if I did not say that his decision
devastated Wendy and me – even though we genuinely believed he had
made the right decision for the business and for his wife and children.

As a result, there came the decision delivered to a hushed gathering of
journalists and analysts in the boardroom of Pick 'n Pay on 19 April 1999.
We announced the appointment of non-family-member Sean Summers as
CEO of Pick 'n Pay. I was to remain Executive Chairman, with Gareth as
my deputy in a non-executive capacity.

It was clear from the atmosphere in the boardroom that April afternoon
that the assembled journalists realised they were witnessing a moment of
rare drama in the history of South African business. The rarity was there
because, as the godfather of a retail giant, I was not handing over the day-
to-day running of the empire to one of my family. The drama was there
because my announcement signalled the end of a long period during which
I had struggled to come to terms with the inevitable.

The new company structure was well received by financial analysts.
They applauded a difficult decision taken in the best interests of the company, which had been put first before family loyalty. In appointing Sean
Summers to the CEO position, it was acknowledged that we had chosen
the best person to take everyday control of the company in the interests of
shareholders and that we were following a world trend in so doing. As for
Sean, he moved into controlling the company at a time when we had done

better than most analysts believed was achievable in the trying economic conditions prevailing. There were impressive gains in the franchising sector of the business too. Also, without the smallest intention of gloating over the trials of rivals, I can record that the Shoprite triumvirate had reported significant losses.

After Gareth had rounded off the April 1999 briefing with a dignified announcement conceding that the moves announced were aimed at putting the right people in the right places and that he supported Sean as the best person available for the post of CEO, I confess to sharing the pain my son suffered when analysts addressed most of their questions to the new boss. But because of the deep planning that has been put in place, the way ahead for Pick 'n Pay as a company led by efficient and ethical directors and for my family is clearly structured and anchored in waters sheltered from storms.

* * *

My daughter Suzanne, younger son Jon and son-in-law David Robins remained with Pick 'n Pay after the 1999 changes, gaining experience and working their ways up, and Gareth was to help me very much with all kinds of issues relating to the family structure while he pursued his own business endeavours. I still also had the mainstay support of Wendy, who had carried the daunting portfolio of employee liaison and benefits and social responsibility on her slender shoulders for 32 tough years. During that time the company's increasing investment in education and literacy programmes, housing, self-help schemes, child welfare, parent support groups, feeding schemes, relief programmes, cultural and theatrical projects, sport development and environment programmes had made enormous demands on Wendy's time and emotions.

From the time in her early twenties when she sidelined her chiefly artistic leanings in favour of promoting and supporting my commercial interests, she has been cardinal to my success and a solace for my failures. Her keen skills at assessing people and situations, her clear head and well-developed instinct for identifying the right course remain invaluable aids to me. In the company, she has often been severely critical of me, has warred with me over points of difference, but it is the fact that she will challenge anyone when her conscience so dictates as well as her brilliant work that makes her the real jewel in our executive crown.

On the subject of crowned heads, with the CEO crown placed on the head it best fitted for the time being in April 1999, it was time to move on. You learn in life to make your choices, and not regret them; so I sat up, took a deep breath and a long look around and began energetically clearing up vestiges of the past still clinging like limpets to the rock of our business. We put the finishing touches to deals, finally winding up our connection to the 7-Eleven franchise and terminating the venture in the Philippines with Shell. Neither had proved successful nor, fortunately, expensive as mistakes.

As though a line was being drawn under Pick 'n Pay's past, at this time I received the sad news that my close friend Des Lurie, a business associate for fifty years, had died in London after a long illness. As the doyen of County Fair, Des and I had squared off over the chicken price wars in memorable tussles that had become part of South African retail legend, but we had always remained deeply respectful of each other and close friends.

Circumstances also contrived to take my thoughts out of the past when, one Saturday morning, I read that the rugby heroes of the Western Province, the Stormers, were threatening to strike and not play against Australian side Otago that afternoon because of a money dispute. I could just imagine how disappointed all the Stormers' fans – myself very much included – would be if the game was cancelled, so I decided there and then to try to do something to resolve the situation. With Pick 'n Pay staffers Nick Badminton and David Smith, I set off for the Vineyard Hotel in Newlands, where the Stormers players were locked in combat with their team management. The situation at the hotel was very tense. Taking a deep breath, I went up to the Stormers' coach, Alan Solomons, and simply said that we had come to help. Everyone then trooped into a conference room, where I took the role of referee and got each side to state their case. Although I am used to the cut and thrust of business negotiation, it was novel to be wringing concessions on both sides from a group of sportsmen noted for their high levels of aggression when challenged. Time and again they went down head-to-head until I was able to throw in an offer of cash to bridge the gap between them. By 10.00 a.m. everyone had agreed and shaken hands. The Stormers went off to their Newlands home ground to prepare for the afternoon's match, and Nick, David and I, well pleased with the morning's work, went back to our office.

Still feeling I had entered a new era of my own, and consequently feeling in great need of fresh horizons, I celebrated the birth of our tenth grandchild – Gus Aaron Robins – born to my daughter Kathy and her husband David – by initiating the collapse of a cumbersome share structure – Nshares – which seemed part of the baggage psychologically slowing us down in our stride towards the future. Then, in the company of David Robins and Adrian Naudé, I set off on an African adventure.

We travelled to five East African countries on a fact-finding mission. We wanted to test the waters, sniff the commercial air, see if there was somewhere we could settle on as a destination for a more ambitious sortie into Africa. We were in Zimbabwe and Botswana and quite a few small places with Score franchised stores, but now we wanted to look further north towards the heart of Africa. The little journey we took in 1999 was, from a commercial point of view, a trip into a world of stark contrasts.

In Europe and America at that time, supermarket selling was poised to move into a futuristic world. Massive chains were investigating the possibility of setting up giant distribution centres situated on outer-city farmlands which would take orders for delivery to central city collection points to increase efficiency while decreasing overheads. There was a concerted and huge movement towards supplying the 'eat at home' trend – it was becoming absolutely basic for supermarkets to provide customers, who had neither the time nor the inclination to cook, with ready-made meals they could sweep up in a quick dash into the supermarket on their way home from work. Electronic shopping, which was on our programme as our next innovation, gained greater sophistication on an almost daily basis.

In a hot street in the Tanzanian capital of Dar es Salaam, I was looking at a scene in which people picked up grubby-looking offerings of food from displays set out on rickety tables unprotected from heat, flies or human hands. Here, serving a city population of five million, was one little supermarket in the middle of town. There was no access to any central supply of cheap, clean food for traders to sell. People had to make do with conditions Europe had left behind a century ago.

All this is, of course, a familiar story. There are still places in South Africa where similar conditions prevail. But large numbers of South Africans are able to buy food from efficient, clean outlets through the sophisticated systems food retailers have planted, nurtured, grown and sustained in South Africa.

At the turn of the last century my grandfather turned his eyes to southern Africa and set the scene for my life's endeavours. At the turn of the next century, my eyes turned north. The day the three of us – David, Adrian and I – stood in the sunshine in Dar es Salaam, we were so taken with the feeling of standing on virgin supermarketing territory. Even though I was scared stiff by the possibility of a journey into such an unknown, I thought that if we did not start to seize the unexploited retail opportunities of Africa now, as sure as eggs one of the big overseas chains would do so within the next five years.

It was subsequently decided to set up a first supermarket in Tanzania. Difficult as it is bound to prove, there is a market of millions upon millions up and down Africa who need our expertise in food distribution as much as the franchise owners whom we plan to launch will need their custom.

In Pick 'n Pay, we have made the corporate decision not to look for overseas investments at this time, but to concentrate instead on extending our expertise in distributing food efficiently and at good prices more widely. I once made the mistake of disregarding a deep instinct that told me not to take Pick 'n Pay into Australia; in the twenty-first century I am heeding another instinct that tells me to keep primarily within the continent where our heartbeat has always been heard. I think we can play an important role in improving the lives of millions more and I believe we can do very well out of concentrating on Africa.

The company that I will one of these days hand on has been subject to such intricate planning for the future that it has one of the best chances of any leading world enterprise to remain at the top while retaining its ethics. I am filled with confidence by the structures built around keeping the company cohesively and equitably in the hands of my family while it is run by the best, professional, non-family managers. Something of real value has been built, something of real value will survive and go on getting stronger. This is the legacy I shall leave.

Conclusion

In the last year of the twentieth century I had tea in London with Freda, my 92-year-old stepmother, who reminisced about the misgivings she had felt about taking on my father's three children when she married him. Being with her, then a very weak old lady although with all her faculties intact, was a poignant reminder of how far I had travelled since the time I longed for her warmth as a small boy confused by the harsh removal of my own mother from my life. There is much truth in the saying 'My joy is my sorrow unmasked'. Through my early, well-suppressed sorrows I developed the love for my own family, which is the main joy of my life. Wendy and the four children, their husbands and wives and our ten grandchildren matter to me above anything else in the world.

As for the adventure of building Pick 'n Pay, I am still amazed at how the simple philosophy of balancing the business on the four legs of a table – administration, merchandise, sales promotion and people – with the consumer on top, and sticking rigidly to these fundamentals, has provided pillars of wisdom strong enough to support a giant. Balanced on our table in the twenty-first century are 273 stores, 176 franchised stores and a staff complement of thirty thousand.

What's more, all of this has happened to a founding couple – Wendy and me – who have truly never seen profit as the main motive, however many hollow laughs this truth may cause. Maximising return on capital has never been of primary importance either, and we have shaken our heads, been baffled, over the fact that the less attention we paid to profits and the more we gave away to staff, charities and social responsibility projects, the more the profits piled up. A strange but true phenomenon, and one that I would advise anyone with their eyes set on building an empire to note as a sound tip.

When the inevitable lists appeared prior to the start of the new millennium, I was incredibly flattered to receive, with Anton Rupert (of the Rembrandt group) and Aggrey Klaaste (of the *Sowetan*), the Millennium Award for our efforts as ambassadors for South Africa and for having produced worthwhile enterprises which had stood the test of time. I was also thrilled to find myself featured in a book, *They Shaped Our Century*, which listed the most influential South Africans of the twentieth century. But, in my seventieth year and fiftieth as a retailer, I have to say that it is South Africa and my fellow South Africans who have shaped *me*.

Where else in the world would a mere grocer have encountered such diversity, known so many great people of differing political persuasions and been able to contribute to changing political policies which affected the lives of ordinary people who shopped in my stores? Where else could I have had the honour to receive a magnificent, silver-topped staff, the coveted symbol of Xhosa chiefs and elders, from a luminary such as Mr Mandela, as I did on the occasion of my seventieth birthday? Is there anywhere else in the world where, as the Chairman of a retail food chain that had gone head-to-head with unions in the past, I could receive a letter in the year 2000 from an extremely militant, stalwart black unionist, in which he thanked me very much for 'not appealing your unfair dismissal at Checkers because you follow your dreams and vision to establish this organisation, lashed out on apartheid to come to an end and made an organisation where South Africans, communities of all races, know each other'?

Where else would I hear a story like the one Sylvester Mofokeng, one of our managers, told me recently? Sylvester, who resides in a house in a part of Johannesburg that was once reserved exclusively for whites, said that when he was a child living in great poverty he used to wander up the road to look at the clean brick-and-mortar houses which made up a Pick 'n Pay staff housing scheme. He saw the fathers and mothers leaving for work, some in the unbelievable luxury of their own cars. He saw the children, who didn't seem to be wanting for anything, going off wearing the uniforms of good schools.

In the crammed, ramshackle house he shared with too many others, his mother, as the only person employed, was the sole breadwinner. She received her weekly pay on Fridays, but by the following Wednesday the money had run out and everyone went without for two long days. Sylvester said that as a barefoot, hungry child watching the patently better-off residents up the road, he made up his mind that he would one day work for Pick 'n Pay, as indeed he now most successfully does as a General Manager and Director.

There is so much merit in the people who make up the population of this weird, wonderful, unexpected, unpredictable southernmost part of Africa. I am so very glad that I decided to stay and have had the privilege of building something of value in this, the most unique nation on the face of the earth.

Viva South Africa, viva!

Index

A

Abad, Miguel 272–4
Ackerman, Bruce 23, 32, 87, 129
Ackerman, Esther 14–15, 26–7
Ackerman, Freda (née Feinstein) 23–5, 34, 44–6, 52, 334
Ackerman, Gareth 52–3, 97, 119, 137–8, 172–4, 181–2, 207–8, 213, 250–1, 276; Deputy Chairman 323, 327; heading Pick 'n Pay Group Enterprises 316–17, 319–20, 323; joint MD 283, 316–17; non-executive Deputy Chairman 328–9
Ackerman, Gustave (Gus) 14–16, 17–18, 20–6, 44, 70, 77; and Ackermans 17–20, 29–30, 70–1; aversion to borrowing money 20, 29–30; relationship with and influence on sons 19, 24, 26–7, 30, 43–5, 52, 62, 89, 135
Ackerman, Jonathan (Jon) 76–8, 172, 205, 208, 217, 284, 319, 324, 329
Ackerman, Kenneth (Ken) 18–19, 21, 23, 26–7, 32–3, 43–4, 76, 169
Ackerman, Meyer 12–14
Ackerman, Mitchell (Mick) 14–15, 25
Ackerman, Rachel (née Margolis) 17–23, 108–9
Ackerman, Raymond 83, 90, 105, 140–1, 143–5, 269, 285, 307, 327; Cape Town's Olympic 2004 bid 3, 5, 259, 261–75, 278, 291–2, 298, 301–3, 304; dealings with Ramsamy 3–4, 265–7, 269–72, 288–91, 295–8, 300–5; paying bid accounts 3, 267–8, 296, 298, 302–3; working relationship with Balfour 270, 292, 296–7, 305;

family: childhood 15, 18–19, 26; family man 10, 46, 151, 334; grandchildren 213, 319, 324, 331; homes 18, 20–1, 23, 82, 97–8; in child custody battle between parents 20–2, 108–9; relationship with and influence of father 10–1, 19, 24–7, 30, 43–5, 62, 70, 89, 135; relationship with mother 19, 22; relationship with siblings 24, 26–7, 32–3, 87; relationship with stepmother 23–5, 45–6, 334; relationship with Wendy 10–1, 22, 44, 47–8, 52–4, 56–7, 61, 67–8, 70, 75–6, 79, 82, 104, 108–9, 128, 141–2, 144, 174, 201, 206, 280, 288–9, 300, 304, 320, 328–30, 334–5; succession plan 323–7, 333;
   general: at Bishops 27–8; 31–6; at UCT 37–45; awards 213, 260, 335; beliefs 28, 36, 38–40, 47–8, 62, 64, 68, 92, 96, 114–15, 149, 152, 206; death threats 3, 208, 285; keeping a diary 31–3; love of simple life and pleasures 319–20; loyalty 114–17; passion for sport 25–6, 32, 34, 41, 44, 220, 241, 253, 263–4, 320, 330–1; pros and cons of leaving SA 67–8, 76, 238; relationship with Denise Rock 45–6; respect for principles of unionisation 234, 285, 313; special interest in education 42, 47, 277–8; use of media opportunities 86, 105, 145, 158, 192–3, 203, 206, 216–17, 221–2, 281, 305; vision for SA 57, 313–14;
   politics 59–60, 64, 146, 149, 165, 193–5, 198, 200–1, 206, 230, 249, 252–4,

Index

280–1, 311–12; Business Initiative
199–203; General Sales Tax 105, 192,
229; homelands 149–50, 158, 165, 211,
214–15; in repercussions of Information
Scandal 41, 149, 157–8; intertwining of
business and politics 91–2, 105, 147–8,
150, 154–5, 208, 240–1, 254, 260–1; land
tenure for blacks 159–60; meetings with
De Klerk 238–9, 245–6, 248, 286, 311;
meetings with Mandela 248–51, 256, 258,
284–5, 293–4, 299–300, 322; member of
CIES 4–5, 174, 177–8, 260–1, 308, 320–2;
on sanctions 149, 151, 174, 235, 248–50;
on the ANC and SA's future 312–14;
SAFF 149–52, 154–5, 157–60; South
African Forum 158, 164–5, 191; tackling
issues of subsidies, price control,
regulation and collusion 84–6, 105–6,
132, 191–3; Urban Foundation 146–7,
153–4, 234; Value Added Tax (VAT)
105–6, 229–30, 278–80;

    working career: business philosophy 4,
20, 38–40, 50–5, 62–3, 67, 69, 95, 117–18,
178, 185, 220, 222, 277–8; buying Pick 'n
Pay 77–90; dismissal from Checkers 10–1,
70–1, 75–7; encounter with Kakouris of
Trevenna 103–5; Hutt's influence 38–40,
46, 62, 106, 184, 223; Trujillo's influence
39–40, 53–4, 61–2, 96, 121, 184; wanting
complete control and fear of losing it 78–9,
87, 169–72, 220, 228; working for
Ackermans 46–7; working for Checkers
51–6, 58–9, 61–3, 66–9; working for
Greatermans 48–9; working relationship
with Goldin 68–9, 81–3, 89–90, 116;
working relationship with Greatermans
Board 52, 54–6, 58, 63, 66, 68–9; working
relationship with Hugh Herman 180–1,
189, 213–14, 282–3; working relationship
with Lawley 84–6, 90, 96, 98–9, 107–8,
110–5, 118; working relationship with
Norman Herber 54, 58, 60–1, 63, 66–7, 69
Ackerman, Samantha (Sam) (née Drummond-
Hay) 319, 324
Ackerman, Wendy (née Marcus) 10–1, 22, 44,
47–8, 52, 56–7, 61, 63, 67, 70, 82, 108, 111,
142, 147, 151, 173–4, 177, 201, 206, 208,
212, 269, 280, 320, 328; Cape Town's
Olympic 2004 bid 262–5, 269, 288–9, 292,
295, 297, 300, 304–6; disagreement with
Raymond about Constantia site 144–5;
grandchildren 319, 324, 331; handling of
human resources and social responsibility at
Pick 'n Pay 90, 96, 106, 124, 128, 140–1,
144–5, 194, 209, 219–20, 228, 277, 285,
329–30; in the USA with Raymond 52–4;
support for Raymond after his dismissal
75–6; teaching in Soweto 57, 68
Ackermans (the chain) 17, 19–20, 22, 28–30,
45–47, 143
Acts. Bantu Education Act of 1953 42–3;
Group Areas Act 9–10, 90, 150, 161–2,
226, 234, 238; Immorality Act 152;
Monopolies Act 127; Population
Registration Act 251; Terrorism Act of 1967
65; Urban Areas Act 204
African National Congress (ANC) 189, 206,
235, 237; and the Olympic bid 265, 267;
armed struggle 193, 247–8; as government
312; banning of 60; conflict with Inkatha
247, 254, 256–8; economics 209, 312–13;
Lilliesleaf Farm (Rivonia) 64–5; 1994
election 259, 309; talks with 202;
Umkhonto weSizwe (MK) 64–5; unbanning
of 240, 245; Youth League 281
Ahlström, Krister 326
Anglo American 171, 202
Angolan War 140, 239
anti-Semitism; at Bishops 27–8, 32–5; at
Clovelly Golf Club 25–6; at Mowbray Golf
Club 25; during and immediately after
World War II 28–9, 32–3; during 1994 Pick
'n Pay strike 285; in Australia 185; in
Lithuania 12–13; taken into consideration
when naming Ackermans 17
apartheid 13, 39, 59, 66, 88, 107, 152, 154, 165,
251; border industries/homelands 211–12,
214; business community's role in
dismantling of 240–1; education as key to
re-regulating society 37–8, 42–3; impact on
business 208; killing the economy 39–40;
legislation 3, 9–10, 13, 59, 65, 150, 152–4,
175, 177, 234, 238, 240, 251; under
D. F. Malan 33, 37; under P. W. Botha
163–4, 177, 203; see also Acts
Arthur Andersen 271
Asmal, Kader 298

B

Balfour, Ngconde 269–70, 288, 292, 296–7, 305
Ball, Chris 207, 292, 302–3
Barclays National Bank 202, 207
Barnard, Christiaan (Chris) 86, 277
Barry, John 107, 111
Battle, Charlie 272–4

Berman, Paul 324
Berman, Suzanne (née Ackerman) 61, 172, 195, 319, 324, 329
Bishops (Diocesan College) 27–8, 31–6
Black Sash 175
Bloom, Tony 200, 207
Blumgart, Keith 71, 83
Board of Trade and Industries 218
Boesak, Allan 199
Boipatong 254, 269
Botha, P. W. 91, 162–4, 175–7, 191, 194, 196–7, 199, 202–5, 207–8, 210, 214, 226, 233–40
Botha, Pik 157–8, 164–5, 195–6, 203–4
bread price 191–3
Buirski, David 115–16
Business Against Crime 322
Business Initiative 199–203
Buthelezi, Mangosuthu 91, 151, 200, 237, 249, 256–8

C
COSATU 227, 234, 286–7
Campbell, Jane 284
Cape Town's Olympic 2004 bid 259, 263–5, 268, 270, 274, 287–9, 291–4; campaign to destroy relationship between Bid Committee and City Council 3, 295–8; City Council's role in 263, 265, 267–8, 270–1, 299–303; funding of 267, 271, 293–4, 296, 298, 300; impact of political issues on 304–5; loss to Athens 4, 304, 306; national competition 1–2, 270–5; see also National Olympic Committee of South Africa (NOCSA); Ramsamy, Sam
Carrard, François 264–5, 268–9, 290
Carrefour 120–1, 123
Chase Manhattan Bank 196–7
Checkers 9–11, 51–5, 58–60, 63, 66–7, 92–3, 95–6, 100, 105, 163, 178, 222–3, 284, 323
Clicks 89–90, 188
Clovelly Country Club 25–6, 32, 161–2
Coates, John 272–4
Cohen, Jack 84
Cohen, Sam 30, 172
Conservative Party 177, 208–9, 240, 252, 254–5
constitutional negotiations 255–6
consumer boycotts and stayaways 199–200, 247
control boards 131–2, 135–6, 212, 215, 230

D
Daling, Marinus 71
de Beer, Zach 41–2

de Klerk, F. W. 177, 210, 226, 231, 235–6, 238–40, 245–6, 249, 251–3, 256, 310–1; and the Olympic bid 265, 267; meetings with Ackerman 238–9, 245–6, 248, 286, 311; 1994 election defeat 259; relationship with Mandela 2, 247–8, 255, 258, 310–1
de Kock, Eugene 311–12
de Kock, Gerhard 197
de Wet, René 118–19, 205, 228, 283, 316–17, 323, 327–8
Deforrey, Denis 120–1
Democratic Party 41–2, 236, 240
Diederichs, Niko 149, 156
D'Oliveira, Basil 107
du Plessis, Johan 265–6

E
Easton, Rita (née Levetan) 26
Eglin, Colin 200
Eiselen, Werner 43
elections, all-race (1994) 2, 210, 256–9, 309; whites-only (1987) 208–9

F
Feinstein, Peter 23–4, 32, 43, 129
Fine, Issy 44, 77–80, 129, 169, 207, 280
Fine, Moyra (née Ackerman) 18, 21, 23–5, 44, 82, 129, 280
Fonn, Martin 49–50

G
Galombik, Arnold 88, 129, 319
Gentry, Grant 170
Genus Resources 324–7
Goldberg, David 181, 188
Goldberg, Issy 230
Goldfields 102, 110
Goldin, Jack 69–70, 77–83, 89–90, 115–16, 187–8
Goldreich, Arthur 63–5
Gorvy, Harold 78–9, 88, 129, 169–70
Government of National Unity 259, 310–1
Greatermans 10, 22, 30, 45, 49–52, 54–6, 58, 63, 66, 68–70, 76–7, 89, 93, 100–2, 143, 172
Grocery Manufacturers' Association (GMA) 105, 134

H
Hani, Chris 255–6
Hawke, Bob 182–3
Heard, Tony 148
Hedley Byrne 115–16
Herber, Harry 22, 30, 48–50

Index

Herber, Norman 10, 22, 50–6, 58, 60–3, 100–1;
 Ackermans-Greatermans deal 30; dismissal
 of Ackerman 10–1, 69–71, 77
Herber, Robert 56, 173
Herber, Somah 22, 30
Herman, Hugh 4, 119, 141, 180–3, 189, 201,
 213–14, 228, 276, 282–3
Heunis, Chris 111, 134, 138, 159
Horwood, Owen 40–1, 106, 163, 192
Hutt, W. H. 38–40, 46, 106, 184, 223
hypermarkets 120–2, 127–30, 140–1, 180,
 185–6, 188–9; *see also* supermarkets

I

Information Scandal 40–1, 149, 154–7, 162,
 164; *see also* Rhoodie, Eschel
Inkatha Freedom Party (IFP) 2, 247, 254,
 256–8, 309; *see also* Buthelezi, Mangosuthu
International Association of Food Chains (CIES)
 4–5, 174, 177–8, 260–1, 308, 320–2
International Olympic Committee (IOC) 4, 107,
 262, 265, 268, 278, 289–90, 304, 306;
 officials evaluating SA cities 272–3; winning
 support of members 274, 291–2, 295

J

Johannesburg Stock Exchange 87–9, 163, 171,
 225, 252, 325
Junior Chamber of Commerce (JAYCEE) 69

K

KWV 215
Kakouris, Mimie 103–5, 107–8
Kennedy, Edward (Teddy) 197–8
Kennedy, John F. 61–2
Kevany, Kevin 269, 288
Kirsch, Sam 16–18, 25, 29
Kissinger, Henry 152, 175
Klaaste, Aggrey 335
Koornhof, Piet 107
Kotze, Fanie 133–4
Krok, Abe *and* Solly 110, 114

L

Lawley, John 81, 83–6, 90, 96, 98–9, 104,
 107–8, 110–5, 117–18
Lazarus, Ivan 77, 79
Liberman, Jack 179–82, 188–90, 213

M

Macmillan, Harold 59, 66
Macmillan, Russell 292–3, 306
Maisels, Isie 101

Malan, D. F. 33, 37, 49
Mandela, Nelson 196, 203, 235, 238, 248–51,
 256, 264, 302, 310, 322, 324; and the
 Olympic bid 265, 293–4, 297, 299–301,
 304; concern about 1994 Pick 'n Pay strike
 284–6, 309–10; meeting with P. W. Botha
 236–7, 240; meetings with Ackerman
 240–1, 249–51, 258, 284–5, 293–4,
 299–300, 322; 1994 election victory 259;
 relationship with De Klerk 2, 247–8, 251,
 255, 258, 310–1; release 1, 206, 210, 245,
 248, 262; sentenced to life imprisonment 9,
 64–5; supporting sanctions 248–9
Mandela, Winnie 237, 249
Mangope, Lucas 214, 257
Marais, Jan 116–17
Marcus, Dr 48, 52, 169, 319
Marcus, Pamela 47, 52
Mauerberger, Morris (Morrie) 16–17, 20, 29–30
Mbeki, Thabo 209, 310, 312
Mboweni, Tito 284–5
McCrystal, Lawrence 105–6
Metrowich, Redvers (Red) 157–8
Miller, Michael 30, 172
Miller, Sam 95
Mofokeng, Sylvester 335–6
Motsuenyane, Sam 150
Mulder, Connie 150, 156, 159, 162
Mulholland, Stephen 76–7
Mutwa, Credo 285–6
Myburgh, Tertius 202

N

NAFCOC 150
National Alliance Convention 200–1
National Business Institute 147
National Cash Registers 52–3
National Olympic Committee of South Africa
 (NOCSA) 107, 265, 267, 270, 288–9,
 299–301, 305; campaign to undermine
 Cape Town's bid 4, 291–2, 295–6; dispute
 over funds 296, 298–9; national
 competition for a bid city 268–9, 271–4;
 see also Cape Town's Olympic 2004 bid;
 Ramsamy, Sam
National Party 37, 42, 106, 152, 154, 177, 232,
 236, 239–40, 309, 311
National Sports Council (NSC) 265
National Union of South African Students
 (NUSAS) 42–3, 45, 111
nationalisation, call for 45, 246
Nkomati Accord 195

O

O'Dowd, Michael 57, 60, 68
OK Bazaars 20, 22, 28, 30, 49, 67, 89, 92–3,
    95–6, 101–2, 105, 122–3, 133–4, 140, 172,
    221–3, 284, 323
oil industry 136–8, 215–17
Oliver, Gordon 263, 265, 267
Olympic Games 254, 265–9, 306–7; see also
    Cape Town's Olympic 2004 bid; National
    Olympic Committee of South Africa
    (NOCSA); Ramsamy, Sam
Operation Hunger 198
Oppenheimer, Harry 146, 175, 202, 234
Overmeyer, Freddy 90–1

P

Pan-Africanist Congress (PAC) 60
Parkinson, Cecil 151–2
Pevsner, Michael 25
Pick 'n Pay 11, 71, 81, 90, 134–5, 170, 228,
    233, 254, 258, 264, 279, 303; advertising
    97, 116; allocation of shelf space 125–6,
    128; awards 213; banking 117; bought by
    Ackerman 77–90; built on bedrock of
    courtesy, avoiding debt and Trujillo's
    philosophy 40, 62, 91, 142, 184–5, 277,
    334; bursary scheme 209, 224, 229, 277,
    329; buying strategies 83–6, 92, 112–13,
    132, 221–2; caring for employees 38–9, 62,
    92, 106, 130, 277, 279, 318, 329; consumer
    boycotts and stayaways 247; consumer
    sovereignty 38–9, 62, 82, 86, 95, 105–6,
    113, 127, 132, 135–6, 140, 142, 184–6, 217;
    contribution to Business Against Crime
    322; copycat stores 100–1; donations 39,
    62, 219, 266, 255, 277, 279, 309; expansion
    94–6, 98–101, 106–7, 111, 124, 129–30,
    142, 163, 211–14, 231, 331–2; extensive
    press coverage 3, 86, 88, 92, 126–8, 188;
    first black manager 90–1; franchises 130,
    213, 318–19, 322, 329–32; going public 89,
    92, 96, 170; growing people into senior
    positions 118, 142; housing schemes 161,
    163, 177, 194, 224, 229, 329, 335–6;
    hypermarkets 118–30, 131, 133–8, 140–2,
    176, 181–9, 217, 220, 223; international
    recognition 174; literacy and numeracy
    programmes 318, 329; military conscription,
    effect of 140, 219; opposition 89, 92–3,
    95–6, 102, 108; outside consultants 4, 119,
    316; overseas operations 140, 165, 178–84,
    186, 188–90, 213, 322, 330; Pay Net system
    237; Pikwik (pyramid scheme) 170–2, 174,

179; political violence at stores 206, 324;
    profits 3–4, 20, 96, 125–6, 185, 199–200,
    218, 225–6, 228, 276–7, 281, 286–7,
    315–16; promotions 84–6, 92, 96–7, 136–8,
    198–9, 215–20, 223, 281–2; property
    matters 140–1, 144, 220; regulated
    payments to suppliers 132; restructuring
    316–17, 321, 323, 326–7; school-feeding
    schemes 198, 329; share incentives 321;
    share price 225, 287; social responsibility
    184–5, 192, 212, 219–20, 249, 277; strikes
    and wage disputes 2–4, 29, 176, 224–5,
    227–9, 254, 281–7, 308–10, 315–18;
    supermarkets 3, 90–1, 94–6, 98–101, 103,
    107–9, 118–19, 144–5, 150, 164, 206,
    211–15, 227, 247, 257, 278–9, 284;
    turnover figures 220, 229, 321, 323; unions
    3, 283–7, 313; Vuselela programme 317–18,
    320–1; wine licences 212, 215
President's Council 176–7
Private Sector Fund 252

R

Ramsamy, Sam 265–7, 287–9, 291, 304;
    national competition for a bid city 271,
    273–4; problems with Chris Ball 303;
    working relationship with Ackerman 3,
    265–7, 269–72, 288–92, 295–8, 300, 302–3;
    see also Cape Town's Olympic 2004 bid;
    National Olympic Committee of South
    Africa (NOCSA)
Reagan, Ronald 91, 199, 201, 205
reconciliation 234, 246, 273, 310–1
Red Cross Children's Hospital 24
Relly, Gavin 202, 209, 234
Rembrandt Group 84, 170–1, 202
Resale Price Maintenance (RPM) regulations
    83–6
retailing 81, 83, 222, 318, 320–1, 325; food
    49–50, 318
Rhoodie, Eschel 148–9, 154–7, 162, 191;
    see also Information Scandal
Rivonia trial 9, 65
Robins, David 329, 331–2
Robins, Kathy (née Ackerman) 56–7, 172, 319,
    331
Rocke, Denise 45–6
Rosen, Martin 219, 317
royal visit (1947) 31
Rupert, Anton 146, 170–1, 249, 335
Rupert, Johann 177
Ryan, Billy 94–5

Index

S

Sainsbury, *Sir* John 325
Samaranch, Juan Antonio 265, 268, 296–7, 303
sanctions and disinvestment 151, 157, 184, 187,
    197–8, 201, 203, 205, 235, 245–6, 248
Sanlam 60, 71, 172, 202
Saunders, Chris 202
Saunders, Clarence 15–16
Schuitema, Jerry 217
Sebe, *Chief* Lennox 165, 211–12, 215
Segal, Leon 16–18, 25, 29
Sharpeville (1960) 9, 59–60, 67, 88
Shoprite 222–3, 323, 329
Shultz, George 201, 205
Sisulu, Walter 240
Slabbert, Frederik Van Zyl 200, 204
Slovo, Joe 255
Smith, Ian 106
South African (Anglo-Boer) War 14
South African Broadcasting Corporation (SABC)
    128, 188, 233
South African Communist Party 286
South African Defence Force 204, 214
South African Forum 158, 164–5, 191
South African Freedom Foundation (SAFF)
    149–152, 154–5, 157–9
South African Non-Racial Olympic Committee
    (SANROC) 265
South African Reserve Bank 180, 197
South West Africa/Namibia 157, 164
Soweto (1976) 139–40, 147, 157
Space Theatre (*Cape Town*) 24–5
Steyn, Joep 105–6, 134, 137
Students' Health and Welfare Organisation
    (SHAWCO) 42, 47
Summers, Robin 115
Summers, Sean 115, 118–19, 205, 283, 316–17,
    320, 323, 328–9
supermarkets 49–50, 95, 130, 134–5, 153,
    188–9, 321, 331; allocation of shelf space
    125; confidential discounts/incentives
    112–13, 221–2; in Australia 180; in South
    Africa 49, 51, 177–8; in the USA 54–6,
    177–8; *see also* hypermarkets
Suzman, Helen 41

T

Tambo, Adelaide 300
Tambo, Oliver 64, 193
Terre'Blanche, Eugene 247
Thatcher, Margaret 151, 174, 199, 236–7
Treurnicht, A. 177
Trevenna 102–5
tricameral system of Parliament 194–5
Trujillo, Bernardo 39–40, 53–4, 61–2, 76, 96,
    121, 184
Truth and Reconciliation Commission (TRC)
    311–12
Tshwete, Steve 253–4, 265, 299–301
Tulbagh earthquake (1969) 97
Tutu, Desmond 151, 198, 235, 237, 254, 259

U

unions 2–3, 40, 176, 224–9, 234, 283, 287, 310,
    313
United Democratic Front (UDF) 201, 227, 234
United Tobacco Company 84
University of Cape Town 37–8, 41–2, 277–8
Urban Foundation 146–7, 153–4, 162–3, 234

V

Verwoerd, Hendrik Frensch 9, 43, 59–60, 65–6,
    257
Vorster, B. J. 9, 40–1, 91, 107, 111, 148–50,
    152, 156, 159–62

W

Walton, Sam 121
Watts, Derek 305–6
Weil, Clive 112, 220–2
Wienburg, Arthur 299
Wiese, Christo 223
wine industry 212, 215, 228
Wolpe, Harold 65
Woolworths 20, 67, 105, 133–4, 172, 199
Worrall, Denis 202, 206